BULBS FOR WARM CLIMATES

THAD M. HOWARD

BULBS

FOR WARM CLIMATES

University of Texas Press ■ Austin

First edition, 2001

Requests for permission to reproduce material from
this work should be sent to Permissions, University of
Texas Press, Box 7819, Austin, TX 78713-7819.

∞ The paper used in this book meets the minimum
requirements of ANSI/NISO Z39.48-1992 (R1997)
(Permanence of Paper).

Library of Congress Cataloging-in-Publication Data

Howard, Thad M. (Thad Monroe), 1929–
    Bulbs for warm climates / Thad M. Howard.—1st ed.
        p.   cm.
Includes bibliographical references (p.   ) and index.
    ISBN 0-292-73125-6 (alk. paper) — ISBN 0-292-73126-4
(pbk. : alk. paper)
    1. Bulbs—Sunbelt States.   I. Title.

SB425 .H75   2001
635.9'4—dc21

00-008893

DEDICATED TO
MARCIA CLINT WILSON

CONTENTS

The genus *Agapanthus*, formerly considered part of the family Amaryllidaceae, has recently been moved to a new family, Agapanthoideae. This change was overlooked until too late to include it in the text of this book.

ACKNOWLEDGMENTS

I wish to thank Jo Ann Trial, who helped guide me through the ginger family and who furnished some of the slides used here. She also helped me with other slides and gave me a crash course in the Zingiberaceae, allowing me to do in a couple of years what would normally have taken much longer. I would also like to thank Larry DeMartino, who also helped me with the gingers at this critical time, and Wm. R. P. Welch for his excellent help with the tazetta narcissi.

I'd also like to thank John Fellers for the use of some of his slides.

Belated posthumous thanks are extended to the late Katherine Clint and her daughter, the late Marcia Clint Wilson, for the use of their slides. Their spirit lingers. The slides from their collections were priceless in helping to illustrate this book.

I'd like to thank former students Chris Abee, Jim Bauml, Charles Curtis, Wayne Curtis, Jeff Fields, Dylan Hannon, Reggie Jackson, and Steve Lowe for their help in collecting the bulbs of Mexico.

Thanks also to companions David Jordan, James Giridlian, Les Hannibal, Jane Kersey, Herb Kelly, Scott Ogden, and David Lehmiller, who accompanied me on various trips and also assisted in collecting many of the bulbs mentioned here.

Thanks too, to the authors of other books on bulbs, for helping me keep in focus when I found myself foundering. At times we must lean on the experiences and observations of others if we are to go forward.

And finally I would like to thank Matt Cady and Orlando Renaud for their help with the computer. After several false starts in which I lost parts of my manuscript, they were able to find them again and get me back on the right track.

BULBS FOR WARM CLIMATES

INTRODUCTION

This book is devoted to plants growing as monocotyledonous geophytes, a fancy way of referring to bulbs. Generally the word "bulb" means a swollen underground rootstock. Botanically, rootstocks are defined according to their morphology. They are true bulbs, corms, rhizomes, tubers, or tuberous roots. The onion is the most familiar example of a true bulb. Others in this book are bulbs of *Calochortus, Crinum, Erythronium, Hippeastrum, Hyacinthus, Narcissus, Tigridia,* and *Tulipa.*

In this book, little space is given to certain bulbs for one reason or another. Some bulbous plants, such as *Gladiolus, Iris,* and *Dahlia,* deserve books of their own, as do orchids. Many herbaceous perennials, including *Hemerocallis, Hosta,* and *Kniphofia,* are sometimes considered "bulbs," but they are not covered here. This book includes a broad spectrum of bulbous plants for warmer areas, particularly favoring the long-neglected bulbs of the Americas along with many bulbs from other countries.

I write about gardening in central, south central, and southeast Texas, an area that includes San Antonio, Corpus Christi, Houston, Beaumont, Austin, Waco, Tyler, and the Dallas–Fort Worth metroplex, in USDA zones 8 and 9. These zones also extend through the Southwest to the West Coast, as well as to the southeastern United States and Florida. Some plants discussed in this book can be grown farther north, in zone 7, while others can be grown in zone 10, but when I state that plants grow "in our area," "in our climate," or "here," I am speaking principally of zones 8 and 9, where we get some winter frost each year. It is too cold for plants that need a frost-free environment but not cold enough for those that require a minimum number of chill hours.

Bulbs are composed of old leaf bases and enlarged scales arranged concentrically. The roots and shoots develop from basal plates. The terminal shoots may contain only leaves, or leaves and flower embryos. They can be easily identified by slicing the bulb longitudinally.

Many though not all true bulbs have tunics, which can be useful in identification. Some bulbs are multitunicated, while others have a single layer. Some have papery tunics, and others have net-like, reticulated tunics that appear to have been woven. Non-tunicated bulbs consist of overlapping scales; some examples of these are *Lilium, Fritillaria,* and some *Oxalis* species.

True Bulbs versus Corms

In spite of older literature, *Calochortus, Erythronium, Tigridia,* and their allies (*Alophia, Cypella, Eleutherine, Gelasine, Herbertia, Nemastylis,* etc.) produce tunicated bulbs, not corms. The rootstocks of *Erythronium* are similar to the tunicated bulbs of species tulips. They are fleshy bulbs with several fleshy tunics, some of them forming what looks like the fang of a dog. Thus we have the term "dog's-tooth violets." To my knowledge, there are no cormous native irids in the Americas, but there are some that grow from rhizomes (*Iris, Neomarica*) or fibrous roots (*Sisyrinchium*).

Corms resemble true bulbs but are solid in structure, with the growing bud atop the center or off to the side. The corm itself acts like an enlarged basal plate, producing roots from the sides or the bottom and a growing bud at the apex or the sides. Often corms are enclosed in tunics, just like true bulbs. Many plants annually form a new corm above the old corm; the old corm shrivels and is absorbed into the new one prior to dormancy. A few corms, such as those found in *Ferarria,* are not absorbed and will form a corm-chain. If the corms in the chain are separated, the slumbering old corm can be reactivated into growth and will in time produce a new mature corm that will flower once more. Examples of true corms are to be found in many plants of the Old World, such as *Colchicum, Crocus, Freesia,* and *Gladiolus,* and in New World plants such as *Brodiaea, Bessera, Milla,* and *Tecophilaea.* Some early taxonomists were careless in classifying the rootstocks, as many true bulbs were said to be corms. It is time to set the record straight.

Bulb Refrigeration

Bulbs are sometimes refrigerated to hold them back and extend the season. Tazetta narcissi can be retarded by planting at intervals until early spring, so that they will be in bloom over a long period. The same retardation works for lilies and gladioli, which can be held back for later planting. Tulips are refrigerated in warm climates to provide an extended winter situation, without which they will not bloom. Most bulbs do not need refrigeration and should be planted in the ground as soon as possible, so as to prevent deterioration. They are safer rooting in the ground than in a state of enforced limbo in a refrigerator.

Bulbs in the Landscape

Bulbs may be used to fill temporary needs. Once they have fulfilled those needs, we can then move on to something else. For instance, a bed of tulips can give way to gladioli, which in turn can give way to summer annuals. In this way one can use a given space several times during the year. Or one can naturalize or perennialize a given space for a show for a short period of the year and then allow this space to rest.

Bulbs for Dry Areas

Xerophytic bulbs, which are perfect for dry areas, include *Iris albicans, Cooperia drummondii, C. pedunculata, C. morrisclintii, Schoenocaulon drummondii, S. texanum, Hymenocallis glauca, H. arenicola, Manfreda* spp., *Rhodophiala bifida, Zephyranthes lindleyana, Habranthus concolor,* and *Crinum album.* These bulbs need little care and can be left to fend for themselves. In extremely dry situations they may need occasional watering. Most bulbs will want a bit more care than this. If you don't mind dragging the garden hose around during dry spells, you can try *Allium, Brodiaea, Cooperia, Crinum macowanii, Hymenocallis acutifolia,* and *Sprekelia,* as well as many *Zephyranthes.* These bulbs will get you through hard times.

Bulbs with Scented Flowers

Among the most fragrant bulbs are *Cooperia, Crinum, Hedychium, Hyacinthus, Hymenocallis, Muscari, Narcissus, Nothoscordum, Polianthes tuberosa,* and some species of *Schoenocaulon.* If carefully selected, these plants can scent any spot in the garden. Avoid ill-smelling flowers such as some of the aroids, unless you just don't care. Their scent does not last very long (only a day), but it is enough to startle an unwary person.

Potpourris

Many small bulb flowers are well suited to being dried for potpourris. Put bulb flowers into a container along with some borax and work it in carefully around the flower, positioning the tepals the way you want them, and allow to dry for a few days. When you have enough of them dried, add some scented oil, and you then have the makings of a potpourri. This works especially well with small flowers such as crocuses and narcissi.

Inexpensive Bulbs

The monetary costs involved in accumulating a collection of bulbs cannot be ignored. Those finding it necessary to start off modestly should begin with simple things. Generally one will want to start with Dutch irises, anemones, and ranunculuses. With these you can have a nice little bulb garden the first year without straining the budget. At this point, you need to know how to go about enlarging your collection. At times it may be necessary to broadly hint to neighbors or strangers in order to obtain some treasure. The worst that they can do is to say no. If you offer to buy the plant or offer another plant in trade for it, the other party can decide if he or she wants to part with one. Often you will find that people are willing to share generously. In the past, this has been a strategy of mine, and it nearly always works.

Bulbs on Sale

Another strategy in collecting bulbs is to wait and see if they go on sale. The problem here is that you need to find a dealer who is willing to sell them at a discount when the demand for them drops off at the end of the season. A good dealer knows when to do this, but there are always a few die-hards who hang on to the bulbs until they are all dead. Such dealers make careful buyers wary of buying from them in the future.

Another problem in waiting for bulbs to go on sale is that the selections are smaller, and many bulbs perform poorly when planted late. You should inspect bulbs thoroughly to determine if they are still firm and succulent. Often they are hard and dead.

Collecting Bulbs in the Wild

If you happen to be fortunate enough to live in an area rich in wild bulbs and the opportunity arises, you might consider collecting them, provided that you can give them a chance to survive in their new environment, and provided that the local laws allow it and that you obtain permission. By all means collect them if they are in the path of future development, such as the widening of highways, and development involving bulldozers. Otherwise, take care to collect only seeds or bulbs that are plentiful, as we must conserve bulbs known to be rare. The best time to collect is when the plants have finished flowering. Then one may (preferably) collect seed. Growing new plants from seed takes a little longer, but in time there should be a good supply.

Bulbs from Specialists

In time you may want to look around for rarer bulbs not usually found in catalogs, and you may want to get in touch with other gardeners. These gardeners may be willing to sell some of their bulbs, or they may wish to trade for things that they don't have. Either way, a new bulb collector benefits. Many bulbs which otherwise would be unavailable are available from collectors in seed form. Joining a bulb society is a good way to get in touch with experienced collectors and growers.

Hybridizing Bulbs

One way to obtain bulbs that no one else has is through your own hybridization. Normally hybridization works only with members of the same genus, such as a *Zephyranthes* with another *Zephyranthes,* or a *Crinum* with another *Crinum.* This can start you on the road to a lifetime hobby. If you care to embark on this route, you must first obtain a variety of bulbs that will set seed. Accumulating them can take many years. Flowering the new plants from seed takes time, and the first hybrids may not amount to much. And finally one must learn to cull them ruthlessly in order to select only the best.

Geophytes from Hell: Weedy Bulbs

Most bulbs are a challenge for us to grow and keep, so it comes as a surprise that some bulbs are weeds and hard to get rid of. Some bulbs are tolerable and rarely become a problem, even though they can stray from where they were originally planted. We don't mind seeing a few bulbs reseeding themselves here and there about a garden as long as they don't get carried away with it. But within the genera *Allium, Nothoscordum,* and *Oxalis* are monsters that are waiting to get a foothold and are nearly impossible to eradicate. Perhaps the worst is *Nothoscordum inodorum,* a lovely fragrant thing with the tenacity of a bulldog. There are plenty of decent nothoscordums that mind their ways, so we don't have to deal with these rough ones. If you are so unfortunate as to have them get into your garden, you can deal with them with certain weed-killers carefully applied.

Mulches

In warm climates, mulches are valuable in winter and summer. They stabilize the soil temperature, but more importantly they help retain moisture during dry spells and protect bulbs against cold or heat. Almost any kind of mulch will do, but ideally it should be a covering of leaves an inch or two deep in summer, and deeper in winter. An occasional light dressing of bug bait will discourage sowbugs, snails, and cutworms.

Withering Leaves

The most critical time for bulbs is when they have finished blooming. It is then that they must ripen their foliage in order to bloom the following year. While doing this they turn from green to yellow and become unsightly. Gardeners may want to conceal this process and permit the poor things to ripen in peace. It's the price that one must pay in order to keep them healthy. It's a tough time for them, but it doesn't last long. Some gardeners bind the ripening leaves or weave them into bunches, but to my mind this only draws attention to them. Actually the longer the ripening process, the bigger are next season's bulbs. Under no circumstances should the leaves be cut.

Diseases and Pests

Basal rot is caused by a *Fusarium* fungus that attacks dormant bulbs during warm, damp weather. Some bulbs are more resistant than others. The disease can be devastating, and explains why a successful planting sometimes fails to return a second season. It is best to avoid susceptible cultivars, while concentrating on cultivars known to be resistant to the fungus. *Rhizoctonia, Sclerotium,* and *Sclerotinia* are other forms of rot, and can also be treated with Benlate, a systemic fungicide and the chemical of choice.

Viruses. A number of viruses (mosaic, yellow stripe, white streak, and chocolate spot) can attack all amaryllids, irids, and many other bulbs. Virus diseases are easily spread by sucking and chewing insects, along with contaminated tools and the contaminated hands of gardeners and unthinking visitors who seem obsessed with handling and rubbing every leaf of every interesting plant that they see. Like the classic "Typhoid Mary," such visitors inadvertently transfer diseases as they go from one plant to another (including suspected virused plants), rubbing and feeling leaves. My advice for them is to look, but not touch, unless they are willing to wash their hands between plants. That should stop them. Virused plants generally do not recover from their ailment and should be destroyed. On the other hand, there are plants that show virus-like symptoms, but later seem to recover. This leads me to believe that some stresses often mimic viruses, but the plants outgrow them.

While aphids, mealybugs, grasshoppers, slugs, and snails are usually blamed for the spread of viruses, I find that thrips (see below) are equally guilty. They can fly and are very active and so tiny that they easily go unnoticed, but they can disfigure flowers and disseminate virus diseases faster than any other insects but grasshoppers. They seem particularly attracted to white flowers, where they gather in large numbers. Spraying regularly with insecticidal sprays is the best method to keep them in check during the warmest months. When they are not busy bothering daffodils, they will be found on *Crinum, Hippeastrum, Hymenocallis,* and *Gladiolus,* to name but a few flowers in their diet. Being so active, they can travel from virused plants in your neighborhood to your garden and back again. Perhaps the solution to viruses is to breed plants resistant to them.

Nematodes can be commercially devastating to daffodil growers, particularly in sandy soils. Formerly nematodes could be controlled by sterilizing the soil with the chemical Vapam, but it has been outlawed by the Environmental Protection Agency and is no longer available. It may help to plant nematode-deterring plants such as marigold and rye, which can later be turned under.

Bulb mites are pests that attack plants already under stress. They rarely bother healthy plants, but woe to a plant that already has problems. They multiply rapidly and can kill a plant in a short time.

Red spider mites are particularly attracted to irids. Spraying or dusting with insecticides works. There are all sorts of sprays, but powdered sulfur is also valuable in treating them. One must begin early; by the time you have discovered that you have spider mites, it is already late.

Snails and slugs. These slimy things are noxious, but can be controlled with bug bait. Beer is also recommended for snails and slugs, but I have never tried this. It is said to work.

Thrips. Tiny black insects. Sometimes a problem with crinums, which they can defoliate. Spray with a systemic poison. See also *Viruses* (above).

Grasshoppers are killed by liberal dusting, or with baits.

Mealybugs and *aphids* are controlled by spraying with insecticide, but it must be repeated frequently as they can be very bothersome.

Mammalian pests. Deer and rabbits can temporarily be kept away from bulb plantings with applications of blood meal. They hate it. But it must be reapplied after each watering or rain. This can get to be a bit of a nuisance in rainy spells, but it is a harmless way to add extra fertilizer to plants at odd times. One can also get similar results with sulfur powder or a mixture of blood meal and sulfur.

Garden Tools

There are many kinds of garden tools for digging, but my favorites are a good sharp shooter spade and a sturdy garden fork, preferably with all-metal handles. These can be hard to come by and cost a bit more than those with wooden handles, but they are well worth the extra effort. For lesser hand work, I prefer aluminum trowels and forks. The kinds with wooden handles don't last long. You will find good quality tools paying for themselves many times over in money saved by not buying new ones again and again. I always place a bit of fluorescent tape around the handles in order to find them quickly should I leave them lying about.

Because this book employs a mixture of common and technical terms, a glossary has been included to smooth over the rough edges. I hope that you find it useful.

AGAVACEAE

Polianthes x *blissii*

The genera *Manfreda, Polianthes,* and *Prochnyanthes* differ from *Agave* in being herbaceous and bulbous. Some authors combine *Manfreda* with *Polianthes,* but they are distinct.

Manfreda is a genus of robust herbaceous plants with rosettes of mottled, often thick, succulent leaves, and tall scapes with one flower per node. The stamens are exerted and brownish, greenish, yellowish, or whitish in color. The underground structures are cormous or rhizomatous.

Polianthes plants have bulbs with well-developed basal plates, rosettes of thin herbaceous leaves, and racemes of white, purple, red, green, or yellow flowers, usually with two, sometimes fragrant, flowers at each node. The stamens are not exerted.

Manfreda Salisbury

Twenty or more species of *Manfreda* are native to the southeastern United States, Mexico, and Central America. These are bulbous herbaceous perennials mostly with dull white, yellow, green, or brownish flowers solitary at the nodes, on a tall raceme or spike. The flowers are generally tubular, with long-exerted filaments, and generally have some kind of scent. Manfredas usually grow from slender corms or bulbs with very large basal plates or rhizomes and have succulent or thin leaves that are plain green or mottled. They do best in full sun in a dry part of the garden.

When collecting manfredas, I generally prefer to look for specimens with the greatest number of spots on the leaves, as these are the most attractive and accentuate their best features. About the only problems with *Manfreda* are grazing deer and root-knot nematodes. Avoid the use of river sand, which might contain nematodes, and give the plants a warm, sunny spot.

M. longiflora (Rose) Verhoek-Williams. A rare species from the upper Texas Rio

Manfreda maculosa

Grande Valley and adjacent Mexico. The fall-flowering scapes are 18–24 inches tall and have pinkish flowers which turn purplish red with age. They are not as tall as the other species and have striated rather than spotted leaves. Unfortunately, overgrazing and over-collecting have made finding them increasingly difficult.

M. maculosa (W. J. Hooker) Rose. A fine succulent-leaved species from south Texas, with stems about 2 feet tall. The racemes of flowers open greenish white and turn reddish with age. They have a peculiar fragrance that some people find unpleasant and medicine-like. The leaves are often spotted and are toothed along the margins. This species has been crossed with *Polianthes tuberosa*, resulting in very good waxy white-flowered hybrids which turn reddish with age.

M. potosina Verhoek-Williams 1975. Mexico, in the sandy northern desert of the state of San Luis Potosí. The flowers of this small plant look like those of *M. virginica*, but the striated, succulent leaves are more like those of *M. longiflora*.

M. sileri Verhoek-Williams. Upper Rio Grande Valley of south Texas, usually found growing under shrubbery. A handsome plant with wide glaucous flaccid spotted leaves and tall racemes of chartreuse-yellow flowers. Needs dry conditions. This plant has become rare.

M. variegata (Jacobi) Rose. South Texas and northeastern Mexico. This is a large plant with spotted or unspotted succulent foliage. The tall scapes of olive-green flowers have long chocolate stamens with the peculiar scent of menthol. I have grown this plant for many years, and it continues to increase in spite of occasional setbacks from the predations of deer.

M. virginica (Linnaeus) Salisbury ex Rose. This is the most easterly species in the United States, with racemes of sweet-scented green tubular flowers on tall scapes. Unfortunately the tepals are much reduced, but the long protruding stamens try to make up for it. It does well in the lower half of the United States, from zone 7 southward.

A few years ago Susan Verhoek-Williams crossed *M. virginica* with the tuberose (*Polianthes tuberosa*), obtaining tall (to 6 feet) hybrids with large greenish white flowers and thin, spotted leaves. Planted outside, they at first thrived but were eventually lost, but not before we learned some positive lessons in hybridizing manfredas with tuberoses. They easily set seed. Since the original cross has been lost, it should be repeated. Does well in pots.

Polianthes **Linnaeus**

Polianthes (syn. *Bravoa*) is somewhat like *Manfreda,* but the flowers are paired (except for *P. howardii* and *P. densiflora*) and showier, with thinner leaves and often well-developed ovoid bulbs. Besides the ones listed here, there are five or more additional species of white-flowered *Polianthes* species found in Mexico, each different, and from different regions and elevations. But the existing information and descriptions are confusing and of little value in determining their nomenclature. When tuberoses are crossed with the more colorful species, the fragrance is usually diluted, but the colors are enchantingly enhanced.

P. densiflora Rose. Native habitat not known, but probably Chihuahua. Formerly thought to be a separate genus, *Pseudobravoa,* because the flowers were unpaired, it is now placed in *Polianthes,* along with *P. howardii.* The tubular flowers are yellow, closely spaced, single at the nodes, and produced on short scapes.

P. geminiflora (La Llave and Lexarza) Rose 1903. A widespread, variable species found in central Mexico. It has a rosette of glossy basal leaves and paired tubular flowers in shades of red, rose, and orange. When in bloom, the plants glow like miniature Chinese lanterns. If it has a fault it is that there is too much space between the paired flowers. Were they more closely spaced they would be much more effective. *P. geminiflora* hybridizes freely with other species.

P. geminiflora var. *geminiflora* (Rose) McVaugh 1989. The type form. The flowers are in shades of pink, orange, and red and are easy to grow and flower.

P. geminiflora var. *clivicola* McVaugh 1989. Jalisco. A large form from steep, shaded slopes, barrancas, and gullies, in oak or oak-pine woods in the mountains of the Pacific slopes of Jalisco. Although it has the appearance of *P. geminiflora* in the flowers, the plant is easier to grow, and taller, with wider leaves and larger bulbs. It is usually confined in Jalisco to subtropical wooded areas where the habitat is often encircled by *P. geminiflora.* There is disagreement that this form belongs with *P. geminiflora,* and it may deserve status as a separate species.

P. graminifolia Rose 1903. Aguascalientes, Jalisco, Zacatecas. McVaugh lists this as another form of *P. geminiflora* because it has pendant red flowers, but there is strong disagreement with this treatment. In addition to the obvious foliar differences, *P. graminifolia* has slightly larger flowers. It comes from a drier part of Mexico, and it has small hairs along the leaf margins. I regard it as a separate species.

P. howardii Verhoek-Williams 1976. Colima and adjacent Jalisco. A recently discovered plant endemic to southwestern Mexico. *P. howardii* grows in partially shaded tropical deciduous forests at mid-elevations. The pendant tubular flowers are on a long raceme, solitary at the nodes, with blackish interiors and red exteriors separated by yellow, ending in green. The bulb is narrowly elongated. As the bulbs enjoy

Polianthes tuberosa

growing shallowly, they need protection in winter if left in the ground.

P. tuberosa Linnaeus 1753. Tuberose. This is an antique Mexican plant without a place to hang its hat. It probably ceased to exist as a wildflower before the coming of the conquistadores, having long been in cultivation in the gardens of the Aztecs. When grown from seed, it can be variable and more nearly approaches what can be construed as a link to wild forms. It does well in pots. Currently in cultivation is a variety known as the "Mexican Single," plus a variegated leaf form and several double forms, including one called "Pearl." All are grown for their sweet, heady fragrance. Of the older forms, one had closely spaced paired flowers, and looked somewhat like a hyacinth, but this one has ceased to be listed. *P. tuberosa* hybridizes easily with other *Polianthes* species.

Five white-flowered species are listed (Rose 1903): *P. longiflora, P. nelsonii, P. palustris, P. platyphylla,* and *P. pringlei.* At various times I may have collected them, but based on the skimpy descriptions, could not identify them.

P. sp. #1. Oaxaca. A red-tubed, green-tepaled species from Oaxaca with Christmas colors. Unfortunately the colors fade in hot weather. It is now nearly extinct due to overgrazing, over-collecting, and activities by the Mexican Highway Department. What a pity, as the nodding red-and-green tubular flowers are enchanting.

P. sp. #2. Oaxaca. A reddish-tubed smallish species from around Huajuapan de León. Bulbs similar in appearance to *P. tuberosa.* It enjoys growing at low elevations on low, sloping hills. One of the best.

P. sp. #3. Oaxaca. A tall red-tubed, yellow-tepaled species, from the Miajuatlan area of Oaxaca. Nearly extinct.

P. sp. #4. Guanajuato. A lovely roadside species with waxy flowers, shaped like a tuberose, but smaller. The flowers may be white, yellowish, or pinkish.

P. sp. #5. Nayarit. A low-elevation species, looking like a tuberose, with smaller white flowers tinged pink.

P. sp. #6. Jalisco. Found at mid-elevations with a few large white zygomorphic flowers and slender foliage and bulbs. The flowers are placed singly or in pairs at the nodes.

P. sp. #7. Durango. A slender species with white flowers, tinged purplish, flowering in August. The flowers are placed singly or sometimes in pairs at the nodes.

P. sp. #8. Guanajuato. Intermediate between sp. #4 and *P. geminiflora*. The flowers run from pure white to red. Found in the mountains north of the city of Guanajuato. Rare.

Hybrids

P. × *blissii* (*P. geminiflora* × *P. tuberosa*) combines the tuberose with the drooping orange-red flowers of *P. geminiflora* to give horizontally held pink flowers with a subtle fragrance. The flowers are paired at the nodes.

P. × *bundrantii* ('Mexican firecracker') is a modern hybrid between *P. howardii* and *P. tuberosa* that has paired flowers more closely spaced at the nodes, marked internally in shades of wine or purple and externally in red or rose and green. The bulb resembles that of a tuberose, and the plant is quite vigorous.

P. 'Sunset.' *P.* sp. #2 × *P. tuberosa*. A modern hybrid with pinkish or reddish exteriors and yellow interiors. The faintly fragrant flowers are paired at the nodes. The bulbs resemble those of tuberoses and multiply rapidly. Easy to grow in full sun.

Prochnyanthes S. Watson

A small genus allied to *Manfreda* and *Polianthes*. Found in grasslands, hillsides and rocky ravines, and pastures, commonly in oak or pine forests. Though attractive, it does poorly at lower elevations. The nodding *Fritillaria*-like flowers are paired on long pedicels on stems to 6 feet high.

P. mexicana (Zuccarini) Rose 1903. Although said to be a single species, it is found in far-flung areas within Mexico in several distinct color forms. All forms are currently lumped together, but perhaps they are in need of further revision.

Pseudobravoa Rose

P. densiflora is now considered to be in the genus *Polianthes*.

Prochnyanthes mexicana

Allium mobilense

ALLIACEAE

The onion family (Alliaceae) differs from the lily family in having the flowers produced in umbels, and from the amaryllis family in having superior ovaries. The rootstock may be a bulb, corm, or rhizome. Some species possess a characteristic alliaceous (garlic) odor when the plant tissues are bruised. Examples of the Alliaceae are *Allium, Ipheion, Leucocoryne, Nothoscordum, Tristagma,* and *Tulbaghia.*

Allium Linnaeus

The large genus *Allium* contains the culinary species such as chives, garlic, leeks, shallots, and onions, along with numerous ornamentals. There is no agreement as to the total number of species, with workers placing the number anywhere between 500 and 1,000. More than likely the number approaches the higher mark, as new species continue to be discovered. They are found around the globe in the northern hemisphere to Central America and North Africa. In South America they are replaced by the allied genus *Nothoscordum.*

Nearly all *Allium* species share the characteristic alliaceous odor of sulfur in the plant tissues when bruised. Surprisingly the flowers of many of them are delightfully fragrant, including scents of honey, hyacinths, and cloves. The Old World members of the genus are found across Europe and Siberia and around the Mediterranean in North Africa, to Asia Minor. In our warmer climates, some of these succeed while others fail, either because they need colder winters or cooler summers or because they rot if given moisture while dormant. They are well represented in North America, and the number of species found in Texas and Mexico has seen an upswing as the list continues to grow. The southernmost known *Allium* species is reported from Central America. (I have found *A. glandulosum* in the mountains of Oaxaca, Mexico, but it is also known from Honduras.) No blue-flowered species have been reported from the New World, but one yellow-flowered species (*A. coryi*) occurs in the Davis Mountains of west Texas. The vast majority of species are in shades of pink, lavender, wine-red, or white. Natives of the U.S. Southwest and Mexico are most successfully grown where there is ample moisture while growing, followed by a long dry spell when dormant. Listed below are some of the alliums that I have tried.

A. altaicum Pallas 1773. Siberia and Mongolia. This is closely allied to *A. fistulosum* but is slightly smaller. It is easy to grow and flower, but is treated here as an annual or biennial. The stems and leaves are hollow, while the umbels are torch-like, with crowded heads of creamy-white flowers. It makes a very effective accent in the border in early summer but does not last long.

A. ampeloprasum Linnaeus 1753 (syn. *A. porrum*). Wild leek, elephant garlic. Introduced from Europe by early settlers and now widely naturalized as a roadside and pasture wildflower. The bulb tastes something like garlic but is too mild to be of use where a serious garlic flavor is wanted. The dense umbels are composed of mauve florets on tall, twisting stems in early summer. Aside from culinary uses, the umbels can be used for dry winter arrangements and are particularly realistic when sprayed with mauve paint, matching the original color.

A. atropurpureum Waldstein & Kitaibel 1800. The Balkans. Firm, healthy bulbs were planted in a sunny, well-drained spot in good dirt but still failed to appear. This suggests that they are unsuited for cultivation where winters are too mild.

A. bulgaricum (Janka) Prodan. A synonym for *Nectaroscordum siculum* subsp. *bulgaricum.*

A. caeruleum Pallas 1773. Steppes of Russia. A medium-blue-flowered species, lovely and inexpensive, but unsuited to our warmer winters. They may flower the first year but will often melt away from bacterial rot even while in full bloom.

A. caesium Schrenk 1844. Siberia to Central Asia. Somewhat similar to *A. caeruleum,* but shorter, and with paler, grayish blue flowers. This is less easily obtained than *A. caeruleum.* It performed satisfactorily in a well-drained bed the first year but failed to reappear the next year.

A. canadense Linnaeus 1753. Wild garlic. Eastern half of the United States. The plants have starry white or pink florets mixed with many bulbils on stems a foot or more tall. This first New World *Allium* discovery was found in Canada around the Great Lakes, but the bulk of its population is in the lower eastern half of the United States. Usually the inflorescence consists of bulbils alone, or mixed with a few flowers, but a few modestly attractive forms have colorful red or wine bulbils with an almost respectable ratio of flowers (about 8) to the umbel. They are especially ornamental when the colorful bulbils are topped by green leaflets, giving a striking illusion of a red-and-green "Christmas" effect. One will want to avoid forms with few or no flowers. With the exception of rare floriferous forms, most are too invasive for anything but the wild garden, and likely even there. Some taxonomists recognize several related, wholly floriferous species as "varieties," such as *A. canadense* var. *ecristatum,* var. *fraseri,* var. *hyacinthoides,* var. *mobilense,* and var. *lavendulare,* but such wholesale "lumping" has been rejected by other botanists, as each form has its own geographical divisions and subdivisions. Realistically, each "variety" differs in enough separate characters (i.e., bulb, bulb coat, leaf form, umbel, flower form, habits, and habitat) to merit separate species status.

Allium canadense var. *florosum*

In the course of looking for forms with higher bud counts, a rare floriferous clone of *A. canadense* was discovered within a large colony of otherwise normal bulbiliferous forms east of Waco, Texas, and was found to be particularly decorative. It was dubbed "White Flag" for the impression it made as it waved within the large population of normal forms. It is many-flowered, with 30–60 florets of typical *A. canadense* form and a few (1–6) bulbils, and is seed-fertile. Otherwise it is identical to the normal forms. Correctly it should be designated as *A. canadense* var. *florosum,* but it has not been published as such. It has continued to maintain its amazing floriferous behavior without any invasive tendencies for more than a decade and is quite handsome.

A different form with grayish leaves and whitish or pinkish flowers was found in a ditch in the middle of bulbiliferous forms near Denton, Texas. The leaf color reminds one of *A. hyacinthoides,* but it is later-flowering and taller, with flowers more like *A. canadense.* The flowers of this one usually lack the bulbils of its bulbiliferous kin. Although a handsome plant, it is less impressive than "White Flag." Clearly these special forms have earned a prominent place in the garden and prove that if one looks long enough, one can find that elusive needle in a haystack. Perhaps they are throwbacks to a more primitive time when all alliums were seed-fertile.

A. carinatum Linnaeus 1753. Keeled garlic. Europe. I have only tried subspecies *pulchellum* and have yet to flower it or keep it for more than one season in our heat. Bulbs that I obtained showed virus mottling in the foliage. It seems to need cooler conditions than we can offer.

A. cernuum Roth 1798. Nodding onion. This allium is widely distributed across

North America, including the mountains of west Texas and northern Mexico. As might be expected from a hardy species with such a wide range, it is variable in time of bloom, color, and height (it can be 4–30 inches tall). The flowers of the nodding onion occur in shades of pink, lavender-purple, or white, appearing from late spring to fall, depending on its place of origin. In hot climates it is best grown in some shade, since it likes cool, moist situations. It makes an excellent pot plant. The nodding character is accentuated by a "crook" at the base of the umbel and repeated at the apex of the pedicels, creating a very graceful effect.

A. christophii Trautvetter 1884. Central Asia. This has failed repeatedly for me, but I once saw it flowering in the planted landscape at the local zoo. I doubt if it persisted, as it belongs to a group that routinely fails in our climate.

Allium coryi

Allium drummondii

A. coryi M. E. Jones 1930. Golden garlic. Native to the Davis Mountains of west Texas. The bulbs are small and have loose, open meshes. One of the brightest and most unusual spring-flowering North American alliums, it is becoming endangered by livestock overgrazing. In cultivation the golden garlic will occasionally extend its flowering season into the summer if precipitation and sunlight are to its liking. One can never be certain. It requires spring moisture and careful summer watering. *A. coryi* will hybridize freely with *A. drummondii*, yielding some of the loveliest color combinations within the genus, e.g., white with yellow centers and midribs, maroon-red with golden yellow centers, lavender with yellow centers, etc. The hybrids are easier to grow and maintain in a garden than *A. coryi*, as they tolerate moisture better, and they remain fertile. The trick is to get both parents to flower together, not an easy task, as *A. coryi* normally flowers several weeks later than *A. drummondii*.

A. cowanii Lindley 1823. Europe. Believed to be a selected commercial form of *A. neapolitanum*. The flowers are white. It is said that this plant came full circle when it was exported to Peru, where it escaped, naturalized, and then was re-collected and imported into Europe as a new species. See *A. neapolitanum*.

A. cyaneum Regel 1875. Northwest China. An enchanting little blue-flowered miniature with thread-like leaves, thriving in cool conditions in moist, peaty soils and unsuited to our hot, dry summers. I once obtained a small clump and was able to see it flower before it finally expired in our relentless summer heat.

Allium ecristatum

A. drummondii Regel 1875. Prairie onion. Texas, New Mexico, western Nebraska, and northeastern Mexico; prairies and hillsides in limestone areas. In its best forms this is one of the showier native species for cultivation, with loose umbels of starry flowers in pink, white, or the rare wine-red. The small bulbs have tightly meshed tan-colored tunics and increase by division. They require good drainage and full sun and will withstand average summer precipitation while dormant. When planted near *A. coryi,* it will hybridize, yielding some of the finest and most colorful *Allium* hybrids.

A. durangense Traub 1968. Mexico, state of Durango, in grassy pastures and gentle slopes east of the city of Durango. A rhizomatous species with slender, spiraling leaves. The 10–20 whitish starry flowers with pinkish crested ovaries are produced in a loose umbel in July.

A. ecristatum M. E. Jones 1935. Endemic to the Texas coastal prairie. This flowers in spring and when well grown is particularly fine, quickly forming showy clumps. The scapes are about 10 inches tall, and although the umbels are usually few-flowered (5–20), in cultivation they can become many-flowered (30–40), but will revert to their normal few-flowered condition if left alone. The starry campanulate flowers are in shades of lavender-pink, or rarely white, and have a faint fragrance. They prefer growing in moist alkaline soil in full sun but will tolerate some shade and will tolerate moisture while dormant. Although nearest to *A. hyacinthoides, A. ecristatum* has been lumped as a variety of *A. canadense,* but it differs sufficiently in all of its characters to be a different species.

A. elmendorfii M. E. Jones 1935. Sand onion. South Central Texas. *A. elmendorfii* performs best in an acid soil, as all the sand onions detest alkalinity. The bulb coats are membranous, with the outer coats having broadly spaced, reticulated, vestigial tunics, which normally do not persist. Many stalked bulblets form around the base of the bulb. The pinkish or whitish urn-shaped flowers have the fragrance of hyacinths. *A. runyonii* is identical, save that the reticulated bulb tunics are layered and persist. Since the same characters that apply to *A. elmendorfii* apply to *A. runyonii* as well, it would make more sense to make the latter a variety of *A. elmendorfii*. It is an instance in which two related geographic sandy-land forms, separated by a 30-mile band of black, alkaline clay soil, differ only in the degree of reticulation in the bulb tunics. Some workers might explain this as parallelism, but common sense suggests that both plants share a single ancestor. Where both forms overlap, it becomes impossible to determine which is which, as bulb coat characters merge.

A. eulae T. M. Howard 2001. Central Texas. Endemic to rocky outcroppings on granite hills near the Colorado River, seeking seepy places or saucer-like basins and flowering in late spring. This species enjoys full sun and is similar to *A. fraseri*, but has erect, somewhat spiraling slender gray-green leaves appearing in late summer and early fall, several months before *A. fraseri* begins leafing out. The globose bulbs of *A. eulae* may or may not have reticulated bulb coats, depending on whether they grew in wet or dry situations. Their reticulated tunics may not persist in wet situations, which they seem to favor. The umbel of starry white (rarely pinkish) flowers is scentless and many-flowered (20–90) and blooms here in late April or May on stems 18–24 inches tall. Often the flowers of *A. eulae* have spoon-shaped segments, giving them a distinct appearance from other alliums.

A. eulae, *A. texanum*, and *A. zenobiae* are among the last spring-flowering alliums to bloom in central Texas. *A. eulae* is well suited for gardens, as it is not fussy, tolerating moisture, heat, and drought with equanimity, unlike *A. fraseri*, which must have a well-drained situation.

A. fantasmoense Traub 1968. Mexico, San Luis Potosí, at Valle de las Fantasmas, flowering in autumn. Closely related to *A. glandulosum*, with which it is said to be sympatric, it is said to differ in having smaller mahogany-red flowers with more slender pedicels in a fewer-flowered umbel, and in having caniculate leaves. More likely they are the same species. A similar form has been collected in the state of Tamaulipas, with slightly paler, reddish brown flowers. All of these probably represent variations within *A. glandulosum*.

A. fistulosum Linnaeus 1753. China and Japan. Japanese bunching onion. An edible onion closely allied to *A. altaicum*, but slightly larger, with attractive torch-like heads of densely packed cream-white flowers. As the name suggests, the leaves and stems are hollow. It is widely cultivated as a vegetable and is underappreciated as an ornamental, but its many white torches can serve as a pleasing accent in a border. It is easy to grow and flower in cool weather but is not permanent during our hot, humid summers.

A. flavum Linnaeus 1753. Southern and south-central Europe. A variable evergreen species. The flowers are mostly in shades of yellow, but other colors are known, including white, orange, and reddish, with the lemon-yellow form being the most sought after. Some forms are said to be quite fragrant. The species should be a favorite in warmer climates, were it not for the fact that it will flower the first year and then die. It may be better suited as a container plant if given afternoon shade and not allowed to become too dry during dormancy.

Allium fraseri

A. fraseri (Ownbey) Shinners 1951. Central Texas, in the Edwards Plateau and hill country. The narrowly linear leaves are dark green, suberect, and spreading, and appear in winter from ovoid bulbs with heavy grayish tan reticulations. The starry campanulate flowers are faintly scented or scentless, and a greenish cream-white color, in many-flowered (16–80) umbels. They are easily grown in well-drained alkaline soil if kept reasonably dry while summer-dormant, in full sun or light shade. This form was inadvertently made the type form for the species by Marion Ownbey, who failed to note the major differences between it and *A. pseudofraseri*. Several other white-flowered Texas species (*A. eulae, A. pseudofraseri, A. texanum,* and rare white-flowered forms of *A. hyacinthoides*) are confused with *A. fraseri,* but each has its own distinctive characteristics and habits.

A. giganteum Regel 1883. Central Asia, Iran, and Afghanistan. A large, spectacular onion in the North but usually a failure in the lower South. This is lamentable, as the tall scapes support densely packed spherical umbels with hundreds of starry violet-purple flowers. The few times that I managed to flower them, the scapes were stunted and the umbels disappointingly small. I knew they were not happy here. In every case they failed to reappear the following year.

A. glandulosum Link & Otto 1828. Mexico, in states of San Luis Potosí, México, Michoacán, and Oaxaca, in wooded mountainous areas. One of a small group of alliums that form bulbs at the end of lateral rhizomes. This is a fall-flowering species with fragrant mahogany-red starry flowers. They have a small gland at the base of each segment. Several other stoloniferous Mexican species have been confused with this one but grow in wet meadows in full sun and have whitish or pinkish flowers, while this species grows at higher elevations on hillsides and mountain slopes and has brown-red flowers later in the season. It tolerates partial shade and is excellent for pots.

A. guatemalense Traub 1967. Guatemala, near Huehuetenango, on dry grassy slopes, flowering in July. A tall, robust plant bearing pale pinkish stars in loose, many-flowered umbels. The leaves are gray-green, channeled, and rather thick. Propagation is from seed, as the bulbs increase slowly by division. *A. guatemalense* is very rare in cultivation and is becoming scarce from overgrazing. It is suitable for pot culture.

A. howardii Traub 1967. West Texas, New Mexico, Arizona, and northern Mexico, on sunny hillsides and mountains. This species has membranous-coated bulbs and narrowly linear, gray-green channeled foliage. The starry white flowers are in bloom in late summer on stems less than a foot tall. Sometimes confused with the related *A. kunthii,* which is native to the central Mexican plateau. Good for pots if watered carefully.

A. huntiae Traub 1969. Mexico, state of Durango, in mountain woodlands west of the city of Durango, flowering in early summer. The membranous-coated bulbs are not rhizomatous. The lax umbel has 10–20 dainty campanulate flowers in pink, keeled darker pink, with pedicels of unequal length and spirally twisted leaves.

A. hyacinthoides Bush 1906. Endemic to north-central Texas and adjacent Oklahoma in calcareous soil. Sometimes classified as a variety of *A. canadense,* but the many-flowered umbels grow on drier chalky hills in north Texas and flower weeks earlier, with urn-shaped florets in pink or lilac, rarely white, and sweetly scented with a hyacinth-like perfume in midspring. The bluish foliage is linear and glaucous with a faint purplish edge, and the bulbs are heavily reticulated. They love an open, sunny upland spot.

A. karataviense Regel 1875. Central Asia. A popular species of modest stature with glaucous tulip-like leaves and round umbels of dingy grayish lavender stars on short stems. It is a curious allium and demurely attractive, but is handicapped by our lack of consistently cold winters and is thus not permanent in the deep South.

A. kunthii G. Don 1827. Mexico in the central plateau region. *A. kunthii* is confused with *A. howardii,* but is said to have flatter, wider, striate leaves and whitish or pinkish flowers with reddish midribs and keels. It flowers in midsummer. As Hamilton P. Traub defined the two species, plants identified as *A. kunthii* north of the Mexican border are really *A. howardii,* and those from central Mexico are *A. kunthii.* Their culture is similar.

A. longifolium (Humboldt, Bonpland, & Kunth) Sprengel 1825, emend. Traub 1968. Central Mexico, in Jalisco and Michoacán, flowering July–August. One of several rhizomatous species. Traub created a tempest in a teapot when he correctly observed that a photograph of the lectotype showed that the specimen was in the process of producing a rhizome beneath the bulb base. He was later challenged by his critics, who claimed that what he observed was not a rhizome, but roots. I have observed that most rhizome-producing bulbs produce new rhizomes in this manner, starting with a thickened, pointed basal protrusion, at first growing vertically downward, then becoming horizontal. *A. longifolium* is a tall, slender plant that has starry pinkish or whitish flowers with pinkish keels. It grows in moist meadows and cornfields in rich soil in midsummer.

Allium mannii

A. mannii Traub & Howard 1968. In poorly drained swaley pastures and ditches in heavy clay soil east of the city of Durango, Mexico, often in standing water following rains. The bulbs increase vegetatively by vertical splitting, and they usually don't form rhizomes. The evergreen leaves are grayish green and spiraling. The tall, slender scapes are nearly 2 feet high and bear 15–25 starry whitish or pinkish florets with purplish keels, opening a few at a time. They will grow well in containers if kept constantly moist in the growing season.

A. mexicanum Traub 1967. Northeastern state of Tamaulipas, Mexico. The oblong bulbs are characterized by producing coarse roots and splitting vertically. They flower in July, with 8–12 pinkish campanulate flowers, keeled purplish.

A. michoacanum Traub 1970. Mexico, state of Michoacán. This very small species is found in woodlands in the mountains east of Morelia and flowers in late summer or autumn. The umbel is few-flowered (4–7) with tiny campanulate white flowers keeled brownish. The bulbs are small and rhizomatous, and there are two to four slender leaves.

A. mobilense Regel 1875. Southeastern United States. Widespread in sandy soils of the U.S. southern coastal plains, flowering in midspring. The small flowers are faintly fragrant and have slender pedicels and small purplish ovaries. The dense umbels are many-flowered and spherical, in shades of pink or lilac. The foliage is narrowly erect, nearly rush-like, and bright green. A bulbiliferous, few-flowered form occurs near College Station, Brazos County, in central Texas, with the same dainty small flowers and slender, erect leaves. The bulbils are quite tiny. Although bulbiliferous, this species lacks the coarser aspect of *A. canadense*. Most forms of *A. mobilense* have bulbs that split into two of equal size, but forms with small basal offsets are known. Because the bulbs of *A. mobilense* are small and the bulb coats are reticulated, it has been lumped as another variety of *A. canadense*, but since *A. mobilense* is distinctive in its own physical characters, it deserves separate species rank.

A. moly Linnaeus 1753. Golden garlic. Eastern Spain and southwestern France. This resident of shady rocky areas ought to thrive in our climate but is usually a total failure. This is a shame, as it has starry golden yellow flowers and is inexpensive and widely available. The flowers are larger and lighter in color than those of our own *A. coryi.* I was successful with it the first time I tried it, but it has consistently failed for me since.

A. neapolitanum Cirillo 1788. Naples garlic. Mediterranean and Iberian Peninsula, in dry, open environs. In the Naples garlic we have an attractive white-flowered European allium, persisting as a perennial, flowering in late winter and early spring, happily reseeding itself and naturalizing in lawns. It is never a problem here, as it flowers early and then becomes dormant before the lawn is in need of its first mowing. This allium lacks the usual alliaceous odor when crushed and is excellent for cutting. Several varieties are known, including an improved commercial selection listed as *A. cowanii.*

A. nigrum Linnaeus 1762 (syn. *A. multibulbosum*). Southern Europe, North Africa, Asia Minor, and western Asia. Usually a species found growing over a wide geographical range is more likely to be adaptable to diverse growing conditions, and thus can endure garden culture better than those species endemic to small regions. *A. nigrum* is one of the few Old World alliums that seems adaptable in the deep South, when given a warm, dry garden situation. The fairly large umbels of whitish (rarely pink) flowers with greenish black ovaries are attractive. The half-dozen or so linear leaves are produced in a basal rosette. This is becoming widely available and affordable, and is worthy of a try.

A. oreophilum C. A. Meyer 1831 (syn. *A. ostrowskianum*). Asia Minor, in screes and dry, rocky places at higher elevations. Like *A. moly,* this is a lovely, inexpensive, easily obtained species, but it is also one that refuses to grow where winters are warm and where summer rainfall and high temperatures go hand in hand. After several attempts I did get to see it grow and flower in my garden, and then it failed to reappear the following year. There were two leaves per plant, and they began withering as the rounded umbels revealed broad, showy carmine-red bells. This behavior is normal for many alliums.

A. ownbeyi Traub 1968. Mexico, state of Nuevo León at the western edge of Monterrey, on the grassy slopes of Cerro del Obispado, in company with *Milla rosea.* Blooms in October, with 7–13 starry lavender-pink flowers. The spiraled leaves are broadly canaliculate, edged and ribbed with tiny denticulations. The scape is also denticulate.

A. ownbeyi shares a similar range and flowering period with *A. traubii* but grows at a lower elevation. Although the flowers of the two are similar, foliage details are slightly different. They may be forms of the same species.

A. paniculatum Linnaeus 1759. Europe and Central Asia. A variable species that is still not fully tested. It seems to go to pieces in a hot, dry situation, but does well as a pot plant if given afternoon shade and some moisture. The many-flowered umbels are hemispherical, with small bell-shaped flowers on slender pedicels of unequal lengths in late spring or early summer. Floral colors vary from pinkish to whitish to brownish or nearly gray. The narrow leaves seem to clasp one another. In my garden grows a related, unidentified form collected in Greece prior to the Second World War by a friend, the late Georgia Harris, which keys out as this species. It produces typically long, bivalved beaked spathes and bell-shaped buff-white flowers with a faint green line on each tepal. Although the flowers are more somber than colorful, it is modestly handsome because of the fluffiness of the spherical umbels. As with many of this group, the foliage begins to yellow as it begins flowering. Having managed to keep this species for more than 40 years, I feel it is safe to say that it is permanent.

A. perdulce S. V. Fraser 1939. North-central Texas, eastern New Mexico, to southeastern South Dakota and adjacent Iowa, in plains and sandy soils, flowering in early spring. The 5–25 large rosy-purple campanulate flowers have the sweet-spicy scent of cloves or *Dianthus* on scapes 4–8 inches tall. Ownbey recognized two well-marked forms, variety *perdulce* and variety *sperryi*. The type form is the most familiar and the favorite because of its bright color and intense fragrance. It prefers sand or sandy loam in full sun.

Var. *sperryi* is a remote form from west Texas with fragrant pale pink flowers and probably deserves the rank of species or subspecies.

A. potosiense Traub 1969. Mexico, state of San Luis Potosí, on dry hillsides and plains around the city of San Luis Potosí. Allied to *A. kunthii*, but smaller. The bulbs are rhizomatous and the narrow subterete foliage is channeled. The umbels of 12–14 starry campanulate flowers are white with pink keels, on stems about 8 inches tall, flowering in July and August. It needs careful watering while growing and no water at all when dormant. Traub published this new species as *A. subteretifolium* in 1968, but a year later switched the name to *A. potosiense* with no explanation. Perhaps the first name was occupied by an Old World species? In a genus as large as *Allium*, such are the possibilities.

A. pseudofraseri T. M. Howard 2001. Central Texas and Oklahoma. This species was one of several that have been lumped under *A. fraseri* (syn. *A. canadense* var. *fraseri*), but differs from that species in several characters. It is a denizen of open woodlands in acid sandy soil. The flowers are sweetly fragrant, much like *A. hyacinthoides* and *A. elmendorfii*, but are urn-shaped, on slender pedicels, like those of *A. mobilense*. The umbels are many-flowered (20–100) on stems 6–12 inches tall. The flowers are usually white, rarely pink, with pinkish or whitish anthers and greenish ovaries. The leaves are bright green, broadly spiraled, erect or suberect. The netted bulb coats are grayish tan and in many layers. The plants flower in midspring in the Post Oak Savannah, Cross Timbers, and prairies of the eastern half of Texas, in sandy soil. The type for *A. fraseri* was based on a different species, but most references to this epithet are misapplied to *A. pseudofraseri*. It makes a fine garden plant where conditions are favorable and will tolerate moisture while dormant.

A. pueblanum Traub 1968. Mexico, state of Puebla, at elevations of 6,000–7,000 feet, on rocky outcroppings in pine forests, flowering in July and August. The umbel is few-flowered (5) with whitish campanulate flowers keeled reddish, above two or three narrowly linear leaves.

A. pulchellum G. Don. A synonym for *A. carinatum* subsp. *pulchellum*.

A. ramosum Linnaeus 1753. Central Asia. This easy-to-grow allium has much the same habits as *A. tuberosum*, but the leaves are hollow rather than flat, and the umbel is funnel-like, with bell-shaped white flowers with red keels. They are said to be sweetly scented, but this has escaped my attention. Culture for this species is easy, and the plant seems permanent, but it is not very conspicuous.

A. rhizomatum Wooton & Standley 1900. New Mexico and Davis Mountains of west Texas, in transition zone in broad wooded valleys on gravelly, grassy exposure. The umbels are few-flowered, with about six campanulate white flowers that have pinkish or purplish keels. The bulbs form slender, scaly rhizomes. Ownbey acknowledged (personal correspondence, 1962), "In *Allium in Texas*, I confused *A. rhizomatum* with the Mexican *A. glandulosum*, but I now find that they are distinct." What was not then understood was that no fewer than a half-dozen distinct west Texas and Mexican *Allium* species have rhizomatous bulbs. These are *A. durangense, A. glandulosum, A. longifolium, A. michoacanum, A. potosiense*, and *A. rhizomatum*.

A. roseum Linnaeus 1753. This species is widely distributed around the Mediterranean and seems much at home in the lower South. In nature it is found in dry open spaces or where soils have been disturbed. It blooms here in spring with pinkish cup-shaped flowers intermingled with bulbils. The best forms are said to have good color and to lack the bulbils, but the ones I have from commercial sources have pale pink flowers and red bulbils. I have not found it to be an invasive weed pest.

A. runyonii Ownbey 1951. South Texas, in sandy soil. Because of its heavier bulb coats, Ownbey regarded this as a distinct species, but in reality it seems to be a variety of *A. elmendorfii* (which see), and identical in all of its characters, except for greater reticulations in the bulb coats.

A. sativum Linnaeus 1753. Garlic. The edible garlic needs no introduction, but is included here because a few forms are marginally ornamental, with many pinkish flowers in the umbel. Also they are easy to grow and can perform double duty as ornamentals and as culinary objects for the kitchen. The rule here is to plant them when the days are shortest and dig them when the days are longest. Unfortunately some people are more sensitive to the odor of garlic than are others. I am reminded of a very old movie in which a cook was instructing a stuffy character to add "a little garlic" to a recipe, whereupon he icily replied, "Sir, there is no such thing as a 'little' garlic!"

A. scaposum Bentham 1840. Mexico, state of Aguascalientes. *A. scaposum* has been confused with *A. kunthii* but is taller and more robust, with the leaves nearly terete rather than flat. The membranous-coated bulbs reproduce slowly by splitting vertically. It is a many-flowered species with starry whitish flowers that have reddish keels.

A. schoenoprasum Linnaeus 1753. Chives. Chives are another familiar double-duty edible herb, widely grown for their mild onion-like leaves, but equally worthy as an ornamental. Few people are aware that this plant's native habitat encircles the northern hemisphere, including Alaska, Canada, Washington state, Maine, and Newfoundland, and that it is quite variable over its extensive range. In addition to the usual lilac color, its flowers are sometimes found in white, pink, purple, and rose. Since they enjoy cool, moist growing conditions, they appreciate regular watering, thriving in pots if watered regularly and given a bit of shade during the hottest weather. The species name is pronounced SKEE-no-pray-sum.

A. schubertii Zuccarini 1843. North Africa and eastern Mediterranean. A personal favorite, in our climate it is inclined to be permanent. *A. schubertii* is a most unusual species with basketball-like umbels loosely composed of starry lilac flowers on pedicels of markedly unequal lengths atop a short, sturdy scape. The leaves form a rosette of about half a dozen bright green, wavy linear leaves 2½ inches wide. Though somewhat rare and expensive, *A. schubertii* is occasionally available, but is considered tender in colder climates. In spite of its price, it is an excellent investment where winters are mild. Autumn-planted seeds germinate well the following spring, and it is amazing to see how deeply the young seedlings will pull themselves into the soil, driving down nearly a foot the first season. Apparently this species likes to be planted deep so that it can revel at a cooler, moister depth.

A. senescens Linnaeus 1753. Europe and Central Asia to Siberia. German garlic. In the North, this variable rhizomatous allium is regarded as an ornamental perennial, but in the deep South it suffers from our hotter, dry summers and warmer winters. It is a pity, since the fluffy pink umbels and the attractive grayish foliage of some forms are highly regarded by northern gardeners. Would that we could grow them all, but the trade-off is that for every species we lose because of climate differences, we gain others, and that is what this book is about.

A. siculum Ucria (syn. *Nectaroscordum siculum*). Southern Europe to Asia Minor, in woodlands. Authorities disagree as to whether this genus belongs with *Allium* or in a separate genus *Nectaroscordum*. Since the differences seem minor (the number of nerves in each tepal), it is convenient to include it with *Allium*. The tall stems are topped by umbels of elegant pendulous flowers, greenish in color, flushed pinkish and edged whitish. Until recently they were commercially unobtainable, but now they are becoming widely available and as a result more affordable. Bulbs usually flower here the first season, but may fail to reappear unless kept perfectly dry while dormant, and so it probably should be regarded as an annual.

A. sphaerocephalon Linnaeus 1753. Round-headed leek. *A. sphaerocephalon*'s tall stems are topped by wine-red umbels of small, closely set, bell-like florets in early summer. These are unusual in that the central florets open first, followed by the outer florets, ultimately giving the umbel an egg-shaped appearance. The first year it flowers unfailingly, but afterward it "peters out" until it is gone. Because of this and the fact that it is readily available and inexpensive, it is worth the effort of replanting every few years. It is only marginally successful where winters are warm and its dormancy is punctuated with high heat and rainfall. The species name is curiously ended with -*on* or sometimes -*um*, depending on the authority, but the consensus is that the -*on* ending is the correct one.

A. stellatum Ker-Gawler 1813. Midwestern United States on prairies, rocky hills, and dry slopes, to north Texas, west to Wyoming and Saskatchewan. It flowers in warm climates in September–October, and the purplish pink rounded umbels are especially attractive at that time. This species is closely related to *A. cernuum*, but though the umbels nod prior to flowering, the starry flowers open widely and face outward. It is happy in a sunny, well-drained situation and is perfectly hardy to extremes of heat or cold.

A. subhirsutum Linnaeus 1753. Native to the Mediterranean in sandy, dry, or stony areas. My personal stock of this dainty allium came from a single unidentified bulb inadvertently mixed with commercially obtained bulbs of *A. neapolitanum* three decades ago. It flowered several weeks after these same *A. neapolitanum*, with two or three basal leaves with hairy margins. The umbels of starry pinkish white florets have greenish ovaries. Thirty years would pass before the descendants from that original bulb would be properly identified as *A. subhirsutum*, emphasizing its durability in the lower South. Although not commercially available, it may occasionally turn up on the lists of specialists, and it is worth seeking because of its dependability.

Allium subhirsutum

A. subteretifolium Traub 1968. Mexico. A synonym for *A. potosiense* Traub 1969. Traub published it as *A. subteretifolium* but a year later renamed it *A. potosiense* with no explanation.

A. telaponense Traub 1968. Mexico, state of México. This is said to be a small alpine species flowering in grassy meadows on the volcanic slopes of Ixtaccihuatl at elevations of 11,500 feet. The umbel is few-flowered with two or three campanulate whitish flowers with purplish keels on very short pedicels (½ inch) in late summer to autumn. There are only two narrowly linear leaves, and it may turn out to be *Nothoscordum bivalve.*

A. texanum T. M. Howard 1990. Central Texas and adjacent Oklahoma. Many-flowered (60–100) umbels of white starry flowers with greenish ovaries appear in late spring on scapes nearly 2 feet tall. The bulb coats are poorly reticulated, often lacking or not persisting, and may be membranous. The robust foliage is distinctive, being flat, about ½ inch wide, glaucous, and spiraling. This species grows in seepy, wet situations in alkaline clay soil where *A. fraseri* cannot grow, and can tolerate water while dormant. It needs to be kept well watered while flowering, or the buds will abort. Along with *A. zenobiae,* this is one of the largest-flowering Texas wild onions. *A. texanum* was previously included in *A. canadense* as variety *fraseri,* but it is obviously a distinct species with a distinctive set of physical and ecological characters.

A. traubii T. M. Howard 1967. Mexico, near the border of Coahuila and Nuevo León, in the dryish mountain peaks west of Monterrey, flowering September through October. This is a charming species with starry flowers in light pink with a darker keel. The leaves are grassy, and this species appears to be allied to *A. stellatum* and *A. cernuum,* but the flowers are upfacing. The bulbs increase by division and require a sunny, dry situation. It belongs in collections with other autumn-flowering alliums. Its cold-hardiness is unknown, but as it grew near the top of a tall mountain, with a full northern exposure, it must experience winter cold. Traub recognized two forms, differing only in how well they performed in pots.

A. triquetrum Linnaeus 1753. Lily-of-the-valley onion. England and western Mediterranean in woodlands and damp places in part shade under trees. The gracefully loose umbels are composed of nodding white bells keeled with a fine green line. Said to be invasive. As the name implies, it has a triangular, fleshy flower stem, bending over until prostrate with ripening seed. The fleshy keeled foliage repeats the triangularity of the stem, hence the name. In our climate it fails to reappear after the first season.

A. tuberosum Rottler ex Sprengel 1825. Eastern Asia. Chinese chives, garlic chives. This quasi-ornamental is so invasive that I have resorted to weed-killers to keep it in check, and failed. I finally had to dig it out by hand. The bulb-rhizomes seem impervious to anything but the most aggressive and ruthless strategy, so if you must grow it, be sure to decapitate the ripening seedheads or you may never be rid of them. With this warning aside, it has tall stems of starry greenish white flowers produced from midsummer until fall. Luckily, the foliage is a tasty substitute for chives, and thus it seems to have found its niche as a culinary herb. My advice is to snip away at it on a regular basis and make this weed justify its keep. Never allow it to set seed, for every seed will germinate and grow into more invaders!

A. vineale Linnaeus 1753. Wild garlic, crow garlic. Europe. The common form is a weed pest, widely naturalized in lawns and pastures in the United States and producing overly generous numbers of basal bulblets and aerial bulbils mixed with pinkish bell-shaped flowers. The flavor and scent of garlic predominate, but in my opinion it fails to be a culinary match for true garlic. Rare floriferous forms lacking bulbils have been reported which produce pink to red or even greenish flowers. Such forms may be interesting, but they are just as weedy as the type.

A. zenobiae Cory 1953. East and central Texas. Its discoverer, the late Victor L. Cory, was so impressed with this plant that he dubbed it the "Queen of the Texas Onions" and named it for his wife, Zenobia. Marion Ownbey, another *Allium* authority, considered it to be no more than a robust version of *A. mobilense* and lumped it as a variety within his concept of *A. canadense.* Theoretically the purpose of this concept was to make for easy identifications, but in practice it was awkward and produced as many questions as it did answers. Many of Ownbey's "varieties" were actually distinct species or subspecies, which in turn broke down into their own varieties, making for a top-heavy concept. Cory and Shinners rejected Ownbey's concept, and thus *A. zenobiae* remains in controversy. There is no question that its nearest relative is *A. mobilense,* but they differ sufficiently to justify giving them separate taxonomic rank. *A. zenobiae* is a more robust and later-flowering plant than *A. mobilense,* with larger, paler, rounder, many-flowered (30–175) umbels on scapes 2–3 feet tall. They often grow near one another, but never together. Mature bulbs of *A. zenobiae* produce one to three large, basally attached offsets, whereas most forms of *A. mobilense* split into two bulbs of equal size. The Zenobia onion flowers in May and is one of the easier species to grow, tolerating alkalinity and shade.

Ipheion Rafinesque 1836

A South American genus native to Argentina, southern Brazil, Chile, and Uruguay, and collectively called "spring star flowers," *Ipheion* has a garlic odor typical of *Allium* when crushed. In a nomenclative sense, the genus has been shuffled around and listed as *Brodiaea, Milla,* and *Triteleia,* to none of which is it remotely related, as

well as *Tristagma,* which indeed is a near relative. Early botanists apparently ignored whether some New World bulb members grew from true bulbs or corms, and
whether their tunics were membranous or reticulated. They also ignored whether
the species had solitary or multi-flowered umbels, whether the spathe valves were
split at the top only or down to the base, and whether the filaments were in one or
two rows, etc. Thus we had the seemingly never-ending transfers from one genus to
another. In the case of *Ipheion,* the plants grow from true bulbs, the flowers are
solitary, with spathe valves split only in the upper third, and the filaments are in two
rows. The flowers are often fragrant and are found in shades of blue, violet, and
purple or pure white. Rare pinkish-flowered forms are reported, but are apparently
not in cultivation. There are also species with solitary yellow or white flowers that
are now placed in the genus *Nothoscordum,* since the spathes are bivalved and split to
the base, while the flowers have filaments in a single row, rather than in two rows.
Modern terminology does not allow them to fit into other families, such as the
Themidaceae.

   I. dialystemon (Guaglianone) Crosa. A synonym for *Nothoscordum dialystemon* and
N. filipponei.

   I. hirtellum (Kunth) Herter. A synonym for *Nothoscordum hirtellum.*

   I. peregrinans (syn. *Tristagma peregrinans*). Uruguay. This was sometimes dubbed
"Rolf Fiedler" in commerce before its true identity was established. It is unique in

that it is a true, mid- to cobalt-blue-flowered (sometimes called "electric blue") species with starry,
bluntly overlapping perianth segments. It is also
unusual in that it produces bulblets at the ends of
slender stolons, while also increasing by seeds. It
needs more moisture than the other species while
growing. The flowers of this species are produced in
smaller numbers than those of the others, but they
last well in the garden. Apparently only now becoming commercially available, the blue flowers of
I. peregrinans are most welcome to spring gardens.

Ipheion peregrinans

   I. sellowianum (Kunth) Traub. A synonym for *Nothoscordum filipponei.*

   I. sessile (Philippi) Traub 1953. Chile and Uruguay. The stemless flowers are white,
striped purple, and held aloft by the elongated perianth tube, while the foliage is
low and nearly prostrate. Spring. Rare in cultivation.

   I. setaceum. A synonym for *Nothoscordum setaceum.*

   I. tweedianum (Baker) Traub. Argentina, Uruguay. Now feared to be extinct. The
nearly tubular, darkly striped white flowers were reported to be smaller than *I. uni-*

florum. The margins of the leaves were papillate and the small bulbs were solitary.

I. uniflorum (Graham) Rafinesque. The best-known member of the genus, with several important varieties. The starry, upfacing flowers are an inch or so broad, sweetly scented, and only a few inches tall. Ordinarily they are in shades of violet or whitish, suffused bluish or purplish, with purple keels. Considering their origin, the bulbs are amazingly hardy to cold, thriving out of doors in Denver, Colorado. A newer, darker purple-flowered form is available under the name 'Froyle Mill,' even though it is a seed-grown strain of var. *purpureum* rather than a true clone. This colorful form is showy and appealing as a border plant. A new robust white-flowered form, 'Alberto Castillo,' is listed as a clone but probably is a selection of var. *album,* since it is grown from seed, making it a strain. Such well-intentioned, non-botanical merchandising is frowned upon by taxonomists, who prefer to have names assigned in an orderly, systematic fashion according to the rules of the International Code of Botanical Nomenclature. Another strain receiving similar nomenclatural treatment is a seed-grown strain (a form of var. *violaceum*) widely marketed as 'Wisley Blue.' This strain was first named in the United Kingdom as an "improvement," but while attractive, it is similar to common purplish forms grown here. All colors are attractive and harmonize well, and many gardeners may wish to try them all. They are hardy, permanent, and inexpensive, and if allowed to reseed themselves they will hybridize, yielding interesting color combinations. They love reseeding themselves into lawns, which they will carpet if left undisturbed, and where they really look their best in early spring. By the time the lawn is in need of mowing, the dormant bulbs will be delightful memories.

I. vittatum (Grisebach) Traub 1949. A synonym for *Nothoscordum vittatum.*

Leucocoryne Lindley 1830

About 15 species, all native to Chile, with or without an alliaceous odor, and growing from sea level to 3,000 feet in elevation. They are related to *Nothoscordum* and *Ipheion,* and occur in white, blue, and violet. The leaves are narrowly linear, and the bivalved scape is slender with an umbel of 2–12 more or less showy pedicellate flowers, usually with three functional stamens and three large staminodes. The fragrant species are long-lasting and useful for cutting. They grow in cool weather and are wonderful for pots, or out of doors in a frost-free environment, if kept dry while dormant. They are ideal for Mediterranean climates, as in coastal California, and can be propagated from basally produced offsets or from seed.

L. alliacea Lindley has greenish white flowers with slender tepals. As the name implies, it has an alliaceous odor.

L. angustipetala has small whitish flowers with narrow, lance-shaped tepals.

L. appendiculata has white flowers with purplish appendages at the apex and yellow staminodes.

L. conferta has narrow-tepaled white flowers with yellow staminodes.

L. coquimbensis has three to ten fragrant flowers in tight umbels, pale violet-blue, striped and zoned white with green in the center. The staminodes are deep yellow. A pure white form is reported. Said to be one of the easiest of the genus to cultivate.

L. dimorphopetala (Gay) Ravenna 1978 (syn. *L. oxypetala*). Chile, Atacama and Coquimbo regions in the arid and semi-arid steppe. The flowers have six stamens and three epitepal androecium appendages.

L. ixioides (W. J. Hooker) Lindley. Glory of the sun. The most popular species, with 6–12 flowers in shades of purple, blue, or white. *L. odorata* was once considered a variety but is now regarded as a separate species, which see.

L. macropetalum has up to a dozen large white flowers per scape, with yellow staminodes. The segments are acute and lanceolate.

L. narcissioides Philippi 1860. Chile, Atacama Province. The flowers have six stamens with six androecium appendages.

L. odorata Lindley. This species has smaller, paler flowers on shorter pedicels than *L. ixioides.* These two species are the ones most apt to be encountered in cultivation.

L. pauciflora. A miniature with violet-veined white flowers and white staminodes, on short pedicels.

L. purpurea Gay has five to eight large flowers. It is arguably the most impressively flowered in the genus with its darkly colored flowers centrally marked violet-red and outwardly marked light violet-blue. The beautiful flowers are produced as the leaves begin yellowing in late spring.

L. violascens. The flowers are large, purplish or violet, with orange staminodes.

Nothoscordum Kunth 1843

The onion-like genus *Nothoscordum* replaces *Allium* in the New World below the equator. The name translates into "false garlic," since most species lack a characteristic alliaceous odor. Most have an uninteresting bland flavor, but a few, such as *N. entrerianum, N. hirtellum,* and *N. gaudichaudianum* are reported to have an alliaceous odor like that of onions. The leaves of *N. inodorum* have no odor when bruised but when chewed will leave a subtle garlicky aftertaste. *N. bivalve* is sometimes called "crow poison," an old-timers' myth, since there is no evidence that any members of this family are toxic. That name likely resulted from its being a tasteless (and therefore useless) onion-like weed, "unfit for crows." On the other hand, the flowers of many *Nothoscordum* species are wonderfully fragrant and could be recommended for this reason alone, were it not for the fact that a few are also noxious weeds. Among these are *N. nudicaule, N. inodorum,* and some of the latter's subspecies (subsp. *inodorum* and subsp. *angustius*), none of which should be admitted into civilized gardens. If you must grow them out of doors, consign them far away to the wild garden, where they can do minimal harm. In a greenhouse the weedy ones flower over much of the year, on lax stems that rampantly ripen seeds, scattering them into adjacent pots.

Until recently *Nothoscordum* was considered a small genus of mostly uninteresting weeds, but new discoveries and recollections of rare old species have changed this. There are now over 30 recognized species, some of which are choice and attractive, but many of which are rare and unavailable. This situation may improve as South American collectors become more aware that a demand exists for the smaller "miscellaneous" bulbs. Contrary to popular belief, some *Nothoscordum* species are slow to propagate and make few, if any, offsets. Some have brightly colored flowers in yellow or lilac, but most of them are white, with the keels often striped purple, brown, or green. Unlike many bulbs, they tolerate some moisture while dormant, and as a result they are surprisingly easy to grow and are most enduring. Many of them have two distinct flowering seasons, in spring and fall, and if conditions are to their liking, a few species are nearly evergreen and everblooming. All do well in pots, and some make fine garden plants in full sun, increasing slowly by the few seeds or offsets. On the other hand, one must beware of those few rampant weedy ones (cited above) which have the alarming ability to set copious seeds and numerous offsets no larger than a grain of rice. These offsets detach at the slightest movement in the digging, to contaminate the soil. So determined are they to increase that small seedlings and offsets are already forming offsets of their own! With that warning for the prolific species aside, I will list a few of the more attractive and interesting harmless forms for cultivation. Unfortunately the white-flowered species with contrasting keels predominate, and only a collector would want them all. For this reason we are grateful that there are brightly colored species with jewel-like yellow flowers, often retaining the added feature of a wonderful fragrance. Some examples of these are *N. filipponei* and *N. montevidense* and its subspecies. A potful of these will perfume an entire greenhouse. The golden yellow *N. ostenii* and *N. hirtellum* are equally attractive but lack any perceptive scent. *N. striatellum* is reported to have pale yellow flowers but apparently is not in cultivation. *N. bivalve* var. *lilacinum* has pinkish or lilac-colored flowers, which harmonize nicely with yellow or white sorts.

Nothoscordum flowers are normally produced in umbels, but several species have only solitary flowers in yellow or white. These were once classified with the genus *Ipheion* but are now considered as true *Nothoscordum* because the base chromosome number is 5 (rather than 6), the spathe is bivalved rather than univalved, and the tepals are free to the base instead of being united into a tube, while the filaments are in a single series instead of two. The saucy *N. hirtellum* has scentless golden blooms in autumn, while the equally charming *N. filipponei* has fragrant lemon-yellow flowers in spring. *N. vittatum* has solitary white flowers, keeled with a violet line. All of the solitary-flowered species make outstanding pot plants and are quite rare and scarce in cultivation.

Of the multi-flowered species with white flowers, *N. balaenense* is outstanding, since the snowy white florets are deliciously scented, and flower in spring and fall. The charming *N. castilloi* gives us a change of pace, with waxy white nocturnal flowers broadly banded a rich purple. *N. bivalve* is a reasonably well-behaved sort without the alarming invasive tendencies. There are many others that fit this category. *N. arenarium* increases very slowly for me, only by seed. Casually it looks much like *N. bivalve*, without the yellowish interiors, and with longer pedicels.

The Species

N. andalgalense Ravenna. Argentina, Catamarca Province. A recently described white-flowered species of which little is known, it is likely a spring bloomer, is reported to be somewhat similar to *N. arenarium*, and is probably not in cultivation.

N. andicolum Kunth 1843. Argentina, in Andean northwest, Bolivia, Chile, and Peru, around Lake Titicaca. A small high-elevation (10,000–12,000 feet) mountain species with four to ten funnel-shaped white flowers externally flushed purplish on short (1½–3-inch) scapes. The filaments are united at their bases. The small bulb is usually solitary and conical in shape and when boiled is used for medicinal purposes by natives. Reportedly cultivated as a greenhouse plant in the United Kingdom, where it is considered modestly attractive. There is no report of any fragrance. It may fail in hotter climates but might succeed where winters are colder. Like other alpine bulbs, it may need melting spring snows to complete its growing cycle. Perhaps precooling the bulbs by refrigerating them, as with tulips, and growing them in an unheated greenhouse might facilitate their culture.

N. andinum (Poeppig) Fuentes 1921 (syn. *Zoellnerallium andinum*). Chile, flowering in spring on arid plains. Sometimes confused with *N. andicolum*, it is taller and has one or two scapes of 4–11 florets with erect, oddly twisted, narrow white tepals and broad purplish keels. The flowers do not open wide, and the yellowish filaments are free to their bases. There are no reports of fragrance. *N. andinum* is found at lower altitudes (6,000–10,000 feet) than *N. andicolum* and might be of somewhat easier culture where winters are warmer. This species differs from other *Nothoscordum* species in having bulb coats that turn from white to purplish when dry. Mature bulbs are subglobose with many bulblets and are said to have an alliaceous odor. This plant is more strangely fascinating than beautiful. It occasionally turns up on seed lists as *Zoellnerallium andinum*. Like *N. andicolum*, it would need an alpine culture.

N. arenarium Herter 1937. Argentina. Like most *Nothoscordum* species, *N. arenarium* has tall, wiry scapes in full sun, but these become lax in part shade. There are a dozen or so starry, fragrant white flowers on pedicels of noticeably unequal lengths, produced in spring and autumn. The flowers open in the afternoon and close at sunset. The bulbs make few or no offsets and must be propagated by seed. Attractive, but rather similar to the ubiquitous *N. bivalve*.

N. balaenense Ravenna 1971. Uruguay, at Punta Ballena. This is one of my favorites. The flowers are snowy white, somewhat like those of *Allium neapolitanum*, but they appear in both spring and fall on pedicels of uniform length and are sweetly scented. The stems are not overly tall, so the plant's proportions are all in proper balance. The bulbs seem not to form offsets, but injured bulbs will heal and regenerate when cut into a few large pieces. This species' cold-hardiness is not well established, but it should be considered tender north of zone 8.

Nothoscordum balaenense

N. bivalve (Linnaeus) Britton. The ubiquitous *N. bivalve* is one of the commonest species, as it is found in the southeastern quarter of the United States, northeastern and central Mexico, Argentina, Chile, and Uruguay. The loose umbels of honey-scented flowers have pedicels of slightly unequal lengths, opening in the early afternoon and closing at sundown. The tepals are cream-white, externally striped purplish, brownish, or greenish, and the filaments and style are yellowish. The flowers are not conspicuous unless massed, but a large colony can perfume a neighborhood on warm, sunny afternoons in the spring or fall. The individual flowers open a few at time and last only a few days, so that the umbels are never crowded. As a result they become somewhat unkempt

Nothoscordum bivalve var. *lilacinum*

in appearance, with a mixture of buds, flowers, and rapidly developing seed capsules, looking as if they had slept in their clothes. On the positive side, the scapes are produced in succession in spring and fall, stopping only with winter's cold or summer's drought. Under favorable moist conditions, they may continue flowering throughout the summer. Luckily the bulbs increase with restraint, and thus the main method for propagation is by seed. I have never found their increase to be a problem in cultivation. Several forms are now recognized, with var. *bivalve* being the one most often encountered.

I recently found ultra-rare lilac-colored forms mixed within large colonies of normal white-flowered forms in south Texas. Till then, the existence of such colored forms was unknown. These are being grown as var. *lilacinum,* and they significantly expand the color range. As might be expected, they harmonize nicely with yellow-flowered forms such as *N. montevidense* var. *minarum* and the immaculate white-flowered *N. balaenense,* all being of similar size, height, fragrance, and habits and flowering at the same times in spring and fall.

N. bivalve var. *nanum.* Argentina. A stoloniferous form, otherwise identical to the type. In nature it is supposed to be smaller, but given optimum culture it becomes larger and loses this distinction. Aside from forming short stolons, it is indistinguishable from the common form.

N. boliviense Ravenna 1978. As the name suggests, this is a Bolivian species with five to nine large, funnel-shaped white flowers, sometimes tinged purplish on their outer surface, and carinate leaves. There is no report of fragrance, but this character is often overlooked by collectors and cannot be determined in dried specimens. No mention is made of offsets in the description of the bulb of *N. boliviense,* but often these may shake loose from dried specimens.

N. bonariense (Persoon) Beauverd 1909. Confused with *N. spathaceum,* or perhaps a synonym for it.

N. brevispathum Philippi 1896. Chile, in the Andes near the town of Illapel. Flowers following melting snow, in late winter or early spring, at 6,000 feet in elevation. There are umbels of three to four fairly large white flowers, keeled with a narrow purple line, on scapes 8–10 inches high. The solitary bulbs are small and grayish-coated, and the leaves are narrowly linear. The spathes were originally reported as being short, but this can be variable. There is no report of any fragrance.

N. capivarinum Ravenna 1978. Brazil, in sandy soil on the banks of the Capivari River in the state of Paraná. There are four to eight starry white flowers, keeled greenish or purplish, in the umbel. They are reported as scentless or slightly fragrant, but this may depend on the time of day. The leaves are broad (2–3½ inches), and the bulbs produce many bulblets.

N. castilloi T. M. Howard 1994. Brazil, state of Rio Grande do Sul. This is a night-blooming species that I discovered in southern Brazil in 1986 and named in honor of Alberto Castillo, a plant-collecting companion. The umbels are composed of four to six waxy white flowers, attractively keeled a rich purple. The incurved filaments are broad and flat, touching one another to form what resembles a cylinder-like trumpet. The scent is strange, sometimes sweet but more often rancid, and unusual for this genus. The flowers are crepuscular, opening at dusk and closing by sunrise. The plant's cold-hardiness is not established, but as is the case with so many of these "tender" species, it can take light frosts.

N. dialystemon (Guaglianone) Crosa 1975 (syn. *Ipheion dialystemon*). Argentina and Uruguay. The yellow-flowered *N. dialystemon* is considered a variation of *N. filipponei,* differing mainly in the filaments being free, not connate at the base. Sometimes there are also extra tepals. It blooms in spring and produces basal offsets, and like most members of this small group, it is rare in cultivation.

N. entrerianum Ravenna 1973. Argentina, in Entre Ríos Province, in sandy clay along the Paraná River. Umbels of seven to ten fragrant white flowers lacking the usual (for this genus) purple stripes. The bulbs are said to have an alliaceous odor and produce bulblets. Not in cultivation, but possibly worth growing.

N. exile Ravenna 1978. Brazil. In stony fields at Guarapuava, state of Paraná. There are seven to ten white flowers with purple keels on stems 5–12 inches high. Apparently not in cultivation.

N. filipponei Beauverd 1921 (syn. *Ipheion sellowianum*). Uruguay. A solitary-flowered species with satiny lemon-yellow blossoms and the same honey-like fragrance as *N. montevidense* and *N. bivalve.* It is quite rare in cultivation and is truly one of the crown jewels of the genus. The flowers, no taller than crocuses, open before noon and close before sunset. The leaves form a small, spreading rosette, and the bulbs form offsets slowly while maintaining live roots even when dormant. Because of this, the bulbs should never be dried out completely. Seed forms only if there is more than one clone present, which is a pity, since few people have the luxury of having extra clones.

Nothoscordum filipponei

N. gaudichaudianum Kunth 1843. Argentina and Uruguay. The tongue-twisting epithet is used for a man whose surname was Gaudichaud. Normally flowering in autumn, the plant is said to have narrow leaves and the usual starry white flowers, keeled violet and open during daylight hours. As usual, its fragrance is unreported, and there is disagreement as to whether or not it makes offsets. Perhaps this confusion stems from some taxonomists considering it as a synonym for *N. bonariense*.

N. goianum Ravenna 1978. Brazil, state of Goiás, in calcareous rocky outcroppings. A dwarf type with six to eight campanulate whitish flowers. Probably not in cultivation.

N. grossibulbum Beauverd 1908. Thought to be a synonym of *N. gaudichaudianum*.

Nothoscordum hirtellum

N. hirtellum (Kunth) Herter 1928–1929 (syn. *Ipheion hirtellum*). Argentina and Uruguay. Once considered an *Ipheion*, this solitary-flowered species blooms in autumn with golden yellow flowers keeled purplish. In flower it looks much like a small yellow-flowered *Zephyranthes*. The suberect rosulate foliage is narrow and grassy. A mature bulb is similar in size and shape to that of *N. bivalve* (½–¾ inch) and may form offsets. It is said to have a strong, near-repellent alliaceous odor when bruised. In order to get seed, there must be at least two clones. There is a variant of *N. hirtellum* with eight tepals instead of the normal complement of six. *N. hirtellum* is a wonderful pot plant, but it is very rare and scarce. Its cold-hardiness in warmer climates has not yet been established. In general, many South American bulbs, including those from Uruguay and southern Brazil, can tolerate more cold than they are credited for, but the limits need to be defined.

N. inodorum (Solander ex Aiton) Nicholson (syn. *N. fragrans, N. gracile*). Argentina and much of South America. Three subspecies are recognized: subsp. *angustius*, subsp. *inodorum*, and subsp. *nocturnum*. Each is very fragrant, interesting, and of modest appearance, but only subsp. *nocturnum* is really worthy of cultivation, since the other two are hopelessly invasive noxious weeds. My introduction to subsp. *inodorum* was initially pleasant enough, as it was taller, larger, and more powerfully scented than *N. bivalve* from Texas, and the chalky white flowers opened in the afternoon and did not close until dusk. The delightful fragrance reminded me of carnations or cloves and was especially pleasing. Some compare it to the scent of heliotrope. Only later would I learn that once planted, you can't be rid of it, short of moving to another address! Years later, in Argentina, I encountered subsp. *angustius* and again was enchanted by charming little clusters of florets colored in combinations of white, tan, and olive, with brown-purple keels. The harmonizing colors were inconspicuous, but unusual, and the powerful fragrance seemed every bit as delightful as that of subsp. *inodorum*. Subsp. *angustius* flowers in spring and fall, opening in the afternoon and closing after sunset. With any sort of good culture it will flower continuously for months, with each scape concluding its performance with capsules of unwanted seed. Unfortunately, like subsp. *inodorum*, it is a weed, fit only for the wild garden. And of course the bulbs have the usual myriads of rice-grain bulblets. It's a variable plant, differing mostly in the size and number of flowers per scape and in the size of the plant. The name suggests narrow leaves, but wider-leaved forms are known.

Subsp. *nocturnum* Ravenna is a robust nocturnal-flowering form of *N. inodorum* that is not a weed, opening in the evening and remaining open until morning, flowering in autumn and spring. It also has a wonderful scent of a different quality and produces large bulbs with a few large bulblets. While currently considered a subspecies, it seems different enough to merit separate species status. Its cold-hardiness is not established, but it probably can take some frost. Unlike other forms of the *N. inodorum* group, subsp. *nocturnum* is worthy of cultivation.

N. macranthum O. Kuntze 1908. Paraguay, at Villa Florida. The umbel has four to six white flowers, with the anthers half the length of the filaments. Probably not in cultivation.

N. mahuii Traub 1973. Chile, Santiago Province. A miniature species with three white flowers, keeled with a thin purple stripe, on scapes 2½ inches high. Said to be fine for pots. No scent reported. Traub once sent me bulbs purported to be this species, but when they flowered I could see no difference between these and *N. bivalve*, save that they were slightly smaller. Traub believed that *N. bivalve* had no scent, but he was mistaken, as it is a sweet-scented species. He either sniffed it at the wrong time of day, or his sense of smell was fading. These things happen with age, as I have learned.

N. montevidense Beauverd 1906. Uruguay, Brazil, and Argentina. Three forms are currently recognized as varieties. They grow in full sunlight in heavy clay soils in lowland fields, meadows, and roadsides, flowering in spring and fall. All are potential treasures for cultivation in our area.

Var. *montevidense* Ravenna. Argentina and Uruguay. This is the type form and is similar to the others, differing in being somewhat smaller in leaf and bulb. In the wild, scapes are one- to three-flowered, with the tiny yellow stars nestling in the grass on short stems a few inches high. When well grown in cultivation, the flowers become surprisingly large and luminous. The thread-like leaves are bright green, and the bulbs are quite small with a few tiny offsets present. They are small enough for ten bulbs to fill a 6-inch pot. With regular water and fertilizing, these can increase to five scapes per season, each bearing three to seven flowers nearly twice as large as the wild forms. This happens twice each year, and sometimes extends well into the next season.

Var. *latitepalum* (Guaglianone) Ravenna 1978. Argentina and Uruguay. This form is distinguished from the other forms of *N. montevidense* by its wider tepals. In itself this might not be a reliable feature, since I collected select wide-tepaled forms from a colony of var. *montevidense,* containing narrow- and wide-tepaled forms growing together in a pasture in the state of Entre Ríos, north of Buenos Aires. When collecting wild bulbs of any given species, one normally expects minor variations. However var. *latitepalum* is reported to have higher chromosome numbers in other parts of Argentina, and this might be enough to tip the scales supporting its status as a separate variety.

Var. *minarum* (Beauverd) Ravenna 1978. Argentina, Southern Brazil, and Uruguay. This variety has larger umbels (5- to 10-flowered) and is quite variable in its own right. In southern Brazil, I collected two forms differing mostly in the foliage. One form had dull green narrow rosulate leaves, and the other had flatter, wider leaves of a brighter green. Otherwise the numbers of flowering, umbels, habits, and bulb characters were similar. Both flower at the same time in spring and fall. The bulbs are larger than those of var. *montevidense,* and offsets are fewer, larger, and formed more slowly. Save for its yellow color, var. *minarum* looks very much like *N. bivalve,* and combines nicely with both the usual white and the lilac-colored forms. A pot filled with yellow, white, and lilac-colored flowers can be impressive, since all are similar in form, size, and fragrance.

All three varieties make wonderful pot plants, and in mild climates they can also be grown in the border out of doors in full sun and will tolerate some frost. If it is unusually cold, they may lose their leaves, but they soon recover when it warms up again. They like mid-temperatures with moisture and grow until it gets too hot. They can outdo themselves with regular watering and fertilizing. Little is known about their ability to hybridize with other species, but color combinations between var. *minarum* and *N. bivalve* var. *lilacinum* could be appealing.

N. nidulum Philippi 1896. Chile, Santiago Province. Said to be common in fertile fields, where it has been misidentified as *Allium roseum* by gardeners. The bulbs are said to be clustered, producing flat rose-colored umbels with up to ten flowers. It is unclear whether this is an *Allium,* a *Nothoscordum,* or a *Tristagma,* but it should be easy to tell.

N. nublense Ravenna 1973. Chile, in the provinces of Ñuble and Valdivia in fields and along seashores. The umbels of three to seven starry flowers are broadly funnel-shaped, often nearly rotate, and said to be intensely white, edged and keeled purple.

No fragrance is reported. The bulbs make offsets. The flowers are considered attractive, and since the plant is native to low elevations, it should thrive as a greenhouse plant in warm climates until its cold-hardiness can be tested. Not known to be cultivated in this country but worth pursuing in seed lists from Chile.

N. nudicaule (Lehmann) Guaglianone 1972. Argentina. This is allied to *N. inodorum* and shares its bad reproduction habits. The starry white, red-keeled flowers are on tall scapes and modestly pretty, opening widely at noon and remaining open until late in the afternoon. They may flower in autumn but are at their best in the spring. They have a delicious fragrance, but since the bulbs make copious offsets, plus the obligatory seeds, they can be frightfully invasive.

N. nudum Beauverd 1908. Uruguay and northeastern Argentina. This is a most unusual species, flowering in autumn from leafless scapes in advance of the foliage. There are three to six small starry white flowers in the umbel. As is the case with so many members of this genus, no fragrance is reported, but this may be an oversight by the collector. As authors often publish from dried material, fragrances are often not available to them to verify. Perhaps more interesting than beautiful, *N. nudum* might make a nice display as a pot plant when grown alongside other fall-flowering members of this genus. The bulbs are solitary, and this suggests that this species is not weedy.

N. ostenii Beauverd 1908. Uruguay. This little-known jewel is endemic to stony hills of coastal Molles. It is one of the finest species in this genus for pot culture, but unfortunately it is quite rare and scarce. There are usually two or three golden yellow flowers in the umbel, somewhat reminiscent of *Allium moly* or *A. coryi*. The flowers last nearly a week, opening in midspring before noon and closing in the evening. Soon a second scape is produced, and perhaps a third. It has been reported as having the lemon-sweet scent of *Freesia*, but mine are usually scentless, and this may be a variable character. Propagation for *N. ostenii* is a serious consideration, as it makes few seeds and no offsets. I have successfully propagated it by accidentally cutting a bulb, but this is an extreme measure for any rare bulb. Truly *N. ostenii* is a treasure to be cherished.

Nothoscordum ostenii

N. serenense Ravenna 1973. Chile, Ovalle region. A distinctive species with 3–12 large white flowers keeled brownish green. The cucullate-convex segments incurve at the tips, giving the illusion that the tepals of the flowers are hooded. Although they appear to be charming, there is a word of caution: their bulbs are said to produce many offsets. This presents no problem, as they are not yet in cultivation.

N. setaceum (Baker) Ravenna 1968 (syn. *Ipheion setaceum*). Argentina, states of Tecumán, Santa Fe, and Entre Ríos. Has solitary white flowers in spring. Formerly listed as *Ipheion setaceum*, it is now regarded as a solitary-flowered *Nothoscordum*. It may be a variety of its nearest relative, *N. vittatum*.

N. spathaceum (Poiret) Parodi 1932 (syn. *N. bonariense*). Argentina, southern Brazil, and Uruguay. A rhizomatous species of damp, low places with three to six white flowers, with leaves shorter than the scapes. The nomenclature and synonymy for this plant are confusing. In a discussion of *N. bonariense*, Ravenna (1971) regarded *N. pulchellum*, *N. gaudichaudianum*, and *N. sellowianum* as synonyms. While agreeing with Ravenna concerning the identification of *N. bonariense*, Guaglianone (1972) considered *N. spathaceum* as a synonym, while retaining *N. pulchellum* and *N. gaudichaudianum* as valid species. Crosa (1974) determined that this plant's true identity is *N. spathaceum* with *N. bonariense* as a synonym. With so much taxonomic disagreement and confusion, this is where its identity remains. It is reported to flower in spring and autumn. Although no scent is reported, it would not be surprising to learn that it is fragrant, as is so often the case in this genus. The bulbs reportedly make either basal offsets or lateral rhizomes. A plant having so much nomenclative confusion is apt to be variable, and perhaps more than one species is lumped under this identification. Taxonomically it is an interesting can of worms, but horticulturally it is too poorly understood to matter.

N. striatellum (Lindley) Kunth 1853 (syn. *N. gramineum*). Chile, from Valdivia to Calbuco. *N. striatellum* is often confused with *N. striatum*, which is a synonym for *N. bivalve*. *N. striatellum* is a rare species said to have pale yellow flowers and perhaps worthy of cultivation, but poorly known. In this respect it may be confused with a similarly colored Uruguayan natural hybrid, intermediate between *N. spathaceum* and *N. montevidense*, and later artificially duplicated.

N. texanum M. E. Jones, reported as being native to west Texas and New Mexico, is characterized by purple keels suffusing the backsides. These don't differ appreciably from similarly colored south Texas forms of *N. bivalve* that gave rise to the lilac-colored forms. Slight color variations within colonies of *N. bivalve*, though interesting, do not merit species status.

N. vernum Philippi 1896. Chile, Conan seashore, flowering in spring. There are two to five white flowers, yellowish in the tepal bases and filaments, keeled violet. No scent is reported, nor is there any report of bulblets.

N. vittatum (Grisebach) Ravenna 1968 (syn. *Ipheion vittatum*). Argentina, Southern Brazil, and Uruguay. The flowers are solitary, rarely twin-flowered, white, keeled violet. Under certain conditions they may sometimes turn pinkish violet. They are usually found growing in company with *N. gaudichaudianum*, flowering from autumn to winter. There are no reports of fragrance or cold-hardiness, but the globose bulbs are said to be solitary. This is a very rare plant in cultivation, but probably worth having as a pot plant.

Tristagma Poeppig

Chile and Argentina, in region of Andino-Patagonia. The mostly whitish flowers are in multi-flowered umbels (rarely one-flowered), with six fertile stamens. The filaments are in one row, and the spathe is bivalved. The bulb is tunicated. It is confused with the genus *Ipheion*, which see, which has solitary flowers and different spathe valves. There are about a dozen species, not especially showy, and mostly not in cultivation.

The following are listed: *T. ameghinoii, T. anemophilum, T. bivalve, T. brevipes, T. graminiflora, T. leichtlinii, T. nivale, T. patagonicum, T. poeppigiana, T. porrifolia,* and *T. subbiflora. T. peregrinans* is regarded as an *Ipheion*.

Tulbaghia Linnaeus

South Africa. Society garlic, skunk agapanthus. There are two or three species of ornamental value in a genus of about two dozen South African species. Two species are notably sweet-scented, but unfortunately some of them have the unpleasant sulfurous odor of skunk mixed with garlic, so they should not be bruised, eaten, or used for cut flowers. In spite of these warnings, some are eaten in South Africa. The umbels are composed of pendulous or semi-erect flowers with a small central crest at the base of each tepal. Only two species are cultivated, both with flowers colored mauve, but other species are known in white, yellow, or muted hues of brown or green and said not to be attractive. Oddly, while most of them have rhizomatous rootstocks, a few have corms or bulbs.

T. fragrans Verdoorn (syn. *T. simmleri*). Eastern Transvaal. The umbels of mauve or white flowers have a delicate sweet scent. They are

Tulbaghia violacea

nearly evergreen, producing broad glaucous leaves which grow from true bulbs. In our climate they persist best as pot plants.

T. violacea Harvey (syn. *T. cepacea*). Called wild garlic in South Africa, where it is native, and sometimes dubbed society garlic. Some might prefer "skunk agapanthus," as the foliage reeks when bruised. The plants are evergreen, and nearly ever-blooming in warm weather, with umbels of lilac flowers on wiry stems above the foliage. In a proper climate, they succeed as permanent garden fixtures in full sun or part shade, enduring neglect if given adequate moisture at regular intervals.

Other species sometimes cultivated are *T. Leucantha, T. capensis, T. cominsii,* and *T. caddii.*

Alstromeria cultivar
PHOTO BY BOBBY WARD

◼ ALSTROEMERIACEAE

Alstroemeria Linnaeus

Alstroemeria is a large, mostly Andean and Brazilian genus with leafy stems and clusters of showy, terminally bracted flowers. The roots are tuberous or fibrous, and the plants range from tropical to alpine regions with cultural needs varying accordingly. One species, *A. pulchella* (*A. psittacina*), a tropical summer-growing sort from Brazil, tolerates hot dry weather. In general our climate is too hot for the Andean species.

    A. caryophyllaea Herbert 1837. Brazil. A fragrant species with pink flowers.

    A. pulchella Linné (syn. *A. psittacina*). Brazil. The culture for this plant is simple, as it soon flowers and makes large clumps. The flowers in the umbel are zygomorphic, with the individual flowers compressed from top to bottom, red with a bit of green on the outside, and spotted with brown on a greenish-white background inside. The plant produces many leafy stems, and the flowering stems appear in midsummer. It is a fine sort for beginners. Perhaps some of the other Brazilian species may do as well.

    A. radula Dusén 1905. Brazil. Has spidery orange flowers.

    A. sellowiana Seubert. Another Brazilian species with fragrant flowers.

Bomarea Mirbel

Bomarea is a genus of over 100 twining leafy herbs, native to the highlands of tropical America, with tubular flowers in drooping bracted clusters. Several species are from the highlands of Mexico, ranging in color from pink, salmon, and orange to red. They are quite showy in tropical settings, vining and twining their way about the understory of trees and shrubs and terminating in brightly colored compound umbels, but they are mostly not for us. They are best grown from seed, as they are difficult to dig. They have deep and fragile root systems with a crown to which are attached long fibrous, tuberous roots, and they like moist, cool situations in which to clamber. *B. acutifolia* is sometimes listed.

Crinum × 'Parfait'

AMARYLLIDACEAE

The amaryllis family is classically distinguished from the lily family (Liliaceae) in that the ovary is inferior and flowers are produced singly or in umbels, subtended by two or more bracts. Some taxonomists have united the two groups, but this is not yet universally accepted. For convenience and practicality, I follow the older, classic treatment. Readers may decide for themselves which concept to follow. The following are some members of the Amaryllidaceae: *Agapanthus*, × *Amarcrinum*, *Amaryllis*, *Ammocharis*, *Brunsvegia*, *Calostemma*, *Chlidanthus*, *Cooperia*, *Crinum*, *Cybestetes*, *Cyrtanthus*, *Eucharis*, *Eucrosia*, *Eustephia*, *Galanthus*, *Griffinia*, *Habranthus*, *Haemanthus*, *Hannonia*, *Haylockia*, *Hieronymiela*, × *Hippeastrelia*, *Hippeastrum*, *Hymenocallis*, *Ismene*, *Ixiolirion*, *Leucojum*, *Lycoris*, *Narcissus*, *Nerine*, *Pamianthe*, *Pancratium*, *Paramongaia*, *Phaedranassa*, *Proiphys*, *Pyrolirion*, × *Rhodobranthus*, *Rhodophiala*, *Scadoxus*, *Sprekelia*, *Stenomesson*, *Sternbergia*, × *Sydneyara*, *Tapeinanthus*, *Urceolina*, *Vagaria*, *Vallota*, *Worsleya*, and *Zephyranthes*.

Agapanthus L'Héritier 1788

African lily, blue lily of the Nile. South Africa. The subfamily Agapanthoideae was moved from the Amaryllidaceae to the Alliaceae and then back to the Amaryllidaceae because of molecular and anatomical data, in spite of the fact that it has a superior ovary and an absence of amaryllid alkaloids. There are about nine blue- or white-flowered species, all with thick rhizomes and fleshy roots. *Agapanthus* is widely cultivated out of doors in tropical or subtropical settings and is ideally suited for tubs elsewhere. The large blue- or white-flowered umbels are decorative, and the plants are somewhat reminiscent of giant alliums with strap-shaped leaves that are handsome in or out of bloom. Gardeners especially welcome the wonderful range of blue colors as cut flowers or as uncommon accents in the garden. Lilies of the Nile are heavy feeders and grow well in moist, rich soil in frost-free situations with warm days and cool nights, as in coastal California or highland Mexico. Perhaps the nights are too warm for them in San Antonio, and they may require more rainfall. All tolerate a little shade but perform best in sun. They hybridize easily, and there are several cultivars from which to choose, including a double-flowered form. There are deciduous and evergreen forms, as well as miniatures and giants, varying from 1 to 4 feet tall. The following species and cultivars are recognized:

A. africanus (Linnaeus) Hoffmansegg (syn. *A. umbellatus*). Dwarf agapanthus. Evergreen, growing 1–2 feet tall, with 12–18 flowers in a smallish deep blue umbel.

A. campanulatus Leighton 1934. Deciduous, hardy, 2–3 feet high. Flowers medium blue to gentian-blue.

A. inapertus Beauvisage 1893. Deciduous, hardy. Subsp. *inapertus* grows 4–5 feet high with deep blue flowers. Subsp. *pendulus* has nodding flowers of a dull blue color.

A. nutans Leighton is deciduous and said to be hardy.

A. praecox Willdenow (syn. *A. orientalis*). Evergreen, 3–5 feet tall. The most commonly grown form, with large heads of good medium blue flowers. Var. *flore pleno* is a white-flowered form with double flowers; *A.* × 'Insignis' and *A.* × 'Peter Pan' are hybrids.

× *Amarcrinum* Coutts 1925

These are bigeneric hybrids between *Amaryllis* and *Crinum*. While I can't recommend the belladonna lily as a reliable out-of-door plant for everyone, I can recommend its bigeneric hybrids, × *Amarcrinum* (syn. × *Crinodonna*), as excellent substitutes for it in the South. Much underrated, these hybrids grow very well in zones 8, 9, and 10 when given *Crinum* culture. They also retain some of the unique spicy sweet fragrance of *Amaryllis belladonna*. There is the potential of much variety as new clones are produced. Initially, *A. belladonna* was bred to *C. moorei*, producing several pink-flowered clones such as the well-known cultivar 'Fred Howard' and the lesser-known 'Lon Delkin.'

Les Hannibal, a California breeder, developed the paler, more graceful 'Dorothy Hannibal,' while Dr. Traub also bred a number of clones: 'Traubii,' 'Donna Schumann,' 'Alma Moldenke,' and 'Vivi Taeckholm.' I have little information about these clones or how they were disposed of following his death.

More recently a new white-flowered garden clone has been discovered and added to the growing list. In this case, *A. belladonna* was insect-pollinated with a nearby *C.* × *powellii* 'Album.' This cultivar has been distributed by Herb Kelly under the name 'Born Free,' in allusion to its spontaneous origin. The flowers are a pinkish white and quite lovely, but not very free-flowering.

Other amaryllid hobbyists have created several new clones of excellent quality. The quest for new and different × *Amarcrinum* hybrids is only beginning. I see little reason why *C. moorei* and its hybrids have any particular advantage over other *Crinum* species. By storing pollen, almost any crinum can be used in seeking new and unusual × *Amarcrinum* hybrids, including those that grow well only along the Gulf Coast. × *Amarcrinum* hybrids may have a great future where crinums are ordinarily grown, as most of them seem more tolerant to cold than *Amaryllis.* New combinations in color forms seem as limitless as the *Crinum* species and hybrids available. They may have to come from California, using pollens available there, and from Gulf Coast growers, as seed production from belladonna lilies grown in the deep South is unreliable.

× *Amarine*

A bigeneric hybrid between *Amaryllis* and *Nerine.* Pink in color and lovely. Best for pot culture, as it is not known to persist out of doors in the South.

Amaryllis Linnaeus 1753

Of all the annoying nomenclature mix-ups found within the Amaryllidaceae, the name *Amaryllis* is the most vexing. Off and on it is applied to what most of us now call *Hippeastrum,* and depending on one's point of view, there are strong arguments that this is where it rightfully belongs. The controversy began with Linnaeus in 1753, when he applied the name *Amaryllis belladonna* to a member of a tropical American genus. According to the International Code of Botanical Nomenclature, the name was valid, and that should have been the end of the matter. Unfortunately, there was confusion as to which plant Linnaeus really had in mind for the name "Amaryllis" among a trio composed of the Guernsey lily (*Nerine sarniensis*), the South African Cape belladonna, and the tropical New World plants, since called *Hippeastrum* by Dean William Herbert. It was argued that *Nerine sarniensis* was the most beautiful plant to be found in the Amaryllidaceae. Later Herbert and Lamarck applied the names *Amaryllis belladonna* and *A. rosea,* respectively, to the South African genus now commonly known as the Cape belladonna. Herbert applied the generic name *Hippeastrum* to the New World plants. The argument continues in that what Linnaeus intended and what he actually did were not in agreement. William Herbert fueled the flames in making the name *Amaryllis* apply to the South African plant rather than the New World plant, to which he gave the curious name *Hippeastrum* ("horse-star").

In the middle of the twentieth century, European botanists J. R. Sealy (1939) and J. E. Dandy and F. R. Fosberg (1954) allied themselves with Herbert, and against Hamilton P. Traub, who argued that the name *Amaryllis* properly belonged to the genus of New World plants. At that point the struggle for power resulted in a stalemate. When Traub died in 1983, his critics could hardly wait to switch the name back to the South African plant, and that is where the argument currently rests. As Shakespeare said, "What's in a name? A rose by any other name would smell as sweet."

Amaryllis is now considered to be a South African monotypic genus allied to the genus *Brunsvegia*. The one species, *A. belladonna* (belladonna lily, naked ladies) is summer-dormant, flowering after the leaves in late summer or early autumn, with exquisite, perfumed flowers in shades of pink or white. It is particularly popular in zones 9 and 10 in Mediterranean climates such as coastal California, where winters are wet and mild. In our area, the flowering of these wonderful plants is not a regular occurrence, so when it does happen, it is very much appreciated. Apparently the trick is to get the foliage through the winter undamaged—not an easy feat when the mercury plunges to below 20° F several times in every decade. In such instances, foliage of *A. belladonna* is damaged, and it can take several successive mild winters for the plants to recover and flower again. But very light frosts don't seem to bother them here. The bulbs should be placed in a warm, sunny position in good soil. Gardeners advise those of us who live on the borders of zones 8 and 9 to give them the sort of treatment that they get in coastal California, with cool, rainy winters and dry summers, but I have seen them grow equally well in the highlands of southern Mexico, where they get mild, dry winters and cool, rainy summers. There, they flower earlier, in July and August. The foliage follows the flowers and remains until spring. They fruit easily, producing many small, fleshy seeds, and will hybridize with various South African amaryllids such as *Nerine, Brunsvegia,* and *Crinum*. Belladonna lilies are suitable for tub culture in zone 8, where winters are colder.

Ammocharis Herbert 1821

Ammocharis is closely allied to *Crinum*. The plants have distichous leaves alternately arranged like a sickle, and large crinum-like bulbs. The scapes are short and stocky, bearing large umbels of starry pale pink flowers, turning darker with age, with spreading segments and stamens. One species, *A. coranica*, is sometimes cultivated. The culture is the same as for *Crinum* in the

Ammocharis coranica

lower South, with full sun in the open garden in zones 9 and 10. Hybrids between *Ammocharis* and *Crinum* are known as × *Crinocharis;* they usually resemble the *Crinum* parent.

Argyropsis Herbert 1837

This genus was erected to include *Zephyranthes*-like plants with very short tepal tubes, with *A. candida* as the type form. Dean Herbert considered this as a mono-typic genus, but Pierfelice Ravenna (1971) more recently demoted *Argyropsis* to a subgenus in *Zephyranthes,* while adding several new species. As they interbreed freely with *Zephyranthes,* and their behavior is similar, it appears that this is where they belong.

Calostemma R. Brown 1810

Australia. The forms grown are *C. album, C. luteum,* and *C. purpureum,* differing from one another mainly in the color. They are somewhat similar, with *Narcissus*-like flowers in small clusters on tall stems. They flower in late summer before the narrow leaves appear, requiring minimal care in the garden, and they can take a little frost with protection. As they easily produce small, fleshy seeds, propagation is easy but slow. Give them full sun.

Chlidanthus Herbert 1821

Peru, Bolivia, northern Argentina. *Chlidanthus* species succeed best if given the cooler summer growing conditions of an alpine greenhouse. They produce umbels of trumpet-shaped flowers in yellow, red, or green striped with pink and tinged purple. Outside of California only *C. fragrans* is likely to be found in cultivation.

    C. boliviensis Traub & Nelson 1957. Bolivia, in semi-arid mountains. Umbels of long-tubed yellow flowers. Closely allied to *C. serotinus* and perhaps a variety of it.

    C. cardenasii Traub 1970. Bolivia, province of Mollevillque. Of modern introduc-tion, the flowers are tubular and green, keeled purple and suffused with pink.

    C. ehrenbergii (Klotzsch) Kunth. Like a bad penny, this name still turns up in the literature, but it is a doubtful plant erroneously ascribed to mountains of Mexico and never verified. Were it not for its (seemingly) sincere and innocent intent, this might be a candidate for a botanical hoax. It is currently believed that the plants described as *C. ehrenbergii* were actually cultivated bulbs of *C. fragrans* grown in a Mexican garden. It is unlikely that out of a group of high-elevation bulbs from the Bolivian Andes one would appear in Mexico, and then never be found again.

    C. fragrans Herbert 1837. Southern Peru. The two to four long-tubed flowers are a bright lemon-yellow with the fragrance of freesias, somewhat resembling a small bunch of *Cooperia pedunculata* flowers. As with *Hippeastrum* and *Ismene,* they were widely distributed early on. They are easy to grow, but our summer heat makes larger bulbs divide into units too small to flower after the first year. Planting them slightly deeper cools them down, but still fails to make them flower. Now nearly unobtainable in the wild because of over-collecting, they are still widely available from Dutch bulb specialists and relatively inexpensive. Perhaps Dutch growers could give us some pointers as to how they flower them and make them reach blooming size.

C. *marginatus* (Fries) Ravenna 1974 (syn. *Castellanoa marginata*). Andean Argentina, Jujuy Province at higher elevations. Each umbel contains about ten funnel-shaped flowers, which are long-tubed, with scarlet exteriors and yellow-streaked interiors. They probably require Alpine culture.

C. *soratensis* (Baker) Ravenna 1971 (syn. *Rhodophiala soratensis*). Bolivian Andes. Tubular erect flowers, two per umbel, in late summer. Closely allied to *C. boliviensis.*

C. × *traubii* Moldenke 1967 (*C. boliviensis* × *C. fragrans*). One of Dr. Traub's hybrids, and reported to be easier to grow and flower than either of its parents. The long-tubed, funnel-formed fragrant yellow flowers were seed-fertile. It is not known if they still exist, and the cross should be repeated.

C. *yaviensis* Ravenna 1974. Argentina, Jujuy Province. Flowers long-tubed, funnel-formed, in multi-flowered umbels, scarlet, banded yellow within.

Clivia Lindley 1828

Africa, in Natal. The plants in this genus lack true bulbs in the usual sense, since most of the structure is above ground and somewhat leek-like. They are bulbous to the extent that the lower part is somewhat like a green leek formed by the overlapping of leathery basal leaves. They are best suited for shade out of doors in zone 10, and pot culture elsewhere, and should be disturbed only when they need division. They need regular feedings. The flowers are in shades of orange, save for a yellow form of *C. miniata.*

C. *caulescens* R. A. Dyer. Eastern Transvaal. An epiphytic form with umbels of 15–20 drooping narrow reddish flowers, tipped green. In forest situations the basal stems can become 6 feet high. In cultivation this should be grown in leaf mold in pots.

C. × *cyrtanthiflora* (Van Houtte) Wittmack. A hybrid between *C. nobilis* and *C. miniata.* The flowers are pendulous, with inner tepals wider than the outer, and foliage wider than in either parent.

C. *gardenii* J. D. Hooker 1846. Natal and Transvaal. Has fewer but larger flowers than *C. nobilis* and narrow foliage. There are 10–14 flowers per umbel, reddish orange, tipped green, and curved downward. Pot culture.

C. miniata Regel 1854. By far the most popular species, with 12–20 spectacular erect to suberect flowers per umbel, bright orange-scarlet with a yellow throat. A yellow form is also grown. Sometimes reported as fragrant, but I have never been able to verify this. Wonderful for pots. In order for plants to reach heirloom status, they will have to be divided every few years.

C. nobilis Lindley 1823. There are 40–60 flowers per umbel, drooping, reddish yellow with green tips. The leaves are long and narrow. Lovely and fairly popular, this species can take more abuse than the others. Best in pots.

× *Coobranthus* T. M. Howard 1990

× *Coobranthus coryi* T. M. Howard 1990. This is a natural hybrid, *Cooperia peduncu-lata* × *Habranthus howardii,* native to Mamulique Pass, state of Nuevo León, Mexico. The plants are intermediate in floral characters, and were initially introduced as the

× *Coobranthus coryi*

"Laredo yellow rain lily" because they were originally found growing in a garden in Laredo. Years later, they were found growing wild at Mamulique Pass, a northern Mexican escarpment between Nuevo Laredo and Monterrey. They are self-fertile and apomictic and therefore must be seed-grown for propagation, as offsets are not ordinarily formed. The erect, lightly scented flowers are a glowing primrose-yellow, with filaments in two lengths, opening around noon. This opening time, intermediate between the two genera, suggests the plant's hybrid origin. The long, glaucous leaves are linear, and the large brownish-black-coated bulbs are somewhat elongated. A planting of these with *Cooperia pedunculata, C. morrisclintii, Zephyranthes lindleyana,* and *Z.* × 'Libra' makes a fine showing of rain lilies in pink, white, and yellow, very early in the season.

× *Cooperanthes* Lancaster 1912–1913

Hybrid crosses between the genus *Cooperia* and the genus *Zephyranthes* initially made by S. Percy Lancaster of Calcutta, India. A few natural hybrids are known to exist where the genera come together, such as × *Cooperanthes* "Labufaroseus," and × *Coobranthus coryi,* found in northeastern Mexico. Also suspect are a few species like *Zephyranthes crociflora* and *Z. refugiensis,* both of which share intermediate traits. Generally they open late in the day, with the reproductive organs centrally recessed and the flowers fragrant and lighter in color. This varies when there are back-crosses. Bigeneric hybrids between *Cooperia* and *Zephyranthes* are known as

× *Cooperanthes* "Labufaroseus"
PHOTO BY JO ANN TRIAL

× *Cooperanthes*, while bigeneric hybrids between *Cooperia* and *Habranthus* are known as × *Coobranthus*. Verifiable trigeneric hybrids involving all three are known as × *Sydneyara*, but few, if any, exist. Dr. Traub, contrary to international rules and trying to cover all of his bets, applied the vague epithet × *Sydneya* (for Sydney, Lancaster's first name) to the hybrids with either or both of the two other genera. In order to use the term correctly, the plants would have to be trigeneric hybrids, but Traub had previously merged *Cooperia* with *Zephyranthes*, weakening the use of the name *Cooperia* as a separate genus. In Tamaulipas, a form has been found that is intermediate between *C. pedunculata* and a pink native *Zephyranthes*. It was given the quaint identification of *Z. labufarosea* for commercial reasons, but the name has no scientific merit. It is obviously a natural hybrid, and has its own characteristics. The name Labufa (not "labuffa") suggests the mountain on which it is found, and *rosea* suggests the color of the flower. Thus the name could be translated as "the pink mountain."

Cooperia Herbert 1836

Cooperia species have long-tubed nocturnal flowers with erect, clustered stamens and are often included with the closely related *Zephyranthes*, but differ in that the flowers are primrose-scented, have whitish or pale yellow pollen, and open in the afternoon or evening. They are considerably hardier than most *Zephyranthes* and usually flower more quickly after rains. *Cooperia* often thrive in drier situations where most *Zephyranthes*, other than some desert species, can't survive.

    C. brasiliensis Traub 1947 (syn. *Z. brasiliensis*). This was collected in the state of Paraná, Brazil, but I can find no difference between it and the Texas form of *C. drummondii*. Except for a difference in chromosome numbers, they are identical.

    C. drummondii Herbert 1835 (syn. *Z. chlorosolen*). Native to much of Texas, Oklahoma, Kansas, Mexico, and the state of Paraná, Brazil. The solitary starry white flowers are fragrant and grow on tall stems held above coarse green leaves. The plants can flower from midsummer until fall and can vary depending on conditions, but are recognizable as a single species.

C. × 'Ivory Star.' A garden hybrid between *C. drummondii* and a yellow rain lily. The flowers look like *C. drummondii* but have slightly shorter tubes and are yellow, though they quickly fade to cream. A similar hybrid has been produced by crossing *C. brasiliensis* and *Z. pulchella.*

C. jonesii Cory 1950 (syn. *Z. jonesii*). From the Texas coastal bend, these resemble *C. drummondii,* save that they are light yellow in color and have orange-yellow pollen. The flowers fade to cream by the next morning. Both small- and large-flowered forms are known, but if you can find them, the largest-flowered forms are preferred for garden use. They are popularly thought to be natural hybrids between *Z. pulchella* and *C. drummondii,* but all of the flowers seem to be sessile, whereas true hybrids between these species would include sessile flowers and flowers with pedicels of varying lengths, paler pollen, and spreading anthers. *C. jonesii* produces starry yellow flowers from August through November, but is becoming rare from habitat encroachment.

C. kansensis W. C. Stevens 1938. Appears to be a form of *C. drummondii* that has extended its range north from Oklahoma into Kansas.

C. morrisclintii (Traub and Howard) T. M. Howard 2001 (syn. *Z. morrisclintii*). Mexico, state of Nuevo León. This is an early pink-flowered form with floral segments opening in two stages. The flower cracks open the first evening, and by the next morning the outer three tepals open wide while the inner trio open only partially. Not until the next afternoon do they open to a crocus-like form. As with other *Cooperia,* the erect stamens stick out from the flower, but the stigma is hidden deep in the throat, making them self-pollinating. There is a faint fragrance. The broad, flat leaves are long and linear, and because the bulbs are usually solitary, they must be propagated by seed. They flower from April to May, and occasionally after that.

Cooperia morrisclintii

C. pedunculata Herbert 1837 (syn. *Z. drummondii*). Giant prairie lily. Texas and Mexico, in states of Nuevo León, Tamaulipas, and Coahuila. This species can flower in as little as 22 hours after a rain, while *Zephyranthes* may be delayed for several more days. Over its wide range, *C. pedunculata* varies only slightly in the width of the leaves and the size of the flowers. The large bulbs eventually form offsets. The grayish leaves are broadly linear, and the flowers are white, with the reproductive structures hidden in the throat. As a result of this, they are self-pollinating, making it difficult to hybridize them without first removing the tepals in advance of opening. They appear in March or April and, depending on the weather, flower again at odd times in the summer and fall. They will grow in sun or shade.

Cooperia smallii
PHOTO BY JO ANN TRIAL

C. smallii Alexander 1930 (syn. *Z. smallii*). Known only from Cameron County, at the southern tip of Texas. The flowers open bright lemon-yellow, but fade overnight to ivory-yellow. *C. smallii* differs from the other yellow-flowered species, *C. jonesii*, in having shorter tubes, shorter pedicels, wider, rounder segments, and paler pollen, and opening earlier in the afternoon. There are several variable forms; the best ones are large and smooth in texture. Thought to be of natural hybrid origin, they put on a fine show from midsummer until fall. They were once common in fields around Brownsville but are disappearing, as more of the land in which they grow has been developed for homes and businesses.

C. traubii Hayward 1936 (syn. *Z. traubii*). Coastal Texas. Similar to *C. drummondii*, but flowering later from smaller bulbs, with narrower leaves and larger flowers that have longer tubes and more reflexing habits. Pinkish forms are sometimes found. The stigma and style frequently tower above the anthers, giving the flower an airy appearance. Perhaps this elevated stigma explains its poor seed set, as it has little chance to self-pollinate.

A similar long-tubed form of *C. drummondii* or *C. traubii* grows in north-central Mexico at higher elevations and begins flowering early, lasting well into the season. It is hard to define as a species. This one has narrow leaves and excellent *C. traubii*–like form and will sometimes cross with other species if hand-pollinated. For lack of a better identification it is called the "Mexican *traubii*."

×*Crinodonna* Ragionieri ex Traub 1961

A synonym for *Amarcrinum*, which see.

Crinum Linnaeus 1753

Crinums are to warmer climates what the genus *Lilium* is to colder climates, replacing true lilies in the tropics and subtropics. Indeed, the word *crinum* comes from the Greek *crinon*, which translates as *lily*. For this reason, it seems redundant to call them "crinum lilies." The genus is cosmopolitan, with species found in tropical and temperate Africa, tropical Asia, temperate Japan, Australia, the Pacific Islands, and tropical and temperate America. There are more than 50 species. Mexico and Guatemala have proved to be a wonderful source for unusual tropical crinums.

J. G. Baker erected three subgenera on the basis of the floral form, position of the filaments, curvature of the tepal tube, and width of the segments. The subgenus *Stenaster* included species with narrowly linear segments, spreading or reflexed, with flowers erectly held. The subgenus *Platyaster* had segments a bit wider at the middle. These two subgenera have since been combined as the subgenus *Crinum.*

In subgenus *Codonocrinum* the perianth is funnel-shaped, the tubes permanently curved, the floral segments oblong and erectly held, the stamens and style contiguous, fasciculate, and declinate, and flowers have a wide range of colors. Some of the loveliest forms are to be found in the hybrids between the subgenus *Codonocrinum* and subgenus *Crinum.*

Culture

In warm climates, crinums are permanent landscape plants living for many generations with minimal care. Because of this, a *Crinum* bulb represents an investment, like a shrub or tree rather than a replaceable annual or perennial. This is just as well, as crinums cost more than most other bulbs, because of labor in digging and (sometimes) slow reproduction.

Except for the *C. asiaticum* group, dividing a clump of crinums can be very labor-intensive, as often the large bulbs grow deeply, with root systems that can easily spread to 6 feet in all directions. Digging requires a lot of muscle and must be done carefully, digging a deep circular trench below the level of the bulb bases and then undercutting the roots so as not to damage the bulbs in the process. It takes time for them to recover and form a new root system. One must have good tools with strong handles for this. A sharp-shooter shovel with a metal handle is best, if you can find one. Broken handles can make the digging costly.

Crinums are gross feeders that appreciate rich soils, and established clumps are wonderful in the landscape, taking the place of small shrubs. Except for a few desert crinums, they do best in climates with high humidity and high annual rainfall or where they are irrigated regularly while in active growth. A few kinds are hardy to zone 7, and nearly all will do well in zones 8 and 9. Most appreciate at least half a day of sun, but a few tolerate some shade.

Soil pH is not too important, as crinums seem to adapt to any soil rich enough to sustain their needs. Mosaic viruses can be a problem, since there is no cure, but most affected crinums are able to coexist with the disease, although it results in unattractively mottled leaves and the affected bulbs may serve as hosts for the spreading of the disease to less-resistant plants. Some crinums seem to recover from the virus from season to season. See the section on diseases and pests in the Introduction.

Crinums usually bloom in the warmer months, from spring until fall, but each variety has its own flowering season. In warmest climates a few are nearly ever-blooming, and mature bulbs of all will produce a succession of scapes for weeks or months.

Hybridization

In order to hybridize crinums, one should gather many species plus hybrids that are known to set seed freely. This can take time. Pollen fertility is a given and hardly worth worrying about. The experience of modern breeders proves that nearly all crinum pollens are fertile, even those from triploids. Only the fertility percentages differ, and not enough to be a problem. The difficult part lies in selecting the proper seed parent, since many hybrids seldom set seed and thus can only be used as pollen parents. But if we use them on known seed-fertile parents, the rest is easy. In order to obtain solid-colored offspring, one parent should be of a solid color, as there are few such species in nature. In any case, many modern complex hybrids are seed-fertile.

Realistically you won't want, or need, too many seeds or seedlings from one cross, as they will eventually require space and individual care to bring them into flower 2–15 years later. In general, most of the species make few, if any, offsets, but lots of seeds. Most of the hybrids make plenty of offsets, but few seeds.

The following species are sometimes cultivated:

Subgenus *Codonocrinum* Baker 1888

C. album (Forsskål) Herbert 1837 (syn. *C. yemense*). Highlands of Yemen. This species has pleasing white trumpets and red-brown tubes. The flowers are fleeting, opening at sunset and drooping by morning. Though slow to establish, once rooted, it increases slowly by offsets and by the very large seeds. It is said to be one of the hardiest species. Its semi-erect foliage is similar to that of *C. zeylanicum*, and several unrelated hybrids have been erroneously ascribed to it. In truth, in spite of similar leaf forms, *C. album* has had a limited effect, if any, in the production of *Crinum* hybrids, whereas *C. zeylanicum* has been widely used in the deep South. At least two forms of *C. album* are known. The first form is described above; the second has a more open aspect, with longer, more narrowly trumpeted flowers. They flower at the same time, and the seeds of both are similar. The second form is sometimes erroneously listed as *C. abyssinicum,* which is really a much smaller, very different plant.

C. bulbispermum (Burman) Milne-Redhead & Schweickerdt 1752. A widely cultivated species with long, tapering glaucous leaves, and always among the first to flower each spring. It is probably the hardiest species. Since it makes many seeds, it has been widely used in the production of many hybrids. The clusters of trumpet-like flowers may be white, white with rose stripes, or (rarely) dark rose-red and often have an odd, chlorine-bleach scent. Offset production, if any, is slow, and it is best propagated from seed. It often makes so many seeds that there isn't enough space to grow them all to maturity.

C. fimbriatulum Baker 1888. West Africa. This is closely allied to *C. scabrum*. It has somewhat similar flowers but with recurving tips, and is taller, with scapes 5–6 feet high and longer, paler foliage. I grew mine from seed, and though it seems to have reached maturity, it has not yet flowered. Photos taken in Africa show it as having beautiful wide-open white flowers with red or pink stripes. It is nearly unknown in cultivation but seems to have a bright future. Keep well-watered while in active growth.

C. flaccidum Herbert 1837. Australia. The leaves are narrow and sprawling above a short "neck," and the wide open flowers vary in number in the umbel. The colors vary from white to yellow, or even pink or amber. The yellow form is unusual and popular in gardens, but the white form has larger flowers. It is said to have a putrid scent; I have not found this to be so in the forms I have grown, but then my aging "smeller" no longer serves me well. This species rarely or seldom makes offsets, but makes many seeds which are fine for production of new hybrids. The name *flac-cidum* is often mispronounced as "flass-idum" but is correctly "flax-idum."

C. graminicola. A species collected in South Africa and grown by Dave Lehmiller in Sour Lake, Texas.

Crinum flaccidum
PHOTO BY MARCIA WILSON, COURTESY OF MRS. ALAN CLINT

Crinum graminicola
PHOTO BY DAVE LEHMILLER

C. jagus (J. Thompson) J. E. Dandy 1939 (syn. *C. giganteum*). West Africa. One of a varied group with petioled, erect thin leaves, all having zygomorphic white-chaliced flowers with a wonderful vanilla-like scent. It was introduced early on in South America, during the slave trade, and since then has been "rediscovered" and re-named several times. My own experience is that it needs an acid sandy soil to grow well. It seldom makes seed, so perhaps several clones are needed. The bulbs of some forms become quite large, forming offsets and making dense clumps.

C. lugardiae N. E. Brown 1903. Southern Africa. A seldom-seen plant, but welcome in southern gardens, where it grows well with ordinary culture. The tight tufts of leaves are erect, narrow, and wavy when very dry. It makes no offsets but is easily propagated by the abundant seeds. The short four- to ten-flowered umbels have white flowers with short pedicels, black anthers, and a pinkish midrib, somewhat resembling *C. macowanii*. Probably of value in producing smaller hybrids.

C. macowanii Baker 1878. A variable southern African species, also found in east Africa to Ethiopia. It makes no offsets but is highly fertile, and several forms are known. They are much varied in size. The variable leaves are in several shades of green, especially in southern Africa. The east African form has good vigor, and glaucous or glaucescent leaves. The buds are balloon-like prior to opening, and the wide-tepaled white flowers may have pinkish keels. Unfortunately the flowers are often fleeting, drooping early in the day. This fault can be bred out in the second or third generation, when the flowers stand up better in the heat and often increase by offsets.

"Mayan Moon." A tropical African crinum related to *C. jagus*, or possibly *C. scillifolia*. It is of unknown origin, is widely cultivated in Guatemala, and was introduced into the United States in 1967. It will tolerate moist alkaline soils to zone 8, producing large white goblets with a greenish yellow center and erect, strap-shaped narrow leaves. It has the sweetly fragrant odor of vanilla and has flowered regularly here for the past 30 years but never makes seed.

C. moorei J. D. Hooker 1887. A southern African species with light to dark pink goblet-like flowers. It thrives in California and the temperate mid-elevations of Mexico. Some pink-flowered forms and the white-flowered var. *schmidtii* do equally well in the humid climate of the South. They become somewhat dormant in the heat of summer but grow actively in cooler weather. *C. moorei* has served admirably in the creation of hybrids, particularly in the *C.* × *powellii* forms.

C. moorei var. *schmidtii* Regel in late 1800's. A vigorous white-flowered form of *C. moorei*, flowering in early summer and useful for hybrid work. The flowers open one or two at a time and are increased by seed or offsets. It is a good breeder.

C. paludosum Verdoorn 1973. Southern Africa. A species that in moist soils rivals *C. macowanii* in size, but has fewer flowers in the umbel. It is hardy and grows well under ordinary garden conditions in the South. The lorate foliage is arched, and each umbel has four to eight large white trumpet-like chalices with a light stripe, aging pinkish. It is propagated by seed, as it makes no offsets. Because of its very small size (8–22 inches), it may be valuable in the development of smaller hybrids.

C. rattrayii hort. 1905. Thought to be from Uganda. This is questionably thought to be a hybrid. It is much like *C. jagus* but has larger, broader, thicker foliage. It blooms a couple of weeks later with slightly smaller flowers than *C. jagus,* and the white chalices have the same sweet vanilla-like fragrance in early summer. Seed production is nearly unknown, but the bulb increases well by offsets. It may be possible to get seed if a different clone is handy. Hardy to zone 8 with protection.

C. scabrum Herbert 1810. Tropical Africa. In its best forms this is one of the finest species to grow and hybridize. In most forms the flowers open wide and are well displayed, but one form from Florida has a smallish trumpet-like flower that fails to open wide. The leaves are low and wavy with scabrous margins; thus the name. With good culture they may grow to 6 feet long. It flowers here in May with four to eight colorful, red-striped white flowers. The floral stripes begin at the inner base of the flower, terminating before reaching the tips. The fragrance is strong, sweet, and spicy. This same pattern is repeated in its hybrids, and this is one way one can tell hybrids of *C. scabrum* from *C. zeylanicum* hybrids, in which the centers are white and the stripes begin at the middle, ending at the hooked apex of each tepal.

C. scabrum is also known for producing solid pink or red hybrids, especially when the other parent is solid-colored. The deep red coloring of the stripe is transferred to the seedlings in the form of a solid rose or red color.

C. zeylanicum Linnaeus 1771. A form found around the Indian Ocean. The plants may vary from short and squatty to tall. Popular in the South about the Gulf rim in zones 9 and 10, where it does well. The leaf margins are smooth. The stripe on each tepal begins about midway and terminates at the strongly hooked apex. Often this same character is repeated in its hybrids. The stripes are darkest on the keels (exterior) and vary from pink to darkest red. The scent is sweet and anise-like. Flowers later than *C. scabrum* and produces a few seeds.

Subgenus *Crinum* Baker 1888

Includes what we once knew as the *Stenaster* and *Platyaster* forms of J. G. Baker. Perianth erect, hypocratiform, segments linear or lanceolate. Stamens spreading.

C. americanum Linnaeus 1752. An American aquatic stoloniferous form, found about the Gulf Coast, from Florida to Texas in coastal and mangrove swamps. The erect leaves are blunt-tipped, and the scapes have four to eight upfacing white flowers of a salver shape. Useful in producing hybrids with wide open forms but which usually need extra water to do well.

Forma *erubescens* Aiton 1780, from Central and South America, is similar to *C. americanum* but is larger in all its parts and has a rust-colored scape and darker foliage. I was able to help resolve the identity of this plant when I made a trip to southern Brazil to collect it growing wild. It turned out that the plant that we were growing back home as *C. americanum* var. "*robustum*," for lack of better identification, was in reality forma *erubescens*, a large dry-land form of *C. americanum*. I have made crosses with it involving *C. scabrum*, resulting in a variety of *C.* × *submersum* forms.

C. amoenum Roxburgh 1807. India. A riverine species with bulbs the size and shape of baseballs. The flowers are similar to those of *C. americanum*, white with narrow segments and red filaments. They are short-lived, opening in the evening and closing before the next morning. *C. amoenum* has been used to make a few hybrids.

C. asiaticum Linnaeus 1732. Tropical Asia. A large plant with upright leaves and large leek-like bulbs, bearing a succession of spidery white flowers on tall scapes. Popular around the Gulf Coast in zones 9–10. There are lesser-known forms with red leaves which are even more attractive but also more tender. Such forms must be grown in tubs north of zone 9. These forms impart the red-leaved color to their hybrids.

Forma *japonicum* Baker 1888. A small version of *C. asiaticum* that grows in marshes and sand dunes on the shores of Japan and tropical Asia and is in cultivation in this country.

C. buphanoides Welwitsch 1878. Southern Africa. A species with arching distichous ensiform leaves and a short scape somewhat like that of *C. asiaticum*. The 20–30 narrow-tepaled flowers are a pinkish white. A few specimens have been introduced around the Gulf states and southern California.

C. cruentum Ker-Gawler 1837. Mexico, states of México and Oaxaca. A Mexican species allied to *C. americanum* and *C. loddigesianum*. The long-tubed, narrow-tepaled pinkish or whitish flowers are found growing in running water of mountain streams, and sometimes choking waterways. A few striped hybrids were made from this species by the late Luther Bundrant.

C. loddigesianum Herbert 1837. Mexico. Similar to *C. americanum* and *C. strictum*, but the narrow-tepaled flowers are white, tipped maroon, and grow in water in coastal Veracruz, Mexico. Rare in cultivation. The species is now under heavy pressure, as its mangrove habitat has been drained to grow bananas. Where *C. loddigesianum* comes in contact with the naturalized *C. zeylanicum*, hybrids can result.

C. oliganthum Urban 1919. Minicrinum. West Indies. A Lilliputian version of *C. americanum*, with the same habits, but the entire plant is less than half as large. There are one to three flowers per scape. It will tolerate growing on dry land if kept somewhat moist.

C. procerum Herbert & Carey 1837. Allied to *C. asiaticum* but said to differ by often having a basal stump, plus many offsets. As with *C. asiaticum*, there are several tender, red-leaved forms which will need pot culture north of zone 10. A few red-leaved hybrids have been made using these, and the progeny is handsome and hardier, maintaining much of the red-leaved color.

C. xanthophyllum Hannibal 1970–1971. Fiji and the South Seas. This one has arching lime-green foliage, turning yellowish with age, making for a very attractive foliage plant. The short 12-inch scape has 20–25 narrow-tepaled white blossoms in the umbel. For pots if grown outside of frost-free areas north of zone 10.

Hybrids

Arriving at the parentage of old hybrids can be a painfully difficult chore. Beginning with Les Hannibal's mini-monograph in 1971, there was a lot of admitted guesswork, some of which was wrong, but which served as a guideline for those seriously interested in the genetics of *Crinum* breeding. Interested students had to work by backcrossing, taking into account major characteristics of each plant. The initial effort took years of serious breeding. Even now breeders are not sure of all parentages. In some cases the results were unexpected, as with the parentage of 'Peach Blow' and 'Ellen Bosanquet.' In all cases the most difficult problems were in ascertaining the parentages where one parent was already a hybrid. It was easier at the

Crinum x *amabile*
PHOTO BY HERBERT KELLY JR.

beginning, when we were dealing mostly with first-generation hybrids. Eventually, as we get into more complex hybrids, it will be nearly impossible to determine parentage without some documentation.

C. x *amabile* J. Donn 1810 and *C.* x *augustum* Roxburgh. Crinum hybrids often exist naturally where the two parental species come together. Perhaps the first known hybrids resulted from forms of *C. zeylanicum* and *C. procerum,* which sometimes coexist around the Indian Ocean. The results in this case were hybrids larger than their parents with huge flowers up to 11 inches across. The hybrids were sterile, but increased quickly by offsets. In the case of *C.* x *amabile,* the leaves are erect, making for a tall plant, but in the case of *C.* x *augustum* the leaves are suberect, spreading at the center, making for a squattier plant. Otherwise they hardly differ. Both have highly burnished scapes, topped by huge umbels of very large, fragrant, patent flowers with narrowish tepals. The flowers of each are purplish rose and pinkish white, and always need staking. They are produced throughout the season. Both forms are tender and are best not grown north of zone 10 except in tubs.

During Herbert's time (1810–1837), hybridizing crinums became fashionable, and many gardeners got into it. This was the first generation of crinum breeders, and most crinum hybrids were given grex names. The next generation of breeders came during the middle to late part of the reign of Queen Victoria, which included the Civil War era. Another bunch of hybrids came near the turn of the century and around the time of the First World War and included many of the popular hybrids we know today. There was then a dearth of hybrids until after the Second World War. But the hobby was revived again in the fifties and sixties. During this period, breeders such as Les Hannibal, Luther Bundrant, Fred Jones, Kitty Clint, Grace Hinshaw, Wyndham Hayward, Hamilton Traub, Herb Kelly, and I got into the act.

Of the earliest hybrids, *C.* × *herbertii* Sweet and *C.* × *powellii* L. H. Bailey in their many forms are still among the best, as they are hardy and of easy culture, but even more wonderful hybrids are now starting to become available. These can be classified according to their colors and floral habits.

WHITE-FLOWERED HYBRIDS

The "Burbank hybrid" came from the late Miss Willie Mae Kell circa 1960. It is mentioned here only because it received wide distribution in the South. It is a large plant with long-necked bulbs, erect foliage, and large white flowers that never fully open. Otherwise the flowers would be enormous. It flowers here in late summer. It is said to set seed easily, but my clone never does. Except for harking back to Luther Burbank's time, it is not really worth growing.

'Catherine,' 'Miss Elsie,' and 'Seven Sisters.' These deserve a grex name, as they are hybrids between *C. americanum* (or *C. americanum* forma *erubescens*) and *C. bulbispermum* and are all somewhat similar. They increase well, with narrow erect foliage and narrow-tepaled, patent white flowers. One will not want them all, but any one of them is worth having.

Crinum × "Christopher lily"

The "Christopher lily" was introduced into Jacksonville, Florida, by the Christopher family. The breeder is unknown. This popular Florida crinum may have resulted from crossing *C. jagus* with the related, smaller *C. podophyllum*. The late Henry Nehrling thought it to be of hybrid origin. A dwarfish plant, it flowers in a very short season in early summer, making many offsets but no seed. The handsome, fragrant white flowers are tulip-shaped. In an effort to modernize the name it was suggested that because of the association of the name Christopher with Christopher Columbus, it must bloom in October, presumably around Columbus Day, and should be called "Saint Christopher." But the fact is that it flowers here in early June, not October, and Christopher Columbus has never been a saint. Thus it is better to leave it as "Christopher lily" for the Jacksonville Christopher family that introduced it. The leaves are thin and erect and tend to be chlorotic in alkaline soils. Moreover, the leaves of those I have seen in alkaline soils look suspiciously virused, and the plant seems happiest in an acid situation.

Crinum × 'Ollene'

'Moonglow' and 'Ollene.' T. M. Howard 1962. These smallish hybrids between 'Seven Sisters' and *C. bulbispermum* var. *album* have well-shaped patent white flowers with wide tepals. The foliage is deep green, narrowly erect, and slightly arched.

'Old Maid' and 'Maiden's Blush.' T. M. Howard 1962. These two siblings are from crosses between *C. moorei* and *C. zeylanicum.* The flowers of 'Maiden's Blush' are white, and those of 'Old Maid' are white with a pale pink stripe. They were introduced to cultivation about 30 years ago, and 'Old Maid' has received wide acceptance. The cross is similar to the one that spawned the pink 'J. C. Harvey,' with similar leaves and habits, but different flower color.

C. × *powellii* 'Album.' Of the pure whites, this is perhaps the best-known for spring and early summer bloom. It is grown by the zillions as a cut flower in southern Mexico for weddings and funerals, and is often seen in churches. The originator is unknown, but it is one of the turn-of-the-century European hybrids and still ranks highly because it has snowy white funnel-shaped flowers. Unfortunately, it rarely bears seed, so it has seldom been used in breeding.

'White Prince' and 'White Mogul' are Les Hannibal hybrids, from crosses involving *C. album* and *C. moorei.* They flower in midsummer and are vaguely similar, rating well among the more recent white-flowered introductions. 'White Mogul' flowers earliest.

'White Queen.' Luther Burbank. Introduced by William H. Henderson, former assistant to Luther Burbank, circa 1936. This one has pure white trumpets sharply recurving at the tips and is really beautiful, being a cross of *C.* × *powellii* 'Album' × *C. macowanii.* It would be even more endearing were it not for the fact that the flowers normally begin drooping at daybreak in our climate, but a cool, wet spell can make them last until noon. It flowers early in the season and increases well, producing quite a bit of seed.

PINK-FLOWERED HYBRIDS

'Alamo Village' is a very old variety of unknown origin. I originally applied the name temporarily as a "handle" for unknown bulbs dug in the early sixties at Alamo Village, near Brackettville, Texas; this shows how temporary names become permanent. The narrow-tepaled flowers are a pale pink and are produced on stems 1½ feet tall. I am stumped as to its ancestry, but suspect that one parent may be *C. americanum.*

'Bloody Mary.' Marcia Clint Wilson, circa 1983. A natural garden hybrid between the red-leaved *C. asiaticum* and *C. × powellii* 'Roseum.' It was one of two seedlings taken from the late Marcia Wilson's garden as red-leaved volunteers. The plant is large, with partially erect reddish leaves. The narrow-tepaled flowers are pale pink, ruffled, and clustered together. Although it increases slowly, it produces no seed. It is hardier and showier than its red-leaved parent. Another person took the other seedling, which had similar red leaves. When it matured, the flowers were a lovely rose color. It was dubbed 'Sangria' and looked much like a pink *Nerine*. Either clone is well worth having.

'Bradley Giant' is a large, well-formed Australian hybrid of *C. moorei* ancestry in a good shade of pink. It produces a few seeds. When the late Luther Bundrant pollinated it with *C. scabrum,* he produced 'Birthday Girl,' one of the prettiest of the new wine-red-flowered hybrids.

'Cape Dawn.' Les Hannibal, circa 1961. One of several polyploid crosses using an F-2 form of *C. burbankii* on a highly colored form of *C. bulbispermum*. A fine large plant with long pedicels, but seldom offsetting. It is probably best duplicated from seed in the form of a strain rather than a clone.

'Cecil Houdyshel.' Circa 1916. The hybridizer, California nurseryman Cecil Houdyshel, thought so much of this one that he named it for himself. It is an attractive plant with rose-colored trumpets and has been grown since early in the twentieth century. A tall tetraploid *powellii* type, its seed-producing ability is small but consistent, and it has yielded several good hybrids. It seems to be in flower throughout much of the summer and is one of those near-everblooming crinums that we would not care to be without, though it is now surpassed in other ways by many newer hybrids.

'Claude Davis.' A large 'Cape Dawn' or *C. × powellii* type hybrid named for its breeder, Claude Davis, a Louisiana nurseryman from Baton Rouge. It has large pinkish rose flowers with narrowish segments and longish petioles in late spring.

C. × eboraci Herbert, early 1800's, in its 'Twelve Apostles' form, is another variety introduced into this country years ago. This form was a cross of *C. bulbispermum* × *C. asiaticum,* but along the way it gained respectability as a garden plant and was given the clonal name 'Twelve Apostles.' In this case the (usually) 12 flowers are pinkish white and of semi-patent form, with somewhat narrow tepals.

'Elina.' Grace Hinshaw, late 1950's. This smallish intermediate cross between *C. ×* 'Cecil Houdyshel' and *C. americanum* has narrow-tepaled pink flowers. It is an interesting hybrid but, like its *C. americanum* parent, needs much watering to do well.

'Emma Jones.' Fred Jones, circa 1950's. A hybrid from Fred Jones which I had the pleasure of naming and introducing in the early 1960's. It has the unlikely parents of 'Peach Blow' and 'Cecil Houdyshel.' It is sweetly fragrant, with large semi-patent rose-colored tepals. Midsummer. It must be staked when it begins to flower, as the very tall scapes always tend to flop.

'Emma Swets.' Hannibal, circa 1980's. One of the newer hybrids from Les Hannibal, and named by Californian Bill Drysdale. The large, fragrant flowers have narrow, recurved tepals. The parentage is unknown but is thought to involve *C. americanum* forma *erubescens* and *C. moorei*. We can't be sure.

'H. J. Elwes.' Cecil Houdyshel. This was one of many hybrids between *C. americanum* and *C. moorei*. On the small side, it could fit in a large pot. With the death of Cecil Houdyshel, its main distribution ceased. If it can still be found, it should do well in the deep South planted out of doors.

'J. C. Harvey.' Circa 1908. The breeder, J. C. Harvey, named it for himself. It was introduced near the end of the last century and because of its great proclivity to form offsets, it became popular. Unfortunately its tendency toward shyness in flowering made for more offsets than flowers. The parentage for it was *C. zeylanicum* × *C. moorei*, and it was initially used for newer hybrids in the early twentieth century. It has dainty pink flowers with a sweet fragrance. Though it sets no seed, it has been used as a pollinator, and in time it was the probable parent of 'Peach Blow' and 'Ellen Bosanquet.'

'Mrs. James Hendry.' Henry Nehrling, circa early 1900's. This rates near the top of any hybrid group, with deep green, blunt-tipped foliage. It reminds one of *C. americanum* forma *erubescens*, which may have been one of its parents. The other parent may have been one of the *C.* × *powellii* forms as the flowers are outfacing, pinkish blush white, with wide tepals and declinate anthers. The plant withstands shade and dry conditions and flowers from late summer until stopped by cold weather.

'Parfait.' T. M. Howard 1980. This is one of the more unusual forms, with large patent flowers having a reddish exterior edged in pink and a pinkish interior, striped reddish. The overall effect is quietly stunning. It came from a cross between *C. scabrum* and *C.* × *powellii* var. *krelagei*, and has the low-growing foliage of the *C. scabrum* parent and a coloring intermediate between the two. It should be in every crinum collection.

'Peach Blow.' Theodore Mead, early 1900's. One of the best of the flowers colored a purplish pink and one of the more unusual crinums, with tall scapes and large flowers of patent form and a very pleasing scent. The lavender-pink flower tepals end in fish-hook tips, suggesting *C. zeylanicum* in its background. The leaves are erect and blunt-tipped. In order to inherit the several unique characters attributed to it, it has to have had *C. zeylanicum* and *C. americanum* forma *erubescens* in its

Crinum × 'Mrs. James Hendry'   *Crinum* × 'Peach Blow'

ancestry. Considering that this cross was made just before the First World War, it could have been done with 'J. C. Harvey' (*C. zeylanicum* × *C. moorei*) as one parent. The tender 'Peach Blow' increases slowly but has potent pollen, as witnessed by its offspring, 'Emma Jones.'

C. × *powellii* 'Roseum' is somewhat similar to the white-flowered version. Flowers range through shades of pink.

'Summer Glow.' Grace Hinshaw, late 1950's. An interesting cross between 'Cecil Houdyshel' and 'Ellen Bosanquet,' and increasing slowly. The flowers are bright rose-pink funnels, and the foliage is dull green.

'Summer Nocturne.' T. M. Howard 1964. This hybrid was achieved by crossing *C. americanum* forma *erubescens* with *C. moorei*. The result is a pale pink-and-white hybrid of a semi-bell form. Its tendency to form many offsets has helped it become quickly popular.

'Tulipan.' Les Hannibal. The year of introduction was around 1978. This one has a declined tulip-shaped form and is self-fertile. The light pink flowers are produced in midsummer. The parentage is unknown but includes *C. moorei* in the mix.

'Virginia Lee.' Cecil Houdyshel. An old hybrid from the early twentieth century still occasionally found in California gardens. The pink flowers are trumpet-like and fertile. It is a winter grower, making it difficult to grow outside except in frost-free areas such as southern California or Florida.

'Walter Flory.' Katherine Clint, late 1970's. This was reported as a cross between 'Ellen Bosanquet' and *C.* × *powellii* 'Album'; it somewhat resembles the *C.* × *worsleyi* hybrids. The funnel-shaped flowers are rose-pink and of moderate size. Increases well.

LIGHT-RED- AND WINE-RED-FLOWERED HYBRIDS

'Birthday Party.' Luther Bundrant 1982. *C. scabrum* × *C.* × 'Bradley Giant.' I was lucky enough to see this the first time it flowered. The flower is large and wide open and is an excellent wine-red. Among the best. Even though it was flowering for the first time, there were already offsets present, so it is a good propagator. This clone has a great future.

'Bradley.' H. B. Bradley. Created circa 1930, using *C. flaccidum* as a parent. The hybrid is of moderate height, consisting of large clusters of wonderful red flowers of *flaccidum* form. It has the fault of having narrow foliage that sprawls about in the untidy manner of *C. flaccidum*.

Crinum × 'Carnival'

'Carnival.' T. M. Howard 1964. A rare red-flowered form of *C.* × *herbertii*. This one is light red, with random stripes in white and pink, since it is a chimera. It flowers in late spring on short, well-displayed full scapes, with as many as nine trumpet-shaped flowers open at one time in a symmetrically radial umbel. In very hot weather the flowers are much paler; however, this normally occurs only near the end of flowering. 'Carnival' was created by using a red-flowered form of *C.* × *herbertii* on an Orange River form of *C. bulbispermum* and has become popular in the marketplace with the increase in stock.

'Circus.' T. M. Howard 1983. This is a hybrid from 'Carnival' and *C. macowanii*. Another chimera, it has umbels with huge flowers which may be light red with a white center or occasionally nearly white with a red stripe. It increases well by offsets, while also making seeds. Unfortunately it is a night bloomer, beautiful when the sun goes down but starting to droop at the crack of dawn.

Crinum × 'Ellen Bosanquet'
PHOTO BY JO ANN TRIAL

'Ellen Bosanquet.' Louis Bosanquet, circa 1915. Rates near the top of the wine-red forms, but there has always been some controversy as to how to pronounce the name. However the Florida Bosanquet family came from England, and they say Bo-san-KWETT. So that is that. Although its ancestry was never revealed, it likely came about from a cross using *C. scabrum* with pollen from 'J. C. Harvey,' at a time when crosses with the latter hybrid were still new. The result was a fine wine-red hybrid with leaves and stems of medium height. Midseason. It would be hard to fault, except that the scape is a bit short, the flowers are produced in a short season, and the bulbs increase rapidly, resulting in too many offsets that compete with one another, reducing the potential number of scapes and size of flowers.

'Elizabeth Traub.' H. P. Traub. This resulted from pollinating 'Cecil Houdyshel' with 'Ellen Bosanquet,' giving a red-wine-colored hybrid on taller scapes and with the flowers better displayed than those of 'Ellen Bosanquet.' It flowers at midseason. Unfortunately, the stems will often flop if not staked.

'Garden Party.' T. M. Howard 1977. This is a *C. × worsleyi* selection. The flowers are similar to other members of this cross, but larger and better formed, and of a deep rose color.

'George Harwood.' H. B. Bradley, circa early 1900's. It carries the genes of *C. flaccidum*, but in this case the bloodlines are more complex, suggesting the genes of *C. flaccidum, C. moorei*, and *C. scabrum*. The large flowers are light red with white centers, opening one to three at a time and well displayed. The narrowish leaves have the typical *C. flaccidum* sprawl.

Crinum × 'Lolita'

'Lolita.' T. M. Howard 1995. A recent hybrid formed by crossing *C. scabrum* with a bright-colored hybrid. In this case it resulted in a watermelon-red hybrid with fragrant flowers. There is a good balance between the radial symmetry of the umbel and the immense green foliage. The scapes are tall and don't flop until near the end of flowering. It has wonderful vigor and will make occasional seeds.

'Louis Bosanquet' was a *C. macowanii* hybrid named for Louis Bosanquet, the originator, after his death, by the late Wyndham Hayward. The trumpets were pinkish, especially on the exterior. Now apparently obsolete, it may still exist in very old collections.

'Mardi Gras.' T. M. Howard 1960. Similar to 'Ellen Bosanquet' in color (dark wine-red) and of trumpet form, but out of 'Cecil Houdyshel' with 'Carnival' as the pollen parent. Thus it is a *C. × powellii × C. × herbertii* cross and a third-generation hybrid with both parents being hybrids. The foliage is similar to that of *C. × herbertii*. A really beautiful plant. Midseason.

'Midway.' T. M. Howard, early 1980's. Produced using 'Carnival' as pollen parent and 'Cecil Houdyshel' as seed parent. It is similar to 'Cecil Houdyshel' of the × *powellii* type, but with glaucescent leaves, darker rose-red flowers, and setting a few fertile seeds.

'Mystery.' Cecil Houdyshel, early 1930's or 1940's. A sterile hybrid between 'Ellen

Bosanquet' and *C. americanum* forma *erubescens* circa the thirties or forties. The flowers are narrow-tepaled and wine-red in color. Unfortunately, it is a shy bloomer, though it makes many offsets. It needs much water to flower well.

C. × *powellii* var. *rubra*. Similar to the white- and pink-flowered versions. The red-flowered form is smaller and increases slowly, which accounts for its scarcity.

'Thaddeus Howard.' T. M. Howard 1950. The rare red-flowered form of *C.* × *herbertii* first flowered in 1954. Because of disease, it has had a very difficult time surviving to the present, except in California, where it is still grown.

C. × *worsleyi* W. Watson 1901. A cross between *C. scabrum* and *C. moorei*. It was initially lost after flowering and was not seen again until 1977, when I succeeded in duplicating it. It is a grand cross with all flowers facing in one direction, in pink with darker red midribs.

STRIPED HYBRIDS

C. × *baconi* hybrids. White hybrids, striped pink, rose, or red. When *C. zeylanicum* was crossed with various forms of *C. americanum*, the result were forms of *C.* × *baconi* Herbert, with patent flowers having red stripes on a white background. Perhaps the best known of these is 'Southern Belle,' which I originally found in a cemetery in Columbus, Georgia. It had wide open white flowers, striped in bright red, with long, overlapping tepals and short pedicels.

'Candy Ruffles.' T. M. Howard 1964. A sibling of 'Carnival' with many small red-striped white flowers open at one time. The tepals are ruffled.

'Carioca.' T. M. Howard 1980. This is a slightly smaller version of 'William Herbert,' with the scape green instead of red, and slightly smaller flowers of the same general form and color.

'Carousel.' T. M. Howard, early 1980's. This hybrid, from *C. scabrum* × *C. macowanii*, has a low-growing habit and many large umbels of radially arranged nocturnal white flowers faintly striped pink. Unfortunately, the flowers droop with the morning sun.

'Carroll Abbott.' This is a fine old striped hybrid from the garden of the late Carroll Abbott. It has some of the characteristics of *C.* × *herbertii*, but more likely is a hybrid of *C. scabrum* and *C. zeylanicum*. The white flowers are broadly striped with a good shade of red. Rare.

'Empress of India.' A hybrid of unknown origin. It was introduced sometime after the Civil War, but no one knows how old the clone actually is. It came from *C. zeylanicum* and one of the Indian riverine species, and it has a number of characters that set it apart from all of the others. The foliage is low and spreading, and the scape is tall and grape-colored with a dull bloom on it. In the evening the white flowers with light red keels open wide and then assume a trumpet shape after a few hours. They pose a spectacular effect during the short hours of their life, but by dawn they are usually finished. Their slight hardiness takes them only to zone 9.

'Exotica.' A beautiful hybrid of *C. scabrum* × *C. procerum*, created and introduced by Dave Lehmiller of Sour Lake, Texas. The flowers are patent, white with rose stripes.

Crinum × 'Exotica' PHOTO BY DAVE LEHMILLER

C. × *gowenii* Herbert. An old cross (circa 1720) between *C. bulbispermum* and *C. zeylanicum*. Time has smiled kindly on it, as it now has a wide distribution in the lower South and northern Mexico. By modern standards the plant is large. Its whitish trumpets have the exteriors keeled in a muddy pale brownish pink. It flowers in mid- to late summer when many crinums are resting, and the scapes may need staking. One of the toughest, and willing to take hot, dry conditions.

Crinum × 'Maximilian'

C. × *herbertii* Sweet, early 1800's. A grex name for popular hybrids uniting *C. scabrum* with *C. bulbispermum*. Many intermediate forms exist, including a rare red one. The usual forms are white, striped pink, or rose. These are widely grown hardy hybrids of easy culture and can take much neglect.

'Marisco.' T. M. Howard 1990. A natural Mexican hybrid from *C. zeylanicum* and *C. loddigesianum*. It is one of several hybrid varieties that I found within a single wild colony in southern Veracruz. Although the foliage is similar to that of *C. zeylanicum*, the narrow-tepaled flowers open wide and are white with red stripes.

'Maurine Spinks.' A *C.* × *baconi* form, it is yet another cross between *C. zeylanicum* and *C. americanum*, but with an informal aspect. Other similar forms are known.

'Maximilian.' A hybrid of unknown origin found in Mexico. It is a *C. zeylanicum* hybrid that I discovered growing in gardens of northeastern Mexico, with medium-sized foliage, glossy burgundy stems, and patent narrow-tepaled red flowers edged in white. The other parent may have been one of the subgenus *Crinum*, as the leaves are erect. The flowers are choice, but they don't set seed. They do well in zones 8–11.

'Royal White.' A natural hybrid, probably arising from a cross between *C. scabrum* and *C. americanum*, and thus a form of *C. × digweedii*. It is a very old hybrid, dating back to the seventeenth or eighteenth century, after the Portuguese began bringing slaves to Brazil. Now common throughout the South, it is the best known of the "milk-and-wine" forms, with large, fragrant white flowers, banded by a light pink stripe. The delicious scent of it flowering on a moonlit August night is unforgettable.

'Southern Belle' is a *C. × baconi* cross between *C. americanum* and *C. zeylanicum*, found in an old cemetery in Columbus, Georgia. It is a smallish plant. The white flowers have vivid red stripes, open wide, and are very lovely.

'Stars and Stripes.' T. M. Howard 1977. A hybrid from *C. scabrum × C. americanum* forma *erubescens*, and thus a new version of *C. × digweedii*. As with *C. scabrum*, the spectacular patent flowers have bright red stripes against a white background. One of the best of the new striped hybrids, it increases rapidly, grows easily, and flowers freely in late summer and fall until cut down by frost.

C. × submersum Herbert 1837. Brazil. A natural hybrid from Rio de Janeiro. *C. scabrum* was among the first crinums brought from Africa to Brazil by early settlers. *C. americanum* forma *erubescens* was a native, and naturally enough, they crossed,

Crinum × 'Stars and Stripes'

Crinum × 'William Herbert'

producing *C. × submersum*. It was at first thought to be a species, when it was found among naturalized *C. scabrum* on the banks of what was then thought to be the River of January (Rio de Janeiro; actually a big lagoon rather than a river) in Brazil. That cross has since been repeated a number of times, yielding a variety of patent, striped hybrids.

'Veracruz.' T. M. Howard. A natural hybrid which I discovered in a patch of naturalized *C. zeylanicum* in southern Veracruz, Mexico. It was the result of random cross-pollinating and backcrossing with nearby native *C. loddigesianum*, and backcrossing onto naturalized *C. zeylanicum*, which was everywhere. As a result, it is intermediate and can set an occasional seed. It is slightly hardier than *C. zeylanicum*, and the flowers open wider, with bright cherry-red stripes against a white background. The leaves are glossy green and suberect. Does well in cultivation to zone 8. Sometimes bothered by red spider mites.

'William Herbert.' T. M. Howard 1978. This has shiny burgundy scapes topped by large patent flowers looking much like those of a modern oriental lily. The

Cybestetes longifolia
PHOTO BY MARCIA WILSON, COURTESY OF
MRS. ALAN CLINT

flowers are large, with a strong band of cherry-red bleeding into the white background. Since the flowers are 8–9 inches across, freshly opened flowers are sometimes damaged in strong winds, but after the first day, the flowers relax and assume the posture of a large pom-pom (all tepals touching).

Cybestetes Milne-Redhead & Schweickerdt 1939

These are South African plants similar to *Ammocharis*. One species is known, *C. longifolia*. It has short umbels with 13–24 flowers, which open white and turn pink with age, and distichous, sickle-shaped, biflabellately arranged leaves. Tender north of zone 9. Does better in zone 10 given *Crinum* culture.

Cyrtanthus Aiton 1789

South Africa. Fifty species are known, but nearly all are tender except in zone 10. Umbels two- to many-flowered. Used elsewhere as pot plants.

C. elatus (N. Jacquin) Traub (syn. *Vallota purpurea*) is sometimes grown, with large red flowers, now hybridized to create a variety of delightful plants, including some with pink or white flowers.

Eucharis Planchon & Linden 1853

A genus of about 16 tropical species from Guatemala to Bolivia and widely dispersed. They are understory plants of primary and secondary lower montane rain forests. The leaves of all are petioled and broad, and the pendant white flowers are produced in umbels of two to ten, with a staminal cup. Most of them are rare and grown out of doors only in frost-free areas. The following are listed:

E. amazonica Linden ex Planchon. Peru.

E. astrophiala Ravenna 1985. Ecuador.

E. bakeriana N. E. Brown. Peru. Has larger flowers and is sweet-scented.

E. bonplandi (Kunth) Traub. Colombia.

E. bouchei Woodson & Allen. Panama.

E. × *butcheri* Traub 1967. Panama. Has one to three leaves and a solitary white flower. A hybrid between *Eucharis* and *Caliphuria*.

E. candida Planchon & Linden 1852. Peru. Has smallish, scentless flowers.

E. casteloneana (Baillon) Macbride. Peru.

E. cyanosperma Meerow 1987. Peru to Bolivia. Has long cups and blue seeds.

E. formosa Meerow 1987. Ecuador, Peru, and Colombia. A widely distributed species with a sour scent.

E. × *grandiflora* Planchon & Linden 1853. A putative hybrid between *E. sanderi* and *E. moorei*. The most common form, which has large, scented sterile flowers on stems about 1½ feet tall. It can be flowered several times per year, but mealybugs can be a problem with it.

E. korsakoffii Traub 1967. Peru, department of San Martín, about 25 miles from the city of Moyobamba. About 11 small white flowers in the umbel.

E. moorei (Baker) Meerow 1987. Ecuador, on both sides of the Andes. A putative parent of *E.* × *grandiflora*.

E. narcissiflora Huber. Peru, department of Amazonas.

E. plicata Meerow 1984. Peru. Umbels of nine or ten pendulous white flowers.

E. sanderi Baker. One of the putative parents of *E.* × *grandiflora*.

E. subdentata Baker. Colombia.

E. ulei Kranzlin. Similar to *E. cyanosperma* in size and number of flowers, but with longer leaves.

Eucrosia Ker-Gawler 1817

Seven species native to northwestern Peru and contiguous area in Ecuador, with petioled leaves and few- to many-flowered umbels. The showy red, orange, pink, greenish yellow, reddish yellow, or bright yellow flowers are hysteranthous, scentless, and zygomorphic, with long, declinate stamens. Primarily in seasonally dry to xeric lowland habitats.

E. bicolor Ker-Gawler 1817. Perhaps the best-known species, with small bulbs and bright orange flowers with long yellow stamens and green veins, produced in advance of the foliage. It can be grown in the garden or as a potted plant. Chromosome numbers: 2n = 46 and 68.

Eurycles

A synonym for *Proiphys,* which see.

Eustephia Cavanilles 1794

A genus of about four species, native to Peru and Argentina. Only one, *E. coccinea,* is under cultivation. Suitable mostly for pots north of zone 10. The umbels of five to eight flowers are orange-red, tubular, and pendant, and the leaves are linear.

Galanthus Linnaeus 1753

Snowdrops. About 13 species, all with small white flowers tipped green. Suitable only for cold-winter climates. Don't bother unless you don't mind using them as doubtful annuals, as they generally fail where winters are warm.

Griffinia Ker-Gawler 1820

Griffinia consists of about seven or eight Brazilian species with thin, lattice-like petioled leaves, flowering in spring and summer. The umbels of these zygomorphic flowers are usually in some shade of lilac or blue, fading to white, and star-like, with the lower tepal pointing downward. Rarely cultivated, but the blue color is welcome in any situation. As they are tender, they are only for pots.

Habranthus Herbert 1824

The genus *Habranthus* has been in existence since 1824, when it was created by Dean Herbert from species removed from *Zephyranthes* and *Hippeastrum.* In recent years Pierfelice Ravenna and others have doubled the number of species. *Habranthus* species usually have hysteranthous, trumpet or funnel-form, declinate, rarely erect flowers which are one- to three-flowered, with tubular spathes, split in the upper part, tubular in the lower part, and stamens declinate, unequal, in four lengths. Chromosome numbers: X = 6, 7. Mostly they are like *Zephyranthes* but with slightly nodding flowers. They do well out of doors in zone 9 and the lower half of zone 8.

H. andalgalensis Ravenna 1967. Argentina, Catamarca Province. Leaves nearly filiform; solitary whitish flowers.

H. andersonii Herbert 1830. A synonym for *H. tubispathus.*

H. barrosianus Ravenna 1974. Uruguay and Argentina, Buenos Aires Province. Prostrate leaves in the spring, after flowering. Flowers solitary, pinkish, brownish at base. Allied to *H. martinezii.*

H. brachyandrus (Baker) Sealy 1937. Paraguay and Argentina, in Chaco regions. A variable species in size, with some forms as large as a small *Hippeastrum*. The solitary, funnel-form flowers, which can be spectacular, are lavender-pink with a wine throat. Easily propagated by offsets or seeds and hybridizes easily with *H. robustus,* resulting in *H. × floryi.*

H. caeruleus Traub. Argentina, Entre Ríos Province, and Brazil, states of Paraná and Santa Catarina. The flowers are solitary and pinkish blue. Rare.

H. cardenasiana Traub & Nelson 1957. Bolivia. The leaves are light green, and the flowers are solitary, somewhat declinate, white inside, and pinkish in the upper third.

Habranthus cardinalis

H. cardinalis (Wright) Sealy 1937 (syn. *Zephyranthes bifolia*). Dominican Republic. Hesitatingly placed here. The correct nomenclature remains in controversy partly because there is disagreement as to the length of the filaments. The leaves are flattened and solitary, and in the forms that I studied the stamens were in four lengths, in increments of 1 mm, with broad, thickened stigmas. The chromosome number is 2n = 60. The flowers are said to be variable, in shades of whitish, pink, orange, or vermilion red, but the latter is the color with which this plant is widely associated. It can be grown out of doors only in zone 10 and requires pot culture elsewhere.

H. carmineus Ravenna 1970. Argentina, Entre Ríos Province, and Uruguay. The flowers are solitary, narrowly funnel-form, whitish, or pinkish with carmine tones. The stigma lobes are narrowly three-cleft.

H. catamarcensis Ravenna 1974. Argentina, Catamarca Province, at the foot of the Andes. Flowers solitary, widely bell-shaped, orange. Allied to *H. tubispathus.*

H. cearensis Herbert. Brazil and Argentina. The leaves are narrow, and the hysteranthous flowers are solitary and whitish.

H. chacoensis Ravenna 1970. Argentina, Chaco Province. The solitary flowers are a very pale carmine-pink, whitish within, purplish at the throat and in the exterior. The inner segments are much narrower than the outer segments.

H. concolor Lindley 1838 (syn. *Zephyranthes concolor*). Mexico, state of San Luis Potosí. Stony, dry hills around the city of San Luis Potosí in full sun. Bulbs black-coated, usually solitary. The leaves are daffodil-like, erect, spiraling, and glaucous. The scape, which is produced in early summer, is a foot or so tall, bearing primrose-yellow flowers with a green throat, erect to nodding, solitary, funnel- to chalice-form, and varying in size. This plant needs xerophytic culture, in which it is dry in winter dormancy with enough water to keep it actively growing in summer. It can take some frost. Slow-growing, and can be difficult. Propagated by seed.

H. concordiae Ravenna 1970. A synonym for *H. pedunculosus.*

H. duarteanus Ravenna 1974. Brazil, state of Minas Gerais. The leaves are narrowly linear. The large flowers are solitary and slightly ventricose below. Ravenna fails to list the flower color.

H. erectus Ravenna 1970. Argentina, Jujuy Province in sandy places. The flowers are solitary, erect, bell-shaped, pink, and carmine toward the base. As with some Mexican *Habranthus* species (*H. concolor, H. howardii, H. mexicanus*), the flowers may be erect or near-erect.

H. estensis Ravenna 1974. Uruguay, near Punta Ballena and Punta del Este; southern Brazil, near Torres. A form of *H. gracilifolius,* with one to three hysteranthous pink flowers, differing in the flowers opening wide and forming shallow goblets. *H. gracilifolius,* which shares the same habitat, has identical bulbs, foliage, and habits, and each easily sets seed when they are crossbred. In my experience, both forms are self-sterile, requiring pollen from a different clone, but when the two forms are cross-pollinated, they give fertile seed. These are hardly grounds to maintain them as two distinct species.

H. × *floryi* Traub 1951. Hybrids between *H. robustus* and *H. brachyandrus,* of easy culture and widely distributed. The trumpets are pink. There are conflicting reports about their fertility or lack of it. Mine never seed. Tender.

H. franciscanus Herbert, early 1800's. Central Brazil, banks of the Rio São Francisco. The leaves are narrow, the flowers solitary and white.

H. goianus Ravenna 1974. Brazil, state of Goiás. The leaves are rather broad and light green, and the flowers are solitary and pink.

H. gracilifolius Herbert 1824. Uruguay. Leaves narrow and nearly cylindrical, with one to three variable pinkish flowers. Occurs in two forms. Those with trumpet-shaped flowers are typically classified as *H. gracilifolius,* while those with shallow, goblet-shaped flowers are now known as *H. estensis.* Aside from these obvious variations, the two forms are identical. Since they share the same leaves and habitat and are self-sterile while easily intercrossing, it is difficult to make a case for two separate species.

H. guachipensis Ravenna 1974. Argentina, Salta Province. The leaves are present at flowering. The flowers are solitary, narrowly funnel-form, and white.

H. howardii (Traub) T. M. Howard 1990. Mexico, states of Nuevo León and Coahuila, at escarpments. The small, round bulbs have brown tunics, and the plant is hysteranthous, with solitary, erect or declinate, primrose-yellow flowers. The pol-

Habranthus immaculatus

len is orange-yellow. This is a rare and lovely locally en-demic species that flowers in early summer. It requires xerophytic culture and is difficult to maintain in culti-vation unless planted in a raised bed of alkaline soil in full sun.

H. immaculatus Traub and Clint 1957. Mexico, states of western Guanajuato and eastern Jalisco. The bulbs are large, with black tunics. The plants are hysteranthous, with large, solitary, white or cream trumpets, sometimes flushed pinkish, and moderately easy in cultivation.

H. irwinianus Ravenna 1970. Brazil, mountains of Minas Gerais. Allied to *H. gracilifolius.* The plant is hysteranthous, with solitary whitish or pinkish flowers.

H. jamesonii Ravenna 1974. Argentina, in sandy soils. Plants hysteranthous, with one to four pinkish or white flowers.

H. jujuyensis (Holmboe) Traub. Argentina, Jujuy Province. Flowers whitish, green-ish in the throat, with exterior grayish lines.

H. juncifolius Traub & Hayward 1947. A synonym for *H. pedunculosus.*

H. leptandrus Ravenna 1978. Bolivia, province of Mizque, in meadows. The plants are hysteranthous, with the flowers solitary, narrowly funnel-form, then expanding. They are carmine at the tips, and whitish at the base.

H. longipes (Baker) Sealy. Uruguay. Flowers solitary. The color is not reported.

H. maasii Ravenna 1978. Argentina, Jujuy Province. Leaves linear. Flowers nod-ding, pink.

H. magnoi Ravenna 1967. Argentina, Córdoba Province. In mountainous areas among rocks or stones. The flowers are solitary and pinkish.

H. maranensis Ravenna 1981. Maranhão, Brazil. Plants hysteranthous, with soli-tary flowers white, pink, or light orange. Related to *H. sylvaticus.*

H. martinezii Ravenna 1972. Argentina, Entre Ríos and Salta Provinces. Also in Uruguay. The flowers are solitary and pinkish, with a brown-purple throat and ex-terior lines. Allied to *H. tubispathus*, but larger. This species has proved easy and popular in cultivation.

H. mendocensis (Baker) Sealy 1937. Argentina, Mendoza Province. Plants hyster-anthous, with the white flowers solitary and declinate.

H. mexicanus T. M. Howard 1997. Mexico, mountains and rocky hills in states of Hidalgo, México, San Luis Potosí, Guanajuato, and Querétaro. The flattened glaucous leaves are a half-inch wide and somewhat twisted, and the flowers are hyster-anthous, usually white, rarely pink. Difficult and tender.

H. microcarpus (Rusby) Ravenna 1978. Bolivia, near Lake Rogagua. Flowers solitary.

H. millarensis Ravenna 1981. Bolivia, department of Potosí. The plant is hyster-anthous and has solitary white flowers.

H. niveus Ravenna 1970. Argentina, La Rioja and Catamarca Provinces in xero-phytic sandy plateaus. The flowers are large, showy, solitary, nodding, and whitish, aging pinkish.

H. nullipes Ravenna 1978. Plateau of Bolivia. The flowers are solitary, funnel-form, and whitish with purplish brown streaks on very short (to ¾ inch) scapes, expanding well only in full sun.

H. oaxacanus T. M. Howard 1997. Mexico, mountains of central Oaxaca. The bulbs are roundish, with leaves with five to eight nerves. The plant is hysteranthous, and the solitary flowers are funnel-form, pink to rose with a green throat, on tall scapes.

H. pedunculosus Herbert 1837 (syn. *H. juncifolius, H. teretifolius, H. holmbergii*). Argentina and Brazil, state of Rio Grande do Sul, growing deeply in sand from elongate tan-coated bulbs. The leaves are narrowly cylindrical, and the scapes are hysteranthous, multiflowered, with pink funnels on long pedicels in mid- to late summer. Although scarce, this species is easy to grow from seed and reasonably hardy if planted deeply. It will easily hybridize with *Rhodophiala bifida*.

H. riojanus Ravenna 1970. Argentina, La Rioja Province on grassy slopes. Flow-ers solitary, pink, funnel-form.

H. robustus Herbert ex Sweet. Brazil, state of Santa Catarina. There are several forms with large, solitary pink flowers. Easily the most popular member of the genus, and hardy through zone 8. Free-flowering and easily propagated from seeds and offsets. This is the same as *Zephyranthes* "*robusta*," which is commonly sold as *Z. grandiflora*, a very different species.

H. ruber Ravenna 1970. Brazil, state of Rio Grande do Sul, in grassy fields at woodland margins. One or two funnel-form red flowers, greenish at base. Closely allied to *H. gracilifolius*, with similar foliage.

H. ruizlealii Ravenna 1974. Argentina, La Rioja Province. Leaves linear. One or two white or pink flowers.

H. salinarum Ravenna 1970. Argentina, Córdoba Province, in sandy, salty places. Flowers solitary, white, and narrowly funnel-form.

H. saltensis Ravenna 1970. Argentina, Salta Province. The plants are hysteranthous, with solitary, nodding, bilaterally symmetrical white flowers.

Habranthus texanus
PHOTO BY JO ANN TRIAL

H. schulzianus Ravenna 1972. Argentina, Chaco region, in northwestern Santa Fe Province. Leaves present at flowering. Solitary white flowers.

H. spectabilis Ravenna 1970. Argentina, Jujuy Province. The plants are hysteranthous, with solitary flowers lilac-pink outside, white inside.

H. steyermarkii Ravenna 1978. Argentina, northeastern Jujuy Province, in sandy soil. The plants are hysteranthous, with solitary white flowers.

H. sylvaticus Herbert. Brazil, near Crato, in dry, open woods. The leaves are ⅛ inch wide and the flowers are hysteranthous, solitary, and purplish red.

H. teretifolius (C. H. Wright) Traub. A synonym for *H. pedunculosus.*

H. texanus (Herbert) Herbert ex Steudel. The Texas form of *H. tubispathus,* with golden yellow flowers flushed reddish on the exterior.

H. tubispathus (L'Héritier) Traub 1970. Uruguay, Argentina, southern Brazil, central and southern Chile, and United States (Texas). Flowers solitary, hysteranthous, bell-shaped, orange-yellow, striped purplish on the outside. Other forms are known.

H. variabilis Ravenna 1974 (syn. *H. tubispathus* subsp. *variabilis,* var. *roseus,* var. *bicolor,* and var. *parvula*). Argentina, Corrientes Province, and Paraguay. The solitary flowers are pink or bicolored.

H. versicolor Herbert 1824. Uruguay. The plants are hysteranthous, with solitary pinkish white flowers and linear leaves.

H. vittatus T. M. Howard 1990. Mexico, state of Oaxaca. Limestone hills and scrub north of Huajuapan de León. The linear leaves are glaucous, and the hysteranthous flowers have a light pinkish background, overlaid with reddish lines.

Habranthus vittatus

Haemanthus Linnaeus 1753

A genus of about 22 South African plants, mostly suitable in zone 10, or for pots elsewhere. The rootstock is sub-bulbous to bulbous, and the leaves are mostly broad, fleshy, and elongate, rarely narrow. The umbel is many-flowered in red, pink, or white. The fruit is a berry. The genus *Scadoxus* has been split off from *Haemanthus* and is listed separately.

Hannonia Braun-Blanc & Marie 1931

H. hesperidium Braun-Blanc & Marie 1931. Morocco, Hercules Peninsula. A charming miniature, with hysteranthous umbels of two small, starry white flowers that have narrow tepals keeled pale green, flowering in late summer or fall. The tepal tubes are less than ½ inch long, produced on short, slender scapes a few inches high. The species is allied to *Pancratium* and *Sternbergia,* and its flowering season is very brief, as each flower lasts but one day. A quaint little mite, but the flowers are too ephemeral to make more than a fleeting pleasant impression in anything but a small pot. It needs a sunny Mediterranean culture and careful watering. *Hannonia* is rare in cultivation and said to be a "rag," but I found it rather charming.

Haylockia Herbert 1830

Some workers consider *Haylockia* as intermediate between *Cooperia* and *Zephyranthes,* but this seems unlikely, as such hybrids (× *Cooperanthes*) already exist and are nothing like *Haylockia* in appearance or behavior. *Haylockia* is most likely a distinct, small, separate genus.

H. americanum Hoffmansegg 1824 (syn. *H. pusilla, Sternbergia americana*). Old World *Sternbergia* is a distant relative.

H. andina Fries 1905. Andean Argentina.

H. cochabambensis Cárdenas 1973 (syn. *Zephyranthes cochabambensis*). Bolivia. Flowers white with greenish throat. Filaments white.

Haylockia pusilla

H. pseudo-colchicum (Kraenzl.) Hume 1914. Bolivia. Likely a *Pyrolirion* (?), as stamens are at two levels and the flowers are brick-red.

H. pseudo-crocus Solms-Laubach 1907. Bolivia.

H. pusilla Herbert 1830. Argentina, Entre Ríos and Corrientes Provinces; southern Brazil in Rio Grande do Sul; Uruguay, department of Tacuerembó, in dry fields or hills. The solitary yellow or white flowers are crocus-like, practically stemless, with long tubes, and the narrow leaves are nearly rotate.

Hieronymiela Pax 1890

A genus of Andean plants with umbels of yellow flowers. Rare in cultivation.

H. aurea. Ravenna 1967. Argentina, Salta Province. Differs from *H. chlidanthoides* in having umbels of pedicelled yellow flowers with shorter tubes.

H. chlidanthoides Pax. Argentina, Catamarca Province. A plant from dry high elevations, it has umbels with four or five funnel-shaped, long-tubed white flowers with spreading tepals. Argentine collectors have widely distributed this relatively untested species of late, but there are no reports of successes in this country. Probably not for average garden use.

× *Hippeastrelia*

× *Hippeastrelia* 'Mystique'
PHOTO BY JOHN D. FELLERS

Bigeneric hybrids between *Hippeastrum* and *Sprekelia.* A clone known as 'Mystique' is marketed. It has two rather wide-tepaled red *Sprekelia*-like flowers on each stem. Oddly, the plant sets fertile seed. It is widely sold as *Hippestralia* [*sic*], but according to the International Code of Botanical Nomenclature, the name for a bigeneric hybrid should be composed of the first part or the whole of one name, the last part or whole of the other, and (if desirable) a connecting vowel.

Hippeastrum Herbert 1821 (syn. *Amaryllis*)

A genus of about 40 species with two centers of distribution, in eastern Brazil and eastern Andean Argentina, Bolivia, and Peru. These are South American plants, called "amaryllis" in the United States. See discussion of the name *Amaryllis* under that topic. In the hands of breeders, *Hippeastrum* has prospered. The large number of *Hippeastrum* species is probably the result of too much splitting based on taxonomic minutiae. They are mostly grown as pot plants and are suitable garden subjects only in the warmest climates. They do best in a friable soil with good growing conditions. Virus is always a problem with them, even in pots, so one must be prepared at any time to give a virused plant the old heave-ho forever. Most are summer-growing and will need a rest in winter. Members of the genus *Rhodophiala* were once grouped as a division within *Hippeastrum* but are now excluded.

While collecting in Brazil in 1986, I was amazed to find *H. vittatum* growing in sandy woodlands at a depth of 6–8 inches. In the United States we tend to plant

Hippeastrum species and hybrids with half of the bulb above ground, for that is the way they grow in pots, but in the garden they can actually go much deeper. Chromosome numbers: X = 11; 2n = 22, 44, and 66.

H. aglaiae Castellanos 1940. Argentina and Bolivia. This has evergreen foliage and trumpet-like yellow flowers and was the among the first of the new yellow species to be published.

H. ambiguum Herbert 1837. Peru. A white, long-trumpet form like *H. elegans* with red lines in the interior.

H. angustifolium Pax 1890. Brazil and Argentina. A spring-flowering stoloniferous aquatic form with linear glaucous leaves and two to four zygomorphic orchid-shaped red flowers, looking much like a many-flowered *Sprekelia*.

H. anzaldoi Cárdenas 1956. Similar to *H. evansiae* and may be a synonym, as they differ principally in pigmentation. The flowers are pale greenish yellow.

H. argentinum (Pax) Hunziker 1890 (syn. *H. fragrantissimum, H. candidum, H. immaculatum,* and *H. tucumanum*). Andes of Argentina and Bolivia. Fragrant long-trumpeted white flowers in April and May.

H. aulicum (Ker-Gawler) Herbert 1817. Brazil and Paraguay. A winter bloomer with hysteranthous spotted scarlet flowers and green centers.

H. brasiliensis (Traub & Doran) 1976. Brazil. These have two to four long-trumpeted white or pink flowers with a heavy fragrance.

Hippeastrum brasiliensis
PHOTO BY MARCIA WILSON, COURTESY OF MRS. ALAN CLINT

H. calyptratum Ker-Gawler (Herbert). Brazil. Evergreen epiphyte. Green orchid-like flowers. Spring-flowering.

H. correiense (Bury) Worsley 1938. Brazil. Flowering in spring, with crimson perianth and a green keel in lower half.

H. cybister (Herbert) Bentham & Hooker 1883. Bolivia. Flowers with an orchid-like form, like that of *Sprekelia*, red and green in color.

H. elegans (Sprengel) H. E. Moore (syn. *H. solandriflorum*). Bolivia. Trumpet-form greenish white flowers.

Hippeastrum calyptratum
PHOTO BY MARCIA WILSON, COURTESY OF MRS. ALAN CLINT

H. equestre Herbert 1821. Synonym for *H. puniceum.*

H. evansiae (Traub & Nelson) H. E. Moore 1956. Bolivia. Flowers light chartreuse or light yellow. With this species came the first of the new yellow-flowered hybrids.

H. forgetii Worsley 1912. Peru. The flowers are a dull crimson with a green base. Autumn-flowering.

H. fosterii Traub 1951. Brazil. The umbel is 5- to 13-flowered and is produced in the spring. The pink tepals are recurved, and the stamens are exerted. Beautiful and distinct.

H. glaucescens Martius ex Schulte 1830 (syn. *H. maracasum*). Brazil. It has a zygomorphic flower with a brick-red perigone of four different sizes.

H. iguazuanum (Ravenna) 1971. Brazil and Argentina at Iguazú Falls. Spring flowers zygomorphic and red-striated.

H. illustris Velloso. Brazil, near Rio de Janeiro. The correct name for a plant previously listed as *H. restingensis.* The tepal veins give a squared effect to the tepals.

H. × *johnsonii* (Bury) Herbert circa 1810. *H.* × *johnsonii* is an old favorite, being among the hardiest, and found in old plantings everywhere that climate permits. The confusion between myth and reality makes its true history obscure. The official story goes that it was first raised by a man named Johnson who had a small garden in Lancashire in 1810. It is now probably no longer in commerce, but there are still plenty of plants around. It is said to be the product of *H. reginae* and *H. vittatum.* It has four to six slightly nodding bold crimson trumpets with a white stripe through each tepal, around the Easter season in our climate. The trick these days is to find virus-free plantings.

H. leopoldii Dombrain 1870. Bolivia. The flowers have regular lobes, white toward the tip, red at the middle, with a two-parted white keel and greenish white throat. A rare species, which originally helped to set the form of the hybrid amaryllis.

H. neoleopoldii Cárdenas 1972. Bolivia, Caupolicán Province. Similar to *H. leopoldii.* It has two flat flowers approaching dinner-plate form with dots and more red coloring.

H. papilio (Ravenna) 1970. A fall-winter bloomer with two large butterfly-shaped flowers streaked maroon on a greenish background. One of the more significant modern species for breeding.

Hippeastrum papilio (foreground) and *H. striatum*
PHOTO BY MARCIA WILSON, COURTESY OF MRS. ALAN CLINT

Hippeastrum correiense × *H. papilio*
PHOTO BY JOHN D. FELLERS

Now available in specialty catalogs. Closely related to *H. aulicum.*

H. pardinum (J. D. Hooker) Dombrain 1867. Bolivia and Peru. Late spring with cream flowers spotted red.

H. parodii (Hunziker & Cocucci) 1969. Argentina. The leaves of this plant are glaucous, and the yellow flowers are of trumpet form.

H. pseudopardinum Cárdenas 1965. Bolivia, Chapare Province. In this species the two flowers do not flare much, but are more cone-shaped and striped, and are not quite as large as those of *H. neoleopoldii.*

H. psittacinum (Ker-Gawler) Herbert 1817. S. Brazil. An odd species, with a distinct incurved corona and lobes with a red edge, green keel, and crimson stripes radiating from the keel.

H. puniceum (Lamarck) O. Kuntze (syn. *Amaryllis belladonna*). Barbados lily. Tropical America. Flowers bright red with green base, followed by the leaves.

H. reginae (Linnaeus) Herbert 1762. Brazil, Peru. Summer-flowering. Bright scarlet with greenish white base. The stamens are as long as the perianth.

H. reticulatum (L'Héritier) Herbert 1824. Southern Brazil. A fall bloomer with three- to five-flowered umbels in bright mauve-red, with cross bars of a deeper shade.

H. solandriflorum (Lindley) Herbert 1821. A synonym for *H. elegans.*

H. starkii (Nelson & Traub) 1963. Bolivia. Suberect pink flowers in spring.

H. striatum (Lamarck) H. E. Moore 1783. Brazil. A popular plant. The flowers are crimson, with a green keel midway down the perianth.

H. viridorchidum (Traub) 1951. Synonym for *H. calyptratum.*

H. vittatum (L'Héritier) Herbert 1788. Southern Brazil. White or pink with red stripes in spring. Fairly hardy.

Hymenocallis Salisbury 1812

The white spider lilies are a genus of about 70 New World species, typified by umbels of one to many flowers, with slender skeletonized segments surrounding a membranous staminal cup. The name *Hymenocallis* literally means "beautiful membrane." They are found in the southeastern United States, Mexico, Central America, the West Indies, and northern South America. They differ from the Old World *Pancratium* in the formation of the seed, which in *Hymenocallis* is round, fleshy, and green, like an olive, while *Pancratium* has thin black seed. All *Hymenocallis* species have somewhat similar flowers, and many have tidy growing habits which cause them to be favored in southern gardens. All of them spring open in the evening and, depending on the species, last for a day or two, but the fragrances differ markedly. Some smell deliciously sweet, while others are spicy or have a chemical smell, depending on the pollinators they want to attract. They have such a heavy root system that they are used for erosion control on some Florida beaches, as some of them are quite salt tolerant.

Most *Hymenocallis* species propagate by offsets, but some of the Mexican species rarely form offsets and must be propagated by seed. Oddly, some of these Mexican bulbs will increase if the basal plate is cored and removed as is done to propagate hyacinths. New bulbs will form in the remaining scales and on the basal plate.

I am listing *Hymenocallis* species with guarded reservations, according to their leaf form or place of origin. Chromosome numbers are given if known. At best this is still a confusing genus and subject to future changes.

Hymenocallis from the Southeastern United States

Generally these are somewhat difficult in cultivation, requiring acid sandy or clay soils and more water than the others. Many of them have small floral umbels and large, beautiful flowers. A number of these are confusing and fall into forms allied to *H. rotata* or *H. caroliniana;* they may need more study.

H. caroliniana (Linnaeus) Herbert 1821 (syn. *H. occidentalis*). Found in Louisiana, Arkansas, Kentucky, Missouri, Indiana, and Georgia. A variable species, and widespread in the southeastern part of the country in acid sandy or clay soil. A medium-sized plant with 5–12 narrowly oblanceolate dull green leaves that appear at the same time as the three to nine large flowers with flat white cups, in midsummer, often in or near running water or on ridges in rocks and native acid loam with excellent drainage. The scape is somewhat compressed. The leaves begin to die off as the fruit ripens. Ovules two to three, rarely one, per cell. Seed is of medium size and mid-green. 2n = (52) 54.

H. choctawensis Traub 1962. Said to come from the Mobile delta and western Florida panhandle. May be a synonym for the eastern range of *H. liriosme.* It has five to nine leaves and four to six fragrant flowers in late spring. 2n = 44.

H. choctawensis is said to differ from *H. liriosme* in that there is said to be a stoloniferous form for *H. choctawensis,* a condition found in certain species which may have both basal offsetting and stoloniferous forms within the same colony, as with *H. acutifolia* colonies in southern Mexico.

H. collieri Small. A synonym for *H. latifolia.*

H. coronaria (Le Conte) Kunth 1850. A form from north-central Alabama and Georgia, growing in and near moving water of rivers and streams in the Cahaba basin. It is one of the prettiest species, with erect, narrow leaves, and is unusual in having three or four large-chaliced flowers with short (to 1 inch) incurved filaments, somewhat like those in the genus *Ismene*. The cup center is yellowish, and the tepals are slightly on the short side, compared to the other species. Flowers in May. 2n = 44.

H. crassifolia Herbert. A synonym for *H. floridana.*

H. duvalensis Traub 1967. Upper coastal plains of Florida, in Duval County, and southern Georgia. Of uncertain relationship to *H. rotata*. It has three or four deciduous strap-shaped leaves, and two-flowered scapes with small cups. Two to four ovules per locule. April–June.

H. eulae Shinners 1951. A synonym for *H. galvestonensis.*

H. floridana (Rafinesque) Morton 1935. Florida. Now considered to be a synonym for *H. rotata*, which see.

H. galvestonensis ([Herbert] Baker) emend. T. M. Howard 1995 (syn. *Choretis galvestonensis, H. eulae*). East Texas, Arkansas, southeastern Oklahoma, western Louisiana, and southern Georgia in sandy upland soil. A distinct plant that has always been steeped in controversy. It has brown-coated bulbs with about eight suberect glaucous leaves that are lanceolate-elliptic and obtuse, emerging with a rush in the spring and dying back in early summer. After the leaves disappear in late summer or fall, it produces tall, naked scapes of showy white flowers in *Lycoris* fashion. The scape is round or oval in cross section. The seed is large, somewhat roundish, and pale green. Hardy, but does not tolerate alkaline soil. 2n = 52.

In 1837, two specimens were submitted to Dean Herbert from Galveston Bay by Thomas Drummond. Later (1888) J. G. Baker examined these two, plus one from a Mr. E. Hall, and selected the Hall specimen from near New Orleans as the type specimen for *H. galvestonensis,* as it seemed to be more complete, having foliage along with the flowers. This was a mistake, as the Hall specimen was a different species, named by C. S. Rafinesque-Schmaltz as *H. liriosme*, unbeknownst to Baker, who apparently was unfamiliar with Rafinesque's work. For a more complete expla-

Hymenocallis galvestonensis
PHOTO BY DAVE LEHMILLER

nation, see "The correct identity of *Hymenocallis galvestonensis* (Herbert), Amaryllidaceae, T. M. Howard," *Herbertia* 50 (1994–1995).

H. godfreyi G. Smith 1994. Florida, Wakulla County in St. Marks marsh. A recently discovered two-flowered marsh form from northeast Florida. Similar to *H. rotata,* and perhaps a variety of it (?), but growing in stagnant marsh situations rather than moving water, and flowering March to May. Culture as for *H. liriosme.* Four ovules per locule. 2n = 48.

H. henryi Traub 1962. Northern Florida. A non-rhizomatous form similar to *H. palmeri,* with erect, channeled, narrow strap-shaped green leaves and two flowers with greenish segments, found in the pine flatwoods but replaced by *H. godfreyi* in the marshes. A form with glaucous foliage, *H. henryi var. glaucifolia,* is known. 2n = 38.

H. humilis S. Watson. A single-flowered Florida form flowering in July and August, and thought to be a synonym of *H. palmeri.*

H. keyensis Small. A synonym for *H. latifolia.*

H. kimballiae Small. Thought to be a synonym for *H. latifolia.* Western Florida. A large late-flowering species having 8–12 small-cupped flowers. 2n = 70. (Note that *H. kimballiae* and *H. latifolia* have different chromosome numbers. This may indicate that these two plants are actually different species.)

H. laciniata Small 1933. A synonym for *H. rotata.*

H. latifolia (Miller) Roemer. A late-flowering species from Florida and Yucatán, Mexico. A large plant with erect, strap-shaped leaves and 5–16 long-tubed, small-cupped white flowers, June–September. The staminal cup is funnel-form. Winter-deciduous or evergreen, depending on location. Allied to *H. pedalis.* 2n = 48.

H. liriosme (Rafinesque) Shinners 1951. East Texas, southern Arkansas, Louisiana, coastal Alabama to Mobile Bay, and the adjacent Florida panhandle. It flowers in the spring from black-coated bulbs. The narrow, acute, bright green leaves are

Hymenocallis liriosme
PHOTO BY THOMAS E. HARDING

erect, and the four to seven flowers have greenish yellow centers. It is often confused with *H. galvestonensis,* which is a different plant. *H. liriosme* requires swamp culture. 2n = 40, 42.

H. moldenkiana Traub 1962. The eastern limit of, and a synonym for, *H. galvestonensis,* as it occurs in southern Georgia.

H. occidentalis (Le Conte) Kunth (syn. *Pancratium occidentalis*). Now thought by some to be a synonym for *H. caroliniana.* See "Observations on the United States species of the genus *Pancratium,*" *Annals of the Lyceum of Natural History of New York* 3 (1836): 142–148. 2n = 54.

H. palmeri S. Watson 1879. Central and southern Florida. The alligator lily is a miniature form with non-rhizomatous bulbs, narrow erect leaves, and one, rarely two, flowers per scape. The tepals are greenish, and the cup does not spread at the margins. Flowers late May to August and likes aquatic culture. Swamp margins and wet roadsides. Eight or nine ovules per locule (3–4 per locule according to some authors). 2n = 42, 46, 48.

H. palusvirensis Traub 1962. North Carolina. It has four or five flowers with cup margins not incised and with four or five ovules per cell. Allied to *H. caroliniana.* 2n = 40.

H. puntagordensis Traub 1962. Gulf side of peninsular southern Florida. A fragrant form blooming in late August or September, with long-necked non-rhizomatous bulbs and five to eight shiny evergreen leaves. The long-tubed flowers have small starry cups with prominent denticulations between the filaments. 2n = 46.

H. pygmaea Traub 1962. South Carolina. A one-flowered species with slender leaves. *H. humilis* may be a synonym.

H. rotata (Ker-Gawler) Herbert 1821. Panhandle of Florida, Georgia, and South Carolina. Perhaps a synonym for *H. floridana* (Rafinesque) Morton 1935. If so, the name *H. rotata* would have priority. A variable but showy stoloniferous species growing in or near running water, with two to four rotate flowers having large (1¾–2 inches wide) cups and long (3–4 inches) segments. Six to eight ovules per locule. 2n = (38) 46 (48).

H. traubii Moldenke 1967. Florida, near Daytona Beach. A two- or three-flowered stoloniferous species found near water and flowering in spring. A small plant with large flowers, similar to *H. rotata,* and perhaps a form of it, but with four or five ovules per cell. Winter-deciduous. Makes a fine pot plant and thrives in aquatic culture. Traub thought so much of this plant that he had Moldenke name it for him.

H. tridentata Small. A synonym for *H. floridana.*

Tropical *Hymenocallis*

Some of these tropicals are widely cultivated. There are petioled and non-petioled leaf forms. The petioled forms are a diverse group, with evergreen and deciduous sorts, and have yellow pollen. They seem to share a tendency toward cold-tenderness. Because of confusion in nomenclature, the chromosome numbers are omitted. The non-petioled forms are more easily managed in garden settings.

H. arenicola Northrop. West Indies. This is one of the finest species for cultivation, as it can take somewhat dry conditions. It has large umbels of showy fragrant white flowers in midsummer. It differs from the other tropical species in having an erect fountain of wide, strap-shaped glaucescent leaves, more or less blunt-tipped. The large, wide bulbs have squared-off shoulders and smallish basal plates. The form in cultivation normally does not set seed.

H. bolivariana Traub 1967. Caicara, state of Monagas, Venezuela. A little-known Venezuelan plant with wide, strap-shaped petiolate leaves and about eight flowers.

H. caribaea (Linnaeus emend. Ker-Gawler) Herbert. West Indies. The true *H. caribaea* is hard to come by, although I have had impostors presented through the years.

Hymenocallis caribaea
PHOTO BY JOHN D. FELLERS

Hymenocallis caribaea var. *plenus*

The plant is evergreen, of average height, with shiny green arcuate, acutely tipped leaves. There are eight to ten large, fragrant flowers with short pedicels in midsummer. A rare double-flowered form (var. *plenus*) sometimes turns up in which the same scape contains both flowers with twice the usual number of tepals and schizoid flowers with split cups. Mixed in the umbels are normal flowers with the correct complement of six tepals and normal cups, making it more of a curiosity than a thing of beauty. There is also a form with beautifully variegated green and white leaves.

H. caymanensis Herbert 1837. "Tropical Giant" (?) Cayman Islands. The correct identity of this plant is still in doubt, but it appears to be the most cultivated *Hymenocallis* around the world. It is often confused with others, such as *H. expansa* and *H. caribaea*. If we must choose but one kind of *Hymenocallis*, then this one is it, as it is Everyman's *Hymenocallis*. It is

not particular as to soil. It got the nickname "Tropical Giant" from the late Cecil
Houdyshel many years ago. The fountains
of evergreen foliage are broad and glossy
and make a wonderful accent in any landscape. In midsummer come the many-
flowered fragrant scapes, with the segments
in two slightly different rows. Cultivated
clones rarely make seed, so it is considered
by some to be of hybrid origin, but this is
unlikely, as some forms do make fertile
seed.

Hymenocallis caymanensis

H. expansa Herbert. West Indies. Related to *H. caymanensis* and *H. caribaea*. The
differences between them are unclear.

H. fragrans Salisbury. West Indies. A tender evergreen tropical species with short,
wide, petioled leaves and an umbel of many open fragrant flowers in the autumn. It
is occasionally cultivated.

H. guatemalensis Traub 1967. Lake Amatitlán, Guatemala. Although I have looked
for it on the few occasions when I was in Guatemala, I have yet to find this plant.
The species is poorly understood. The five to seven flowers are said to be produced
with immature leaves in the spring.

H. latifolia. See in preceding section, "Hymenocallis from the Southeastern United
States."

H. littoralis (N. Jacquin) Salisbury. Central America. It has bright green erect,
strap-shaped leaves and fragrant, long-tubed flowers. The cups are adnate to the
segments at the base, and the pollen is red-orange. A lovely variegated form is grown
in California.

H. miniatum Herbert. Peru. A red-flowered species from the Peruvian Andes.

H. ovata (Miller) Sweet. A poorly understood species found on the Atlantic side
of northern South America, with petioled ovate leaves and short-tubed flowers.

H. pedalis Herbert 1821. Central America. A tropical evergreen species with large
umbels of fragrant, long-tubed, daddy-longlegs-like flowers from mid- to late summer. The leaves are strap-shaped, erect, and acutely tipped, and the 6–15 flowers
have funnel-form cups. It is occasionally cultivated in warmer parts of this country
in zones 9 and 10.

H. praticola Britton & Wilson 1920. Santa Clara, Cuba. A narrow-leaved species
with a four- to seven-flowered umbel. Probably not in cultivation.

H. speciosa Salisbury. A South American tropical evergreen with long petioles.

The white flowers have small cups. Widely cultivated in Brazil and other tropical regions. Unfortunately much of the cultivated stock in Rio de Janeiro seems now to be virused.

H. stenophylla Urban & Fedde 1925. Cuba, marshy savanna, near Jaguey Chico, Santa Clara Province, blooming in August. Related to *H. praticola,* which differs in its linear-lanceolate leaves, which are slightly narrowed below, and its peduncle, which is only half as long. There are five or six flowers in the umbel, with tubes 3½–4¼ inches long with shorter (2¾–3½ inches) tepals.

H. tenuiflora Herbert. Guatemala. Has wide decumbent foliage and slender, fragrant flowers with greenish segments. Blooms in early summer. Easy but tender. Needs plenty of moisture while in active growth.

H. "Tropical Giant." A horticultural name for the most widely cultivated species. Its origin is undoubtedly in the West Indies. It is a magnificent plant with large, shiny leaves and clusters of large, fragrant flowers in midsummer. As it increases rapidly, it is often used as a landscape plant where hardiness is not a factor.

H. tubiflora Salisbury. Northern South America and Trinidad. A tropical evergreen species with petioled leaves and long-tubed perianths. Many flowers are open at one time.

H. venezuelensis Traub 1963. Venezuela, at Estero de Camaguán, state of Guárico. Leaves linear. It flowers in May, with about five white flowers in the umbel and a funnel-form cup.

Mexican *Hymenocallis*

H. acutifolia (Herbert) Sweet 1830. Southern Mexico. A widely cultivated species, flowering in late summer and fall. It is always the last species to flower, beginning in

Hymenocallis acutifolia

early September and sometimes continuing into early December if protected. In the best specimens the filaments spread widely, pulling the cup flat, with the tepals twisting and rolling beneath, making for exceptionally expanded flowers. Lovely. Considering its southern habitat, it is surprisingly hardy, to zone 8 or the southern half of zone 7.

H. araniflora T. M. Howard 1990. Mexico, states of Sinaloa and Nayarit. A recently published species with spreading lanceolate, glaucescent leaves. The small umbels produced in early summer are composed of four to eight flowers with recurved tepals. In order to keep the flower buds from blasting, it needs considerable water prior to flowering. Does not offset, so must be grown from seed.

H. astrostephana T. M. Howard 1981. Guerrero, Mexico. It has costate leaves and two to five long-tubed flowers with small six-pointed cups and spreading segments. Easy, but needs plenty of water while growing.

H. azteciana Traub 1967. Jalisco. A medium-sized species from western Mexico with glaucous petioled leaves and fragrant, small-cupped white flowers with slightly S-shaped floral tubes. Midsummer.

H. baumlii Ravenna 1979. Coastal Veracruz and eastern Mexico. It has erect green strap-shaped leaves and ribbon-like flowers with dangling tepals in early to mid-summer.

H. chiapasiana T. M. Howard 1979 (syn. *H. cleo*). Mexico, Chiapas highlands. It has several medium-sized white flowers and broad, glaucous, petioled leaves in early summer.

H. concinna Baker 1893. Mexico, state of Jalisco. A small plant with erect glaucous leaves and umbels of small white flowers with short, out-curving tubes.

H. cordifolia M. Micheli 1899. Mexico, mountains of coastal Guerrero. Winter-deciduous. It has heart-shaped petiolate leaves and umbels of small white flowers in midsummer. Probably not in cultivation.

H. durangensis T. M. Howard 1978. Mexico, state of Durango. Flowers in early summer, with erect, spiraled bright green linear foliage and outward-facing umbels of white flowers with slightly curved tubes. This one does well in cultivation if given enough water during the growing period.

H. eucharidifolia Baker 1884. Sometimes found in cultivation. Its origin, though unknown, is presumed to be Mexico. A pretty plant with six to eight decumbent subpetiolate leaves. The plant is technically distichous, but the leaves arrange themselves into a rosette. The small umbel has three to five white flowers.

H. glauca (Herbert) Baker 1847. South-central Mexico. Occasionally cultivated, this plant bears about four erect petiolate glaucous leaves and few-flowered scapes with one to six lovely large-cupped white flowers with a yellowish green center. The

*Hymenocallis
durangensis*

flowers, which have a strange sweet-vegetal odor, appear in early summer and last well. Propagation is by seeds, as it seldom makes offsets.

H. graminifolia Greenman 1903. Mexico, state of Morelos. A miniature species with narrow glaucous leaves less than a foot high and two or three small, fragrant flowers with large cups. Grows well in our summers but is difficult to overwinter out of doors.

H. guerreroensis T. M. Howard 1978. Mexico, central Guerrero. A quaint little endemic plant from southern Mexico, blooming early with one to four fragrant flowers and three to five glaucescent linear-elliptic leaves. Very easy, but must be increased from seed, as it makes no offsets.

H. harrisiana Herbert 1840. Mexico, state of Morelos. A widely cultivated species from south-central Mexico with broadly erect glaucescent leaves and umbels of white flowers in early summer. The flowers have small cups and a style that is longer than the segments, often compressed in zigzag fashion in the unopened bud. A nice plant that can take neglect. Semi-hardy.

Another plant sometimes identified as *H. harrisiana* from the state of Guerrero and flowering a month earlier (May) is probably a different species. It has brighter green erect leaves, each with a distinct lateral rib between the central rib and the margins.

H. howardii Bauml 1989. Western Mexico in states of Jalisco and Nayarit. A daffodil-like plant with erect narrow glaucous leaves and umbels of slightly curved short-tubed white flowers in midsummer. Scarcely scented.

H. imperialis Howard 1990. "Big Fatty." Mountains of the coastal bend of south-eastern Mexico. This is a robust tropical plant with long, broadly (to 5 inches) glaucescent leaves and large umbels of fragrant white flowers with the segments

1 mm wide, in early summer. The style is compressed in zigzag fashion in the unopened bud.

H. jaliscensis M. E. Jones 1933. Jalisco, Mexico. A poorly understood plant known only from a single collected specimen. It has been confused with *H. nayaritiana,* which may share some of its habitat.

H. kerseyi T. M. Howard 1999. Mexico, in central Guerrero. A streamside plant with erect narrow leaves and small umbels of non-adnate cupped white flowers. Smaller, but otherwise similar to *H. riparia.*

H. latifolia. See in section "Hymenocallis from the Southeastern United States."

H. leavenworthii (Standley & Streyermark) Bauml 1989. Mexico, state of Michoacán. Has petioled deciduous glaucous leaves and fragrant small-cupped, few-flowered umbels in midsummer.

H. lehmillerii T. M. Howard 2001. Mexico, state of Guerrero. A small coastal species with suberect, glossy strap-shaped foliage and clusters of small-cupped greenish white flowers in early summer.

H. maximilianii T. M. Howard 1981. Mexico, coastal Guerrero. This is somewhat like *H. acutifolia,* with slender, erect, bright green leaves, but the floral segments are not adnate to the cup, and the cups are smaller. Early summer. Becoming widely distributed by seed.

H. nayaritiana T. M. Howard 1978. Mexico, state of Nayarit. A tiny, early (May) flowering species with low, subpetiolate to petiolate foliage and few-flowered umbels with slightly curved tubes. Has been flowered in as little as two years from seed.

H. phalangidis Bauml 1989. Western Mexico. A daffodil-like plant with few-flowered umbels of outward-facing white flowers. Likes at least part shade.

H. pimana Laferrière 1990. Mexico, state of Chihuahua. A species with erect, narrow, spiraled glossy green leaves and large flowers with a yellowish-centered flat cup, remindful of *H. liriosme.* From northwestern Mexico. Early summer.

H. proterantha Bauml & Howard 1979 (incorrectly published as Bauml 1989). Mexico, states of Colima and Jalisco. It has wide, petioled glaucous leaves. The white flowers appear as the leaves go dormant in late summer.

H. pumila Bauml & Howard 1979 (incorrectly published as Bauml 1989). Mexico, states of Jalisco and Colima. A miniature species with low, bright green sword-like leaves. There are one to three large flowers with a small cup above a short scape in early summer.

H. riparia Greenman 1905. Similar to *H. acutifolia* but with a more western distribution and usually flowering several months earlier in the summer. It has slightly smaller, less "arty" flowers than *H. acutifolia.*

H. sonorensis Standley 1937. Mexico, states of Sinaloa and southern Sonora at sea level. It has erect daffodil-like foliage and small umbels of fragrant white flowers with straight tubes. Midsummer. Does not offset.

H. woelfleana T. M. Howard 1978. Mexico, mountains of Sinaloa. It has a short growing season and is winter-deciduous. There are three to six shiny petiolate leaves and three to ten white flowers with small cups in early summer. Somewhat difficult in cultivation.

Hybrids

H. × 'Hispaniola' (*H. traubii* × *H. imperialis*).

H. × 'Invicta' (*H. traubii* × *H. imperialis*).

H. × 'Pirate Queen' (*H. traubii* × *H. liriosme*).

Ismene Salisbury ex Herbert 1812

Ten to fifteen species, native to the Andes of Peru, Bolivia, and Ecuador, differing from *Hymenocallis* in that the leaf bases form a sheathing neck and the flowers are zygomorphic or actinomorphic, declinate or pendulous, with the stamens straight, or in some cases turned inward. *Ismene* was once again segregated from *Hymenocallis* by Alan Meerow in 1990, and appears to be a natural group based on the vegetation, ovary, seed morphology, distribution, and chromosome number.

I. amancaes (Ruiz & Pavón) Nicholson (syn. *Hymenocallis amancaes*). Peru. This is one of only two yellow-flowered species. It does not thrive for very long in our climate.

I. calathina (Ker-Gawler) Herbert (syn. *Hymenocallis narcissiflora*). Andean South America. Though widely grown, this does indifferently in the lower South, but at times survives and flowers.

Ismene × 'Dancing Dolls'

Ismene × 'Sulfur Queen'

I. hawkesii Vargas 1975 (syn. *Hymenocallis hawkesii*). Bolivia, Sandia Province, at 6,000 feet. A dwarf *Ismene* with three to five flowers. Allied to *I. calathina.* Hard to find and harder to keep for long in the lower South, as it is not very hardy and tends to split into smaller bulbs.

I. heliantha Ravenna. Peru, at Cajamarca. A new species with narrow leaves and large solitary yellow flowers. Not in cultivation.

I. longipetala (Lindley) Meerow 1990 (syn. *Elisena longipetala*). Lovely outward-facing flowers with curled tepals and a small, short cup with straight stamens. Hard to find and harder to keep. One of the parents of *I.* × 'Festalis.'

I. macleana Herbert (syn. *Hymenocallis macleana*). A dwarf white-flowered species. Pretty, but does not last long in a hot climate.

I. velardii Traub 1963. Somewhat similar to *I. longipetala,* but has smaller flowers with nearly sessile ovaries and shorter tepal tubes and pedicels. The flowers are a light greenish yellow, the segments are narrowly undulated, and the cup is flattened and small. It is from a lower elevation (1,640 feet) and so may do better for us than some of the others.

Hybrids

I. × 'Dancing Dolls' (*I. amancaes* ×. *I. longipetala*).

I. × 'Festalis' (*I. calathina* × *I. longipetala*).

I. × *lajolla* (*I. calathina* × *Pseudostenomesson vargasii*).

I. × 'Pax' (*I. calathina* × *I. amancaes*). A seedling of Len Woelfle and similar to the one that gave us 'Sulfur Queen,' but this flower is white with yellow tinges.

I. × 'Snowflake' (*I. calathina* × *H. harrisiana*).

I. × *spofforthiana* (*I. calathina* ×. *I. amancaes*).

Ismenocallis × 'Buccaneer'

Ismenocallis × 'Excelsior'

× *Ismenocallis*

A combination of *Hymenocallis* with *Ismene*.
'Buccaneer' (*H. liriosme* × *I. calathina*).
'Daphne' (*H. speciosa* × *I. calathina*).
'Excelsior' (*H. traubii* × *I. calathina*).
'Snowflake' (*H. harrisiana* × *I. calathina*).

Ixiolirion (Fischer) Herbert 1821

A genus of perhaps one species (*I. tartaricum* [syn. *I. montanum*]) found from Asia Minor to Central Siberia and Baluchistan, Pakistan, with tunicated bulbs and an umbel of two to eight light to dark blue flowers. Although widely distributed, it is not known to grow in warm climates.

Leucojum Linnaeus 1753

Snowflakes. About 11 species with umbels of one to five white flowers tipped yellow or green, or tinged with pink. At least one, *L. aestivum*, the summer snowflake, thrives in warm climates, flowering here in spring, with hollow scapes, strap-shaped leaves, and flowers that have club-shaped styles. The snowflakes are related to and often confused with snowdrops (*Galanthus*). Snowflakes have all six tepals the same size, while snowdrops have three short and three long tepals.

L. aestivum Linnaeus. Europe and parts of Asia. This is fine for our climate. 'Gravetye Giant' is the best cultivar, with the largest flowers. The white flowers have a green spot on each tepal. This species will take sun or shade, and will thrive in heavy, damp soils. In the south, it flowers in the spring, in spite of the name *aestivum*, which alludes to summer.

L. autumnale Linnaeus. Portugal. For pots. Thread-like leaves and masses of pinkish-tinged white bells in fall.

L. roseum Martin. A Corsican plant fit for pots, as the crystalline pink flowers are small. Late summer.

L. valentinum Pau. Prostrate leaves and robust spikes of one to six white flowers in autumn. For pots or in the garden.

L. vernum Linnaeus. Southern Europe. This one requires a cold, damp climate and is definitely not for us.

Lycoris Herbert

A genus of showy plants from China, Japan, and Korea, flowering in summer or fall, followed by foliage in autumn or spring. They are particularly amazing in that all of the colors in the spectrum are to be found in the various species and hybrids. This rare feature is shared with only a handful of plants such as *Hyacinthus*, *Iris*, *Polianthes*, and *Primula*. And they choose to flower in what for some are the hottest, driest months of the summer season in late summer and early fall, at which time they bring a decided welcome relief.

Subgenus *Symmanthus* Traub & Moldenke. Perianth fairly regular with tepal tube absent or present, tepal segments little or moderately reflexed.

Subgenus *Eulycoris* Traub & Moldenke. The perianth is irregular, with the tepal tube very short or longer, and the tepal segments much reflexed and waved.

The Species

L. aurea (L'Héritier) Herbert 1819 (syn. *Amaryllis africana*, *A. aurea*, *Lycoris africana*). Hurricane lily. China. Once erroneously thought to have come from Africa (hence that name). Most bulbs commercially sold as *L. aurea* are in fact the related *L. traubii*. Indeed, it is now very difficult to find a commercial source for *L. aurea*. The six or seven flowers face upward at a 45° angle and are a vibrant orange-yellow (cadmium-yellow), with narrow, crisped segments and pedicels ⅗–⁹⁄₁₀ inch long. The floral tubes are straight and ½ inch long. They flower here in early October on stems 2 feet tall. A fountain of relatively tender, almost elliptic glaucescent leaves follows the flowers and will need protection from hard frosts. The plant is seed-fertile and useful for hybridization with a chromosome number of 2n = 12, the same as *L. traubii*. Hybrids between these two are named *L.* × 'La Jolla' and are fertile. Since *L. aurea* is relatively tender, it is best for the lower South, south Texas, and southern California.

L. chinensis Traub 1958. China. The flowers vary in color from chrome-yellow to white. Midsummer. Fertile, but does not do well here. This is one of the putative parents of *L. squamigera*.

L. haywardii Traub 1957. Japan. Flowers orchid-pink tipped violet-blue. Early. Fertile and adaptable to the upper South, but probably not in zones 8 and 9.

L. radiata (L'Héritier) Herbert. China and Japan. Red spider lily. This is the best-known species. Fertile diploid and sterile triploid forms are grown. Radially arranged, recurved red flowers with long exerted filaments on tall, naked stems in August–September.

L. sanguinea Maximowicz 1885. Japan. Blooms early with small scapes of red or orange flowers. Fertile, but rarely blooms in zone 9.

L. sperryi. Chekiang province of China, in hills of Huchow. An orange-yellow large-flowered *Lycoris*. The leaves resemble those of *L. squamigera*, but appear later.

Lycoris radiata   *Lycoris traubii*

L. sprengeri Comes ex Baker 1902. Central China. Flowers carmine, tipped Prussian blue. Fertile. Grows well here, but usually refuses to flower.

L. traubii Hayward 1957. Taiwan. The six outward-facing flowers are saffron yellow, with pedicels up to ⅜ inch long. The tepal segments are narrowly oblanceolate and wider (½–⅝ inch) than those of *L. aurea*. The tepal tubes are ¾ inch long and curved downward, and the spathe bracts are half as long as those of *L. aurea*. *L. traubii* is more cold-resistant than *L. aurea*, and the darker, shiny lorate-lanceolate leaves appear about a month later. Thousands of bulbs of *L. traubii* are annually imported from Japan as *L. aurea*, although they are easily distinguished in several subtle particulars. This is never a hardship, as both species are equally decorative in gardens where climate permits, with *L. traubii* being the hardier of the two by a slight margin. They are easily hybridized, yielding intermediate plants known as *L.* × 'La Jolla,' which are reportedly fertile.

Hybrids

The following are listed as hybrids, due in most cases, to their sterility.

L. albiflora. G. Koidzumi 1924. Japan. August–September. This is probably a natural hybrid between *L. radiata* and *L. aurea*. It is a beautiful plant, and a favorite because of its hardiness, ease of culture, and free-flowering habits, although it is sterile. It increases steadily from year to year, which is important, as it is becoming scarce. The flowers are similar to those of *L. radiata* in form, with slightly larger recurving tepals, opening a lovely pale pastel yellow and turning creamy white with age.

L. × 'Blue Pearl.' Hirao. A Japanese hybrid with umbels of white flowers.

L. caldwellii Traub 1957. China. Flowers pale yellow to creamy white. Probably a hybrid, since it is sterile.

L. × 'Cinnabarina.' A hybrid of unknown origin involving *L. sanguinea* as one

Lycoris albiflora   *Lycoris* × *houdyshellii*

parent. It has glaucous foliage and is easy to grow and flower. The flowers are a lively apricot with burnt-orange tones. Midsummer.

L. × *elsiae* Traub 1958. Probably a sterile hybrid sibling of *L. albiflora*, with which it shares similar habits and cultural requirements, differing mainly in having flesh-pink flowers and less-recurved tepals. Once marketed as "*L. carnea*," and now becoming difficult to find.

L. × 'Hay-jax.' A Sam Caldwell backcross of *L.* × *jacksoniana* × *L. haywardii*. Flowers freely in zones 8 and 9 in midsummer and is self-fertile. The flowers are somewhat similar to *L.* × *jacksoniana* in color and form, rosy-red with blue tips. The umbels are a bit more open at the center and open a week or two later.

L. × 'Hay-sper.' A cross between *L. haywardii* and *L. sperryi*.

L. houdyshellii Traub 1957. China. A lovely and desirable hybrid, though sterile and tender. It flowers early (July–August) and has slightly yellowish or pinkish white flowers turning white with age.

L. incarnata Comes ex Sprenger 1906. China. Perhaps a hybrid (?), as it seems to be sterile. Flowers whitish, keeled pinkish. Grows well in our climate in good exposure but is difficult to flower, as it probably needs colder winters.

L. × *jacksoniana* Traub. A Sam Caldwell hybrid strain between a fertile diploid form of *L. radiata* and *L. haywardii*. A plant with a bright future, *L.* × *jacksoniana* is seed-fertile with us. There are several lovely clones in shades of deep rose with blue tips flowering freely in our late July–early August heat. The stamens are noticeably exerted.

L. × 'La Jolla' (*L. aurea* × *L. traubii*). Traub. An intermediate yellow-flowered strain with both parents sharing the chromosome number of 2n = 12, and with fertile seedlings. This suggests that the relationship between *L. aurea* and *L. traubii* is so close that they may be subspecies of *L. aurea*.

L. × 'Shugetsu.' A free-flowering hybrid of Japanese origin; the parentage is not

Lycoris × 'Shugetsu'   *Lycoris squamigera*

reported. This may be a cross similar to *L.* × *woodii.* There are six or seven large flowers in the large, loose umbel blooming from August to late September. The flowers open pale yellow, overlaid with apricot and pale olive and an occasional red line, turning pastel salmon-apricot with age. The stems are about 1½ feet tall and wine-colored with a powdery bloom. The bluish green autumn foliage is produced after flowering. Although this clone is nearly unknown in this country, it has proved a great success in our climate, increasing and flowering regularly each year, and is apparently as hardy as *L. radiata.*

L. squamigera Maximowicz 1885. Japan. Flowers rose-lilac, tipped bluish. Although said to be a species, it is likely an old, sterile natural hybrid. It was likely based on a cross involving *L. sprengeri* and *L. chinensis.* It grows well in our climate, but usually fails to bloom here, as the embryo buds abort during summer dormancy.

L. straminea Lindley. A tawny yellow form grown in Australia, flowering before *L. radiata.* Reported as a species, but it may be a natural hybrid.

L. × 'Ueki.' A Japanese hybrid that grows well in our climate and sometimes flowers. Perhaps it blooms more reliably where winters are colder, in zones 7 or 8. It flowers in early August with bright rosy red tepals stained halfway to the tips in purplish blue, with exerted stamens. With its unusual markings, it is very lovely. It suggests a parentage involving *L. sprengeri* or *L. haywardii* as a source for the blue markings, with the red color probably originating from *L. sanguinea* or *L. radiata.* I have seen photos of a number of other beautiful red-flowered Japanese hybrids in shades of rose, cerise, and vermilion. All probably involve *L. sanguinea,* which succeeds best in a cooler climate, as one parent.

L. × *woodii* Traub and Moldenke 1957. *L. aurea* × *L. radiata.* The leaves are intermediate between the parents. The flowers are yellow, and its hardiness is assumed to be intermediate.

Narcissus Linnaeus

Narcissi, Daffodils, and Jonquils

"Narcissus" is the Latin name for the beloved daffodil. This name is often applied to forms of *N. poeticus* and *N. tazetta*, as well as all other members of the genus. It has been said that the word "daffodil" is one of the loveliest-sounding words in the English language. "Jonquil" is a synonym for those forms with clustered yellow flowers, and that name is often used in place of "daffodil" in the South. Technically it is applied to *N. jonquilla* and its hybrids that have obvious jonquil characteristics. Currently it is acceptable to use "narcissus" and "daffodil" interchangeably, and either name can also be applied to jonquils.

Who among us is not smitten with Wordsworth's observation:

> *When all at once I saw a crowd,*
> *A host, of golden daffodils;*
> *Beside the lake, beneath the trees,*
> *Fluttering and dancing in the breeze. . . .*
> *Ten thousand saw I at a glance,*
> *Tossing their heads in sprightly dance.*

Daffodil Divisions

Daffodils are currently classified into 12 divisions, based on the lengths of the cups in relation to the perianths, floral posture, whether the corona is doubled or split, and whether the flowers are produced singly or in multiflowered umbels. Members of the first four divisions are difficult to grow and maintain in warmer climates, as they are susceptible to basal rot when exposed to excessive heat and moisture during dormancy. A few are more resistant, and often we must learn this through trial and error as new forms continue to come into general cultivation. Tazetta and jonquil hybrids generally fare better, as do hybrids of *N. triandrus*, *N. cyclamineus*, and some of the other species.

Division 1. Trumpet Daffodils of Garden Origin

One flower per scape. Corona as long as, or longer than, the perianth.

The classic trumpet daffodils of Wordsworth are easily the favorite narcissi, but unfortunately, south of zone 7, they may succumb to basal rot during dormancy.

The combination of high summer temperatures and excessive moisture can be del-eterious to dormant bulbs. There are many clones from which to choose, with the popular 'King Alfred' strains the most widely grown, but not necessarily the most enduring. The best results can be had by choosing from among the earliest-flowering sorts. 'Rijnveld's Early Sensation' is reputed to be one of the earliest of the all-yellow trumpet forms. The two-toned yellow 'Emperor' (William Backhouse, circa 1865) and the bicolored 'Empress' were new around the end of the Civil War. 'Golden Spur' (1885) became popular by the turn of the century and was reputed to flower quite early. It was replaced by the more robust 'King Alfred' (J. Kendall, circa 1899) by the end of the First World War and has lately been considered an heirloom daf-fodil. In the meantime, the original 'King Alfred' has been replaced by a series of look-alikes that have similar color and form but may have improved commercial characteristics, such as larger or earlier flowers, with bulbs that are larger, firmer, better propagators, or have better keeping qualities.

Division 2. Long-cupped Daffodils of Garden Origin

One flower per scape; cup or corona more than a third of, but less than equal to, the length of the perianth. By sheer number of varieties, this group has the largest number of successful varieties for the upper South.

The advisability of selecting the earliest-flowering sorts applies to this division as well. Choose from the older, tried-and-true, virus-free survivors (if you can find them) such as golden yellow 'Carlton' (1937), orange-and-ivory 'Dick Wellband,' yellow 'Fortune' (1924), orange-and-white 'Franciscus Drake' (1921), ivory-and-white 'Ice Follies' (1953), pink-and-white 'Lovenest' (1925), pink-and-white 'Mrs. R. O. Backhouse' (1923), yellow 'Sir Watkin' (1884), or buff-and-white 'Tunis' (1936). Of these, 'Carlton' and 'Fortune' may endure for years, and 'Tunis' and 'Ice Follies' have earned an excellent reputation for permanency. The starry white 'Tunis' with its unusual copper-buff-edged trumpet, is in the "heirloom" category and may now be hard to find. 'Ice Follies,' with its twisted white perianth and large flattish ruffled lemon crown, is popular, widely available, and a reasonably permanent clone.

'Louise de Coligny,' a smallish flower with a long trumpet-like pink cup and white perianth, was promoted in catalogs for its wonderful fragrance. I have tried it on several occasions, and this hidden virtue escapes me. I find that its scent is that of an ordinary daffodil, no more, no less. What amazes is not that an over-zealous catalog writer concocted such flattering purple prose, but that others in the business so willingly follow cattle-like, shamelessly perpetuating the exaggeration. No matter, since this daffodil appears to be of very short duration in warm climates. Better warm-weather choices for pink "trumpet" forms would be 'Mrs. R. O. Backhouse' or 'Lovenest,' if you can find a source for either of them.

Division 3. Short-cupped Daffodils of Garden Origin

One flower per scape; cup or corona not more than a third the length of the perianth segments.

Choose the earliest-flowering forms and the "old reliables" known to be permanent in your own region. Though the list for this division is long, there aren't that many permanent ones in the warmest climates of zones 8 and 9, since the genes of *N. poeticus* are concentrated in the composition of this group. 'Mrs. Nette O'Melvaney,' an heirloom variety with a white perianth and small yellow cup edged orange, was one of the more enduring clones but is now difficult to find. The old 'Barrii Conspicuus' (1869), with its yellow perianth and a small yellow cup edged in red, was popular but became nearly unobtainable during the latter half of this century. 'White Lady' (1869) is a short-cupped daffodil of the old "Leedsii" section, with a white perianth and a small yellow cup, and is reputed to be permanent in the sandy Piney Woods country of east Texas and Louisiana. I have not tried it but am not surprised that it shares the endurance of other old "Leedsiis" like 'Tunis' and 'Ice Follies.'

Division 4. Double Daffodils of Garden Origin

One or more flowers per scape, with doubling of the perianth segments, crown, or both.

The appeal of double-flowered daffodils is due not only to the extra tepals and the doubling of the cups (often in a contrasting color) forming whorls of tepaloids, but also to the extra tepaloids formed by the stamens, which further enhance the flowers. In this respect they are physically different from most other double flowers, and this emphasizes their charm. The tazetta forms do best in our area, and the poetaz the worst, because of the influence of *N. poeticus*. Some of the old generic *incomparabilis* "Phoenix" group are reliable to zone 8, but only marginal in zone 9. Still, they are worth having, as some of them may persist, although the flower buds are apt to abort unless the weather is damp and cool. When they do flower well, they are as lovely as any of the modern double-flowered hybrids. These heirloom *N. × incomparabilis* var. *plenus* forms are variously known as 'Butter and Eggs' (syn. "Golden Phoenix" and "Yellow Phoenix"), 'Primrose Phoenix,' and 'Orange Phoenix' (syn. "Eggs and Bacon"). The same can be said of the old 'Van Sion' (syn. "Tele-monius Plenus"), which was introduced to England circa 1620. This early-flowering antique with its raggedly informal greenish yellow flowers is worth trying and some-times can be a permanent resident although, like most doubles, it is prone to blast if the environs are too warm or dry. Because of this 'Van Sion' is recommended with reservations.

The semi-double primrose-yellow 'Twink,' with its orange tepaloids, was intro-duced in 1926, and was followed by the similarly colored, more double 'Texas' (1938). These were soon joined by a host of newer doubles, as fickle fashions changed. Just as 'Texas' replaced 'Twink,' the yellow-and-orange 'Tahiti' (1956) has since replaced 'Texas.' The all-yellow 'Dick Wilden' is a sport of 'Carlton' and behaves similarly, except that it is cursed by blasting. It is for this reason that I can't recommend it. Unless they are known to flower very early, most doubles share the tendency to blast their buds in warm, dry weather and are not usually recommended.

N. × odorus Linnaeus 'Plenus' ("Double Campernelle") has proved to be a reliable performer in my garden, although a few of its buds may "blast" on occasion if it is grown too dry. Most of the early-flowering double tazettas, such as 'Bridal Crown,' 'Constantinople,' 'Double Roman,' 'Erlicheer,' and 'Golden Rain' are reasonably re-liable. (See Division 8 for more on 'Constantinople,' 'Double Roman,' and 'Erlicheer.') On the other hand, the later-flowering 'Cheerfulness' (1923), a double sport of the late poetaz hybrid 'Elvira,' consistently fails in zones 8 and 9.

Double tazetta forms often produce a few fertile pollen-bearing anthers between the tepaloids, and though they are triploids, it is sometimes possible to obtain seed by applying their pollens to *N. jonquilla, N. papyraceus,* or other species, in hopes of producing double-flowered hybrids.

'Queen Anne's Double Jonquil' is a double form of *N. jonquilla* or one of its hy-brids. (Queen Anne of Austria is commemorated.) Its blasting performance for warm climates is apparently unreported, although it may grow as well as the normal single-flowered forms. The flowers are said to be small golden balls, and there are several flowers per scape. An old engraving shows that it is of semi-double form, with one row of normal perianth segments containing a ball-like corona of tepaloids. An elu-sive jewel, it is difficult to find in modern catalogs or lists in this country. Moreover, it is reported that most stocks are virused.

'Pencrebar,' a very similar all-yellow double *N. jonquilla* form, is occasionally of-fered, but I am unaware of its performance in warmer climates. In *Narcissus,* Michael Jefferson-Brown states that it is very much like 'Queen Anne's Double Jonquil' and may be a minor mutant form of it.

TO SUCCEED WITH DOUBLE DAFFODILS:

1. Select only the earliest-flowering sorts.
2. Select the semi-doubles, as the tendency toward blasting is enhanced by higher numbers of tepaloids.
3. Choose from the yellow-flowered forms, as the white-flowered forms tend to flower later and are more inclined to blast.
4. Keep them constantly cool and moist while in bud and while flowering, since all those extra tepaloids require extra moisture.
5. Keep them cool with a heavy mulch and by providing partial shade in the afternoon.

Division 5. Triandrus Daffodils of Garden Origin

Characteristics of *N. triandrus* Linnaeus obvious. Usually two or more pendant flowers per scape. Perianth segments reflexed.

Because of their tendency to flower late, *N. triandrus* hybrids get mixed reviews in the warmer climates. Some are reasonably permanent, but many are not, probably due to basal rot. A few hybrids, such as 'Hawera' (W. M. Thompson 1938), 'April Tears' (1939), and 'Fairy Chimes' (*N. triandrus* × *N. jonquilla*), have the potential for durability. The tazetta-like umbels of 'Silver Chimes' (1916) (*N. triandrus* × *N. tazetta* cv. 'Grand Monarque') somewhat resemble its pollen parent, 'Grand Monarque,' but the flowers tend to nod and are midseason to late, due in part to genes inherited from *N. triandrus*. In this instance, thanks to the heat-loving *N. tazetta* parent, the worrisome lateness does not impede success. The perianths are white with cream-yellow cups and have a strange but pleasing scent combination from the two parents.

Hybrids from *N. triandrus* × *N. jonquilla* behave much like those of other hybrid jonquils, with clusters of two or three graceful pale yellow flowers. 'Hawera' is popular and reasonably enduring and is currently listed in most bulb catalogs. Only the strange lemony-sweet scent and the two or three nodding flowers betray its *N. triandrus* ancestry.

Division 6. Cyclamineus Daffodils of Garden Origin

Characteristics of *N. cyclamineus* de Candolle obvious. Usually one flower per scape. Perianth segments reflexed. Flowers at an acute angle to the stem, on a very short pedicel.

Although *N. cyclamineus* is not permanent in hot, dry climates, preferring cool, moist situations, some of its hybrids do yeoman duty in hotter climates, outperforming their larger trumpet daffodil counterparts of Division 1, while providing us with their essence. The flowers have much character, demurely glancing downward, with the perianth segments reflexing in varying degrees and cleanly emphasizing the stark beauty of the trumpet. This is a refreshingly attractive pose for those accustomed to old-fashioned daffodils whose perianth segments lean lazily forward, giving the illusion that they aren't quite fully opened.

'February Gold' (1923) is a fine example of a compact, early-flowering yellow *N. cyclamineus* hybrid with a Division 1 trumpet daffodil as the other parent. It has slightly reflexed perianth segments, plus a wonderful tendency to abide in our warmer climates of zones 8 and 9. It is highly recommended.

'Jetfire' (Mitsch 1969) is very exciting, with orange-yellow trumpets and broad yellow perianths, initially flowering freely enough on sturdy stems, but we don't really know yet what its endurance record will be in hotter climates.

'March Sunshine' (de Graaff 1923), a peer of 'February Gold,' is less frequently listed or grown. In spite of their names, the difference in flowering time is only a matter of days.

'Peeping Tom' (1948) is everyone's favorite, and very dramatic, with long, narrow trumpets, looking like an enlarged version of *N. cyclamineus*. It should be as long-lived as 'February Gold,' but is handicapped because commercial stocks have been nearly devastated by virus. Finding healthy stocks is a challenge.

The dwarf 'Tête à Tête' (Alec Gray 1949), like 'Jumblie' (1952), is a fortuitous back-cross between *N. cyclamineus* and 'Cyclataz' (*N. cyclamineus* × *N. tazetta* cv. 'Grand Soleil d'Or'), with one to three small, nodding yellow trumpets on short stems. They are popular with the florist trade for winter forcing, as the little bulbs, if planted early in small pots in little more than a handful of soil mix, are irrepressible in their zeal to flower. Nearly everyone admires the cheery, tiny flowers in the doldrums of midwinter.

I grow an unidentified modern yellow *N. cyclamineus* hybrid whose label I lost long ago. The golden yellow flowers, which are larger than those of 'February Gold,' have slightly reflexing, overlapping segments and large trumpets posed in a horizontal direction. The stems are less than a foot tall. It persists from year to year. It's a shame that I am unable to identify it, as it is the finest of this type that I have grown, increasing well and flowering in early March each year. With such qualities it should be used as a basic landscape daffodil. There are a number of new *N. cyclamineus* hybrids that flower well for a year or two after planting and then fail to perennialize; however, permanency in the newer daffodils is something we must learn through trial and error. Some *N. cyclamineus* hybrids are up to the challenge.

Division 7. Jonquilla Daffodils of Garden Origin

Characteristics of *N. jonquilla* Linnaeus obvious. Usually one to three flowers per rounded scape. Narrow, dark green leaves; spreading, reflexed perianth segments; fragrant flowers.

The early-flowering form of sweetly scented *N. jonquilla* is one of the most enduring of daffodils in warmer climates. Perhaps it is more resistant to basal rot (and other daffodil maladies) than most of the others. Certainly many of its hybrids, such as *N.* × *odorus* Linnaeus (*N. jonquilla* × *N. pseudonarcissus*), inherit a wonderful longevity, flowering in zones 8 and 9 in February and early March. *N.* × *odorus* is the grex name for this group, sometimes called "campernelles," but mostly called "jonquils" in the deep South. There are several different clones, differing in minor ways, but the common *N.* × *odorus campernelli* is best known and most widely grown. Usually there are one to three flowers per scape, but many of them are flawed with split perianths or lacking one or two tepals. A handsome double-flowered form (discussed above under Division 4) is the result of a mutation and is as enduring as the common single that spawned it.

Other forms of *N.* × *odorus*, such as *N.* × *odorus rugulosus* 'Orange Queen' and 'Golden Sceptre,' do variously well. 'Golden Sceptre' is pretty enough, and a very old variety. It usually bears a single flower here, rarely two. By today's standards, it is outperformed by 'Trevithian,' 'Sweetness' and 'Quail.'

The initial jonquil hybrids were between *N. jonquilla* and other wild species, but in later years, modern trumpet hybrids have served as seed parents instead of wild forms of *N. pseudonarcissus*, making for larger-flowered first-generation hybrids. With a few notable exceptions, such as 'Quick Step,' nearly all hybrids of *N. jonquilla* are sterile.

Narcissus × *odorus*
("Single Campernelle")

Narcissus × *intermedius*

N. × *intermedius* Loiseleur ('Texas Star') is the grex name for a yellow-flowered natural hybrid between *N. jonquilla* and a form of *N. tazetta*, perhaps *N. canaliculatus*. This is an excellent plant, given good drainage, for those living where winters are mild. The species name describes the plant, which is intermediate in all ways and very satisfactory for gardens and for naturalizing. It looks like a stocky little jonquil, with loose clusters of yellow flowers nestled within the longer, erect leaves. The cups are a bright golden yellow, while the perianth segments are a shade lighter in hue. When it is viewed more closely, the tazetta relationship becomes more apparent. Since both parents are fragrant, it is no surprise that the flowers of *N.* × *intermedius* are also sweetly scented. The bulbs are rounded, medium-small in size, and tend to grow shallowly. If it has a fault, it is that the stems are not quite tall enough to display the flowers properly above the erect foliage. The plant is sterile like most jonquil hybrids and does not set seed.

'Pipit' (1965) is one of the more enduring popular jonquil hybrids from the late Grant Mitsch of Oregon. There are two to three flowers per scape, with yellow perianths and cream cups that turn white, a reverse bicolor combination.

'Quail' (Mitsch 1974) is a later, improved version of 'Sweetness,' somewhat similar in size and a bronzy yellow, but with two to three flowers per stem. The perianth is composed of broad, overlapping segments with a similarly colored cup. Only a few days separate the flowering of the two varieties. In my garden 'Quail' increases steadily from year to year, flowering regularly, and I can't recommended it too strongly.

'Quick Step' is a highly fertile reverse bicolor jonquil hybrid that should be in the collection of every serious breeder. Fertile clones such as the yellow tazetta hybrid 'Matador' and 'Quick Step' serve to open doors to a future of more varied and improved multiflowered hybrids, uniting the jonquils and tazettas with other daffodil forms.

'Sugarbush.' Modern jonquil hybrids are now found with white perianths and yellow or pink cups. They are quite lovely and initially perform reasonably well, but may not be as eternally faithful as the yellow ones, perhaps because of basal rot and/or virus. Of the ones that I have tried, the most enduring is 'Sugarbush,' which has one or two flowers with white perianths and longish yellow cups. It is as winsome as 'Sweetness,' but daintier and a little later in flowering.

'Sweetness' (1939). The encomiums used to describe 'Trevithian' also apply to 'Sweetness.' One of the older hybrid jonquils, it is still one of the most enduring and best for the garden as the scapes are well displayed above the leaves. 'Sweetness' begins flowering several days earlier than 'Quail' or 'Trevithian,' and the starry, pointed perianths and cups are a brighter, deeper shade of yellow. Mostly there is but a single flower per stem, but a bulb will produce several stems. It is inexpensive and should be freely used in the garden, since it is a durable spring flower in warm climates.

'Suzy' (1954) has several flowers with large yellow perianths and dark orange cups and may perform well if conditions are to its liking.

'Trevithian' (1927) is currently popular, inexpensive, and widely available, since it is as permanent as any members of the jonquil clan. The one to three flowers have rounded lemon-yellow perianths and small flat cups in the same color. The scapes are taller and begin flowering as the campernelles are finishing their display, but they are just as sturdy and permanent in the landscape as the campernelles. Generally you only have to plant 'Trevithian' once in order to always have it.

Many modern jonquil hybrids are not listed here because they did not persist or because my impecunious wallet could not afford the gamble at the higher prices associated with newer introductions. For expensive introductions, a good strategy is to wait for stocks to increase, with the subsequent lowering of prices, depending on supply and demand.

Division 8. Tazetta (Polyanthus) Daffodils of Garden Origin

Characteristics of *N. tazetta* Linnaeus obvious. Usually 3–20 flowers per stout scape. Broad leaves; perianth segments spreading, not reflexed; fragrant flowers.

Like the jonquils, tazettas are excellent daffodils for the Sun Belt, and here we must pause to make some serious selections. As hybrid sources for new warm-weather daffodils, the tazettas have scarcely been tapped. Earlier hybridizing efforts were restricted to hardier forms, but today it would be well to consider the opposite, breeding for forms tolerant of the milder climates of southern California, the south-eastern Atlantic coast, and the deep South, whether hardy or not. Generally our choices have been limited to a few standard varieties, but the options should continue to improve.

Since there are many tazetta forms, the correct identification and nomenclature for some of them can be a minor stumbling block. At this point I wish to acknowledge the invaluable information generously supplied by William R. P. Welch, a Californian and an eminent aficionado and breeder of tazettas, jonquils, and other warm-weather narcissi. Though I have experienced growing narcissi through trial and error in east and south-central Texas, I am deeply indebted to Bill Welch for his scholarly, authoritative guidance in this discussion of warm-weather (Sun Belt) daffodils. Both he and R. A. Scamp of the United Kingdom list many tazetta species and hybrids.

PAPERWHITES AND SIMILAR FORMS

N. papyraceus Ker-Gawler is the common "paperwhite narcissus." Although it is now also correct to refer to "paperwhite daffodils," traditional gardeners of the South may balk and be more comfortable calling them "narcissi."

"Paperwhite" narcissus is found wild in the south of France, Italy, Spain, and North Africa. Some consider it a variety of *N. tazetta,* but this seems unrealistic, as *N. papyraceus* is normally a fertile diploid, easily reseeding itself, with much diversity in the always-fragrant pure white seedlings. This is usually a sure sign of normal species behavior. The flowers are heavily scented, with an odor that some classify as intoxicatingly "musky." Others simply regard it as cloying. It's not a bad smell, but I would not like to be in a small room with a large bouquet of it for any protracted length of time.

As there is quite a bit of variation in *N. papyraceus,* there are selections that flower early, midseason, or late, but all are good in the sunny outdoors in the warm climates of zones 8, 9, and 10. They increase rapidly by offsetting, but this can be deterred by planting the bulbs more deeply, to a depth of 8–10 inches. Bulbs will then become larger, producing fewer offsets and usually yielding more scapes with larger clusters of flowers.

Paperwhites are also easily grown in containers, in fiber, pebbles, or gravel, if kept well-watered. They are best kept in sunlight until the buds begin opening lest they stretch and become top-heavy.

Thanks to their diversity, several recent Israeli pure white paperwhite selections are cultivated under the clonal names of 'Galilee,' 'Jerusalem' ('Shelag'), and 'Ziva.'

A few paperwhites have cream-white cups. Otherwise the cups are typically short

and narrow, like the usual garden forms. Some growers may consider them as "black sheep" among otherwise immaculate pure white forms. Such minor variations are to be expected in any colony of wildlings and
should be considered normal. It is this diversity that
permits selections to be made, for any reason that
pleases the collector.

A number of recent hybrids of the paperwhite with
yellow-flowered *N. tazetta* forms are sweetly perfumed, cream-colored with light-yellow cups, and
have clonal names in English and Hebrew, such as
'Israel' ('Omri'), 'Bethlehem' ('Nony'), and 'Nazareth'
('Yael'). Although sometimes sold as "yellow paper-

Narcissus x 'Omri'

whites," these are not as deeply colored as the familiar 'Grand Soleil d'Or' but are
intermediate offspring between diploid forms of the "Sols" and the paperwhites.
They are sterile, presumably with 21 chromosomes, 11 from the paperwhites and 10
from the "Sols." While lovely in their own right, they don't qualify as true
"paperwhites" in the strictest sense and are genetically similar to the old *N.* x *italicus*.

Theoretically, a double-flowered true paperwhite would be most remarkable, but
none seem to exist, although the popular 'Erlicheer' approaches that goal. Currently
a so-called "double paperwhite" form from Israel is being marketed, but it is actually one of two double-flowered forms of the 'Chinese Sacred Lily,' known as 'Constantinople' and 'Double Roman' respectively. Both clones produce flowers with a
few fertile anthers and may prove useful for breeding improved double tazettas.

'Double Roman,' which is usually semi-double but occasionally fully double,
is the best-known form. The flowers, which are smaller than those of 'Constantinople,' are gracefully carried in a horizontal pose on strong stems. A fine engrav-

Narcissus x 'Double Roman'

ing of 'Double Roman' which can be seen in Peter Barre's *Ye Narcissus or Daffodyl Flowere, and Hys Roots* illustrates the semi-double condition that sets the two clones apart. 'Double Roman' usually has one or two whorls of cream-white perianth segments in which is set a ball-like crown of cream-white and orange-yellow tepaloids. The stamens also acquire tepaloid vestiges, which help fill the cup.

'Constantinople' is a fully double-flowered clone with three or more rows of cream-white perianth segments, combined with many extra sets of small orange-yellow and cream-white tepaloids where the cup should be. Apparently this name is of recent origin, having emerged near the end of the twentieth century in recent bulb catalogs. It is sometimes erroneously listed as a "double paperwhite" even though it looks nothing like the paperwhites. The fragrance has the same pleasing fruity citrus quality as that of 'Double Roman.' Unfortunately the added weight of the larger flowers of 'Constantinople' causes them to droop depressingly. The stems will need staking, as they often are unable to support the top-heavy clusters. Compared to 'Double Roman,' this form makes smaller, rounder bulbs. In spite of flaws, it's an interesting clone deserving of cultivation. Unfortunately commercial stocks have become widely virused, and growers need to clean up existing stocks through meristem culture.

'Chinese Sacred Lily.' This familiar bicolored tazetta occurs in single- and double-flowered forms. It is an old favorite with creamy white perianths and large, orange-yellow cups, but is more tender than most tazettas. The umbels usually consist of six to ten flowers (12 at most) with a heavenly citrus-like perfume reminding one of the scent of a Christmas mixture of tangerines, oranges, and grapefruit—a delightfully exotic, memorable scent. The plant is triploid, and thus mostly sterile, as noted by William Welch: "It would be nice if it were a tetraploid so that one could more readily breed from it, but it is a triploid and self-sterile and its pollen has minimal capacity for function. I don't think there is anything of the 'Chinese Sacred Lily' in anything we grow."

N. canaliculatus hort. is a related miniature species, quite similar to the 'Chinese Sacred Lily' in most respects, save that the smaller, narrower leaves are deeply channeled and the plant is smaller in all of its parts. The smaller flowers tend to have reflexing perianths. It is known to be a triploid with 30 chromosomes. The color and fragrance of the flowers are the same as for the 'Chinese Sacred Lily.' Even when it persists, it has a poor record for flowering reliably from year to year, as the small bulbs are inclined to split into tiny bulbs. It may be of interest to collectors but is not recommended for the landscape.

'GRAND SOLEIL D'OR' AND VARIANTS

A popular old tazetta, the yellow-flowered 'Grand Soleil d'Or' sports an unwieldy name, and is more often referred to as "Sol d'Or" or simply as "Sols." There are two distinct commercial forms, each with its own special merits, and other forms are also recognized, such as 'Autumn Sol's,' and 'Newton.'

The classic Guernsey form has bright yellow rounded perianths with contrasting bright orange-red cups and is sweetly scented. The foliage is comparatively darker, coarser, and more glaucescent. It's a wonderfully lovely tazetta, but stocks are generally virused. Although it seems to be able to coexist with the virus, its performance is diminished.

Narcissus × 'Grand Soleil d'Or'

A second form ("French Sol") has a more pointed perianth, orange-yellow cups, a less sweet, more pungent scent, and paler glaucescent foliage in a lighter shade of green. Foliage usually emerges with virused streaks, even from freshly planted bulbs.

'Golden Rain,' a double yellow-flowered form derived from the "French Sol," has recently been introduced and offered by Bill Welch. It is said to have strong stems supporting 10–15 rich yellow, fully double fragrant flowers, much like a yellow-flowered form of 'Erlicheer,' but even more double. Unfortunately, the unopened buds won't expand if picked and placed in water before they begin opening naturally on the stem.

BICOLORED TAZETTAS

Bicolored tazettas with white perianths and yellow- or cream-colored cups include 'Avalanche,' 'Gloriosus,' and 'Grand Monarque,' plus the closely allied "Pearls," "Primos," *N. ochroleucus,* and *N.* × *italicus.*

'Grand Monarque' is an old favorite, and possibly an old Dutch hybrid at least 200 years old, registered in 1890. The *Journal of the American Daffodil Society* featured 'Grand Monarque' on its cover in the December 1985 issue. Because the pedicels are of varying lengths, the large, informal umbels are somewhat pyramidal in shape. The white perianths contain irregularly shaped lemon-yellow cups. This carefree aspect easily distinguishes 'Grand Monarque' from the more formal, uniformly pedicelled, compact heads and more circular cups of 'Grand Primo,' with which it is sometimes confused. It is more apt to be confused with 'Avalanche,' as they differ mainly in the umbel size, pedicel lengths, and the number and size of the florets. 'Grand Monarque' is known to be both pollen- and seed-fertile, making it useful for breeding tazetta novelties. It is found growing in some California gardens as well as in the United Kingdom. The U.K. bulbs originally came from the Netherlands, while the California bulbs were imported from the United Kingdom, the Netherlands, and Australia.

Narcissus × 'Avalanche'

'Avalanche,' of unknown origin, is sometimes called 'Compressus' and is similarly colored, but the rounded flowers are smaller, and there may be more of them in an umbel. The inflorescence is informal, with pedicels of varying lengths, giving the umbel a somewhat pyramidal appearance. The flowers have creamy white perianths with bright lemon-yellow cups and are sweetly scented. They are known to be pollen- and seed-fertile. The charming 'Avalanche' deserves to be in any collection of tazettas. Its one fault is that the foliage can be overlong for the scape, interfering with the display of the flowers.

'Gloriosus' is rarely seen in this country, but it is a lovely white and orange-yellow tazetta bicolor with slightly longer cups than those of other tazettas, and it flowers at midseason. It is known to be a fertile diploid and is closely allied to the wild *N. tazetta* of the Mediterranean. When crossed with paperwhites, plants of this type give rise to hybrids like 'Grand Monarque' and the various "Primos," "Pearls," and 'Scilly White.' Although each clone is slightly different, they share a remarkable family resemblance, and for the novice they can be confusing unless labels are carefully maintained. The white perianth segments are similar, differing slightly in form, and the cups vary slightly in shades of yellow, cream, or white. Each clone has a distinct flowering time—early, midseason, or late, according to variety. And while their flowering seasons overlap, each is worth having to fully extend the tazetta season from winter to midspring.

'Early Pearl' (registered in 1983; also known as 'White Pearl' and 'French Monarque') is the earliest of these, often flowering in January. It is possibly the form grown in the distant past as 'French Monarque.' It belongs in any warm-winter garden. It is inclined to increase rapidly, so bulbs should be planted deeply to slow them down and keep them of flowering size. This form is reminiscent of the paperwhites, since the cream-colored cups rapidly fade to white, giving the appearance of an all-white umbel.

'Polly's Pearl' is similarly colored, but flowers a month later. It is much like 'Grand Primo,' but the cups are broader and paler, becoming near-white at maturity and suggesting an "improved" paperwhite with darker green foliage. The pedicel lengths are intermediate between 'Grand Primo' and the others. This variety is winsome and certainly belongs in any collection of tazetta narcissus.

'White Pearl' is somewhat like 'Grand Primo' but has paler cups and is lighter overall. Except for the larger size and shape of the cup and the broader perianth segments, it might easily be mistaken for a paperwhite. 'White Pearl' resembles 'Polly's Pearl' in color as the flowers mature, and it is easy for novices to confuse the two. The flowers of 'Polly's Pearl' are slightly larger, while 'White Pearl' produces more scapes per bulb and increases more rapidly.

'Grand Primo' is found wherever tazettas can be grown out of doors and has always been popular. The familiar bicolored flowers have cream-white perianths in which are set medium-sized pale lemon-yellow cups. Though I have never seen this mentioned, the precise, densely compact, rounded umbels give them a hyacinth-like quality, but on taller stems, due to the pedicels being nearly equal in length. The clone has wonderful vigor and thrives even with neglect. When they are grown together, it is easy to see that the foliage of 'Grand Primo' is darker than that of 'Polly's Pearl.' 'Grand Primo' also increases more rapidly than 'Polly's Pearl' and behaves as a perennial in a warm-climate garden. It seems hardier than most tazettas simply because it bides its time before appearing and flowering in late February or early March. Late frosts sometimes damage the flowers of precocious tazettas, but it is rare for this to happen to the tardier flowers of 'Grand Primo.'

Narcissus × 'Grand Primo'

'Erlicheer' is thought to be the fully double-flowered form of 'Grand Primo,' having the same compact umbels (all pedicels are of the same length) and dark green leaves. On rare occasions, 'Erlicheer' is said to lose its doubleness and revert to the single form, but I have

Narcissus × 'Erlicheer'

never seen this. There are also yellow and yellowish forms in the "Primo" group, and thus there is a 'Yellow Primo' and a 'Grand Primo Citronière.' These names were formerly considered as synonyms of one another, but now the latter seems to be a synonym for the usual white-flowered form.

A form with the curious nickname of "Seventeen Sisters" may be found in lists, but this name is often applied to various bicolored tazettas, many of which may carry approximately 17 florets per scape when the bulbs are deeply planted and well established.

Recently a two-toned yellow form was found and christened 'Montopolis,' with the declaration that it has *N. tazetta* and *N. jonquilla* as its ancestors. But it has been suggested that it may be the same as an old form listed as *N. ochroleucus* by the American Daffodil Society.

N. ochroleucus is reportedly scattered throughout the South, including northern Mississippi, where the hardier jonquils replace tazettas. Certainly we have no proof that this is a spontaneous wild form. More likely it is the result of an open pollination in the garden. Genetically it is a triploid, with two parts tazetta and one part *N. jonquilla*. The foliage is narrower and a darker green than that of 'Grand Primo,' and it flowers somewhat later. It has the usual "Primo" appearance, with pale yellow perianths and lemon-yellow cups, fading in strong light to appear somewhat similar to the original 'Grand Primo' coloration. Thanks to the *N. jonquilla* ancestry it is known to survive sub-zero temperatures without damage.

'Scilly White' is sometimes listed and is similar to 'Polly's Pearl' but is said to be less vigorous and is rarely seen in this country. The styles are recessed, when compared to 'Polly's Pearl,' but this insignificant detail would go unnoticed in the landscape.

N. × italicus (Ker-Gawler) Baker. Throughout the deep South may be found a

Narcissus × italicus

tazetta that looks much like a paperwhite, but whose informal clusters of fragrant, starry flowers have wavy cream perianths and small lemon-yellow cups. The perianth segments are narrowly pointed and informally twisted, and the cups are narrower than those of paperwhites, though twice as long. The foliage is a dull glaucescent green. This may be an ancient natural hybrid derived from *N. papyraceus* and another tazetta, which would account for its sterility. It is to be found flowering in great abundance in late January and early February around the Gulf

Coast, though strangely it seems not to be found in commerce. Were it not for its abundance in old gardens and cemeteries, one might lament its anonymity, as it seems not to fit into the general scheme of modern daffodil culture. Some authorities place it as *N.* × *italicus,* while others refer to it as "Minor Monarque," almost a contradiction in terms. Such a nice, enduring, sweet-scented variety deserves more respect and popularity.

POETAZ HYBRIDS

Poetaz narcissi were effected by hybridizing various forms of *N. tazetta* with forms of *N. poeticus* for the purpose of producing cluster-flowered (polyanthus) hybrids with a more cold-hardy constitution. The results were as expected, but many clones flowered rather late and lacked some of the disease resistance and enduring vigor of the tazettas. Some poetaz fail miserably from basal rot, while other, more resistant forms seem reasonably permanent to zone 8.

'Cragford' (1930). This lovely hybrid is remarkable in that it flowers much earlier and is more tender than the bulk of poetaz narcissi. (Because of the *N. poeticus* ancestry, most poetaz hybrids tend to flower later than the true tazettas). The flowers are white with bright orange cups and can be flowered at approximately the same season as paperwhites. For this reason alone, they are worth having, provided that basal rot is not a problem. 'Abba' is a double-flowered sport of 'Cragford' and should behave similarly in zones 8 and 9.

'Early Splendor' is a midseason poetaz hybrid with orange cups and white perianths, and not nearly so early to flower as 'Cragford.'

'Geranium' (1930). A popular late-spring-flowering hybrid with three or four flowers with white perianths and orange-red cups. Because of its late flowering, its reliability in warm spring climates is questionable.

'Golden Dawn' (1958). This is one of the best, because of its totally enduring habits and unusual pedigree, which includes the bloodlines of *N. tazetta, N. jonquilla,* and *N. poeticus.* The flowers have bright yellow perianths with flattish orange cups. This hybrid is proving to be both a reliable, generous bloomer and a permanent perennial, as each bulb will usually send up secondary (and tertiary) scapes following the initial flush. Recommended, but may need frequent division.

'Glorious' (1923) has three or so rounded flowers with white perianths and red cups. It is fairly early and also fertile and thought to be the tazetta parent of 'Geranium' and 'Early Splendor.'

'Laurens Koster' (1906). One of the original poetaz hybrids, with white perianths and golden cups. Though once very popular, it has become a scarce heirloom. It succeeds to zone 8 and the upper part of zone 9.

OTHER TAZETTA HYBRIDS

N. × *intermedius* is a natural hybrid between *N. tazetta* and *N. jonquilla,* described in Section 7.

'Matador' (1958) is an important genetic breakthrough and the darling of tazetta breeders because it is seed- and pollen-fertile and thoroughly charming with its yellow perianth and orange-red cups. Its influence will be felt well into the twenty-first century.

'Minnow' (1962) is a currently popular miniature among the tazetta hybrids with gold cups and cream perianths. It has yet to establish a reputation as a permanent garden plant in the lower South, but the potential is there.

'Silver Chimes' (1916) is a wonderful hybrid of *N. triandrus* × 'Grand Monarque' and can be regarded as permanent in a garden. The slightly nodding waxy flowers are much like those of 'Grand Monarque' in size, but the cups are paler, opening creamy and fading to white. They bloom rather late and have a peculiar fragrance due to the *N. triandrus* parent. Many commercial stocks are reported to be virused.

Division 9. Poeticus Daffodils of Garden Origin

Characteristics of *N. poeticus* Linnaeus. Usually one flower per scape. Pure white perianth segments; corona usually disc-shaped, with a green or yellow and red ring. Fragrant flowers.

N. poeticus is the fragrant white-flowered "poet's narcissus" and has been a cornerstone of daffodil hybridization. Sometimes called "pheasant's eyes," its disc-like bright-red-rimmed green-and-yellow cups have contributed the rich colors of red, green, orange, and pink to the cups and trumpets of modern daffodils. The advent of the poet's narcissi marks the end of another daffodil flowering season. They revel in a cool, moist mountainous environment, and this is their downfall in the deep South and on the Pacific Coast, where the combination of drought and heat is lethal to them. They resent being disturbed and are poor keepers out of the ground. As a result of these problems, only the relatively early *N. radiiflorus* (a closely related species) is tentatively recommended for warm-winter climates. It is said to have a windmill-like narrow perianth that does not recurve and a red-rimmed yellow cup. The leaves are said to be stiffly erect. I have not yet grown it, but it is said to be the only poet suited to the South, at least to zone 8, and well worth a try. If it lives up to its friendly reputation, it might be useful for the development of a new race of poetaz hybrids.

The lovely *N. poeticus* classically conveys one of the essential images of the genus.

Unfortunately its late flowering and requirements of cool weather with adequate moisture in late spring are in conflict with normal environmental conditions of warmer climates. Thus it is apt to fail and is not recommended in zones 8, 9, and 10. A few of its hybrids, such as the poetaz narcissus (discussed in Division 8), are marginal in zones 8 and 9.

Division 10. Species and Wild Forms and Wild Hybrids

All species and wild or reputedly wild forms and hybrids, including wild double forms of these varieties. Among the species can be found miniature trumpet daffodils, as well as some of the more unusual forms, such as the hoop petticoats, autumn-blooming narcissi, green-flowered narcissi, etc. Most of these will reseed themselves if given the opportunity.

AUTUMN-FLOWERING SPECIES

There are several autumn-flowering species, including *N. serotinus; N. viridiflorus,* allied to *N. jonquilla;* and *N. elegans,* allied to *N. tazetta.* It is not fully established that they will persist in the ground in the lower South, but they may very well do so, as they are natives of the Mediterranean, from southern Spain and North Africa. They are easily grown in containers set out of doors under trees, where they can get the needed protection that they deserve. In the coldest weather they will need some protection from hard freezes.

    N. elegans (Haworth) Spach is tazetta-like in its habits and is inclined to have two or more flat leaves. There may be two to ten fragrant white flowers with twisted tepals and small greenish yellow coronas.

    N. serotinus Linnaeus has usually solitary, upfacing flowers; when it is well-grown, there may be a second or even a third flower in the umbel. The glistening 1½-inch white flowers are tazetta-like, with rounded perianths and tiny, shallow olive-yellow or orange-yellow cups. Offsets are not freely formed, but it can be easily propagated from seed, which will germinate shortly after ripening. Although reputed to be fragrant, it is often scentless, depending on the clone. After flowering, the stem functions as a leaf in photosynthesis and should not be cut, as mature bulbs may fail to produce true leaves. Pollen from this species should be tried on *N. viridiflorus, N. elegans,* and various tazettas in order to obtain strains of autumn- or winter-flowering hybrids.

    N. viridiflorus Schousboe has two to five uniformly green flowers with a powerful fragrance which, as is the case with paperwhite narcissus, people either love or dislike. The mature bulbs are leafless, with the floral stem persisting and functioning as a leaf in photosynthesis. The cup is reduced to six tiny lobes, and the relationship to *N. jonquilla* is immediately apparent. Obviously such flowers are not intended for the cut-flower trade, though they last rather well, considering that they can bloom in hot autumn weather! *N. viridiflorus* is rare in cultivation but can easily be propagated by seed, flowering in three or four years.

Hybrids can be created with these autumn-flowering species for gardeners enjoying mild winters, and hybrids between *N. elegans* and *N. viridiflorus* are known. Pollen can easily be stored in order to cross them with spring-flowering daffodils, and certainly there is no reason not to cross them with autumn- and winter-flowering tazettas, aside from reduced hardiness.

OTHER SPECIES AND WILD FORMS AND WILD HYBRIDS

The "Lent lilies" are variable forms of *N. pseudonarcissus* and do very well in the lower South, in the lower half of zone 8, and tolerably well in the upper half of zone 9. It's a shame that anyone would call any daffodil a "lily," but for some people almost anything growing from a bulb is fair game to be called "lily." For all practical purposes, "Lent lilies" are what everyone thinks of when "daffodils" are mentioned. That is to say that they are all yellow in color and of trumpet form. The tepals are swept slightly forward and downward, and they are not very tall (8 inches).

The tiny "hoop petticoat daffodils" are typified by *N. bulbocodium* subsp. *bulbocodium* and its several varieties, plus several related miniatures, typified by *N. cantabricus* and its several varieties, *N. romieuxii*, and *N. hedraeanthus*. All are desirable for collectors, although many are quite rare, expensive, and available only from specialists. One will want to grow these in pans or pots to enjoy indoors during the winter months. Only *N. bulbocodium* will concern us here, as it is hardy, inexpensive, and widely available. It thrives out of doors in the acid sandy soils where pine trees grow in the South. Given such a friendly environment it will cheerfully reseed and naturalize itself. The elfin yellow flowers are bright and cheerful and "look you in the eye." They do best where there is ample rainfall in the cooler months of winter and spring, and can waste away where spring is inclined to be hot and dry.

Division 11. Split-corona Daffodils of Garden Origin

Corona split rather than lobed, and usually more than half the length of the perianth.

Most of these are split-cupped hybrids from the first three divisions, and many of them give the illusion of being semi-double-flowered. The same cultural advice applies as for other plants from those divisions.

Division 12. Miscellaneous Daffodils

All daffodils not belonging to any of the foregoing divisions. There are very few in this division, but it will grow in number as breeders develop new forms.

Overview and Summary

The key to successfully growing daffodils in warm climates is to select forms known to flower earliest, in late winter or early spring, and which are resistant to basal rot. In warmer climates, the first four divisions usually do poorly after the first season, though there are a few notable exceptions in zones 8 and 9. Hot, dry weather combined with scorching winds can be devastating to the flowers. There is nothing as pathetic as the sight of daffodils keeling over and withering on a dry, windy afternoon in late March or April when the humidity drops and temperatures soar. Daffodils simply can't take such rapid dehydration. At such times they need shade and adequate moisture. It is far better to select only those kinds that flower early, before this sudden climate switch inevitably arrives. The worst selections would be double-flowered forms of *N. poeticus*. On the other hand, 'Silver Chimes' is a good choice to wind up the daffodil season in mid-April, before the arrival of late spring's drying wind and searing heat. Generally speaking, the tazettas and jonquils (Divisions 7 and 8) are permanent, because they are earlier, and should be planted as lavishly as space and the budget allow. The *N. poeticus* plants (Division 9) fail, due to their late flowering and the need for a cool, damp environment. Don't waste money and space on such losers. Hybrids of *N. triandrus* and *N. cyclamineus* (Divisions 5 and 6) fall somewhere between, and a few are nearly permanent. Early-flowering species such as *N. pseudonarcissus* (Division 10) are good investments. The doubles (Division 4), in addition to having the usual problems of their single-flowered equivalents, are plagued by the additional burden of nourishing those extra tepals with life-sustaining moisture at a critical time in their development. Thus, there is the tendency to abort their buds during warm weather, but some of the early-flowering doubles, as well as daffodils from the first three divisions, may succeed in a damp, cool spring.

Virused plants are permanently diseased (there is no cure) and, like the classic "Typhoid Mary," have the potential of infecting healthy plants. Fortunately, some virused bulbs can be "cleaned up" with meristem tissue culture, and it is comforting to know that virus-free "Sols d'Or," for instance, are now being offered in England.

Nerine laticoma
PHOTO BY DAVE LEHMILLER

Nerine Herbert 1820

A large genus from South Africa resembling the Asian *Lycoris* and with similar habits. The tunics of *Nerine* will tear apart to a web-like network, while those of *Lycoris* are papery, like those of *Narcissus*. Nerines require Mediterranean cultural conditions and do well on our Pacific Coast. They are mostly unsuitable for the South unless grown in pots.

    N. bowdenii W. Watson is found in shades of pink and is one of the hardiest species, growing well where the others won't.

    N. laticoma (Ker-Gawler) T. Durand & Schinz is summer-flowering with pale pink flowers, doing well in pots or in the ground.

Pamianthe Stapf 1933

Evergreen bulbous epiphytes from Ecuador, Peru, and Bolivia. There are two distinct species.

    P. cardenasii Traub 1972. A synonym for *P. peruviana*.

    P. parviflora Meerow 1984. Ecuador, Peru, Bolivia. An evergreen bulbous epiphyte, with small white daffodil-like flowers that have long pedicels. Flowers in September. Unknown in cultivation.

    P. peruviana Stapf 1820. An epiphyte with large white flowers similar to those of *Pancratium maritimum* from the Mediterranean. Not a garden plant, but does well in the greenhouse.

Pancratium Linnaeus 1753

Sea daffodil. *Pancratium* is a large Old World genus found around the Mediterranean, tropical Africa, and the East Indies. It differs from *Hymenocallis* by the character of the seeds, which in *Pancratium* are black, papery, and flat, and in *Hymenocallis* are green and fleshy. Only three species are generally cultivated. The fragrant white flowers are in umbels of one to several. The perianth tube is funnel-shaped, and the stamen filaments widen at the base, forming a corona. The leaves are strap-shaped, grayish or bluish green, and present most of the year.

P. canariense Ker-Gawler. A native of the Canary Islands, it is about 24 inches high. In autumn it produces 2½-inch flowers that have a corona with a bifid toothed edge. The deciduous leaves are gray-green. Best grown in a pot unless planted in a frost-free area.

P. illyricum Linnaeus. The Illyrian sea lily is a stouter species than *P. maritimum* and grows in rocky places. It has smaller, fragrant, narcissus-like flowers with a shorter tube. It flowers in late spring.

P. landesii Traub 1968. Coastal Muscat and Oman. The flowers are solitary.

P. maritimum Linnaeus. The sea lily has long-tubed flowers like a white daffodil. The spicy fragrance is not unlike that of *Hymenocallis galvestonensis.* Does well in a raised sandy bed in full sun. Will take some frost and is nearly evergreen. July to September.

P. zeylanicum Linnaeus. Sri Lanka and tropical Asia. Has solitary 2-inch flowers with recurving tepals on short scapes. The foliage is short and glossy. Very charming, but strictly for pots.

Paramongaia Velarde 1949

P. weberbaueri Velarde 1949. Peru, north of Lima on steep slopes in scrub, in decomposing granite. It is hysteranthous, flowering before the leaves. The plant produces a large bulb and leaves nearly an inch wide, with flowers somewhat like a large yellow daffodil. It is a pot plant, or a garden plant in frost-free areas. It is now believed in some quarters that the separation of *Pamianthe* and *Paramongaia* may not be justified.

Phaedranassa Herbert 1845

The genus *Phaedranassa* has nine species, six of which are endemic to Ecuador. They have petiolate leaves and bird-pollinated flowers, narrowly funnel-form, tubular, or slightly ventricose, with

Pancratium maritimum

Paramongaia weberbaueri

straight stamens and green anthers. They lack fragrance, but the clusters of some, with Christmasy red-and-green flowers, are quite attractive. Only a few are in cultivation. They should be grown in pots or where winters are dry and warm. 2n = 46.

P. carmioli Baker, a native of Peru, is sometimes grown.

Phaedranassa carmioli

Proiphys Herbert (syn. *Eurycles*)

Two species are now placed in the genus *Proiphys.*

P. amboinensis (Linnaeus) Herbert, from the Malay Peninsula and Philippines to Australia, is the best known. Although rare in cultivation, it does well in a tropical situation in zone 10. It occurs in monsoon rain forests and likes a winter-spring dormancy, when the bulb should be kept dry. The kidney-shaped petiolate foliage is as interesting as the flowers. There are 10–15 scentless white flowers with staminal cups in the umbel.

P. cunninghamii (Aiton ex Lindley) Mabberley. "Brisbane lily." Australia. Summer-flowering in umbels of up to 18 white flowers.

Pyrolirion Herbert 1821

Peru, Bolivia. The "fire lilies" are allied to *Zephyranthes* and are sometimes erroneously listed as such but differ in having an erect perianth, the spathe being split to the base, with erect filaments, incumbent anthers, and seeds with whitish unilateral wings. The style is erect or nearly erect, and the stigma is three-cleft with spatulate segments. There is also better substance in the flowers than in *Zephyranthes.* The plants don't flower until the bulb nearly reaches golf-ball size. Planted in early spring in full sun, they flower in late spring and then leaf out. The bulblets are produced on short stalks beneath the surface of the bulb coats. They require warm growing conditions, as they will lose foliage and roots when the temperature drops below 50°. They have lovely, showy flowers, but they do take up a lot of space for plants that flower only a few days out of each year. They seem not to set seed on their own pollen; perhaps two clones are required for successful pollination.

P. albicans (Herbert) Sprague. A white-flowered form from Peru.

P. albolilacinus Cárdenas 1973 (syn. *Z. albolilacina*). Bolivia. The flowers are white, finely striped lilac.

P. boliviensis (Baker) Sealy 1937. Bolivian plateau. There are one or two leaves. The plant is hysteranthous, with erect, sessile, bell-shaped yellow flowers.

P. cutleri (Cárdenas) Ravenna 1978 (syn. *Z. cutleri*). Bolivia, Ayopatha Province.

P. tubiflorum Baker. Peru. There are three varieties of this species, *P. tubiflorum* var. *aureum* (gold), *P. tubiflorum* var. *flavum* (yellow), and *P. tubiflorum* var. *flammeum* (orange). All are similar in leaf and habits. They are easy to grow in warm weather but will lose their roots when the temperature drops below 50° unless dug and stored. They form stipitate offsets beneath the tunics and will flower when they become about 2 inches in diameter. They won't flower again until the following year. They do not make seed when selfed and may need the services of another clone.

Pyrolirion tubiflorum var. *aureum*

P. xiphopetalum (Baker) Sealy 1937. Bolivia, near La Paz. A synonym for *P. boliviensis*. Sessile, flowering before the leaves with an erect, bell-shaped yellow flower. The one or two linear leaves follow.

Pyrolirion tubiflorum var. *flammeum*

× *Rhodobranthus* Traub 1958

Bigeneric hybrids between *Rhodophiala* and *Habranthus*. The two genera are closely allied, differing principally in the spathe valves, which in *Rhodophiala* are split, or nearly split, to the base, while in *Habranthus* the spathes are split in the upper part and tubular in the lower part.

The number of flowers in the umbel may not be very helpful. *Habranthus* are principally solitary-flowered, but a few South American species are multiflowered (1–3), and while most *Rhodophiala* have multiflowered umbels, a few are solitary-flowered.

Rhodophiala C. Presl 1844

About 38 species of subtropical or temperate South American amaryllids, of which only a few are in cultivation. X = 9, 2n = 18.

It is amazing that a genus so well suited to temperate climates is still so poorly garden-tested, undervalued, and underappreciated. Although formerly included in the genus *Hippeastrum,* it differs in several important particulars and is nearer to *Habranthus* in size, form, and habits. Differences from *Hippeastrum* include being hysteranthous with sessile leaves and bipartite spathes usually tubular in the lower part. Unlike *Hippeastrum,* the mostly Andean *Rhodophiala* species are relatively cold-hardy and have small, long-necked bulbs that grow deeply. They produce smaller solitary or multiple flowers following seasonal precipitation from late summer rains or melting snow. As with *Habranthus* and *Zephyranthes*, they last for several days in hot weather, longer if the weather is cool, opening in the morning and closing at sundown. As with *Habranthus*, their filaments are in four lengths, fasciculate, and usually declinate-ascending.

Hippeastrum is larger in all of its parts, with relatively broader sessile or petiolate leaves, and the flowers generally last longer than those of *Rhodophiala*, remaining open both night and day. No known hybrids have been reported between *Hippeastrum* and *Rhodophiala*, while hybrids are known between *Rhodophiala* and *Habranthus* (see × *Rhodobranthus*).

The similarities between *Rhodophiala* and *Habranthus* can be confusing, and they cannot be distinguished on the basis of the number of flowers per umbel. Each genus contains species producing only solitary-flowered scapes and others with multiflowered scapes. One must examine the spathe valves, which are split or almost split to the base in *Rhodophiala;* partially split in the middle or upper part while tubular at the base in *Habranthus*.

Rhodophiala forms a natural bridge between *Hippeastrum* and *Habranthus*, falling within the tribe Zephyrantheae. It is horticulturally important and deserves wider cultivation.

R. advena (Ker-Gawler) Traub 1953. Coastal plains and hills of central Chile. Three to six flowers of trumpet form, in yellow, orange, red, or white, on 12-inch stems, before the leaves in late summer. Cultivated in Australia and the United Kingdom.

R. ananuca (Philippi) Traub 1953. Chile, Atacama Province. Flowers lemon-yellow or red.

R. andicola (Poeppig) Traub 1953. Eastern side of Andes in Argentina and Chile, in sandy places. Flowers erect, solitary, expanding, carmine-pink, purplish black at the base. Rare.

R. angustifolia. Chile, Santiago, Maipo Valley.

R. araucana (Philippi) Traub 1953. Chile, Andes of Araucanía, Cupulhue. One or two erect flowers in the umbel, reddish to yellow. Rare.

R. bagnoldii (Herbert) Traub 1953. Southern Chile. Four to six yellow flowers, tinged red, on 12-inch stems in summer. This species is cultivated in Australia and the United Kingdom.

R. bakeri (Philippi) Traub 1953. Chile, Cordillera of Talca. Three to six funnel-form yellow flowers. Rare.

R. berteriana (Philippi) Traub 1953. Chile, Rancagua. Five or six purple flowers in midsummer.

R. bicolor (Baker) Traub 1953. Chile. Said to be common around Valparaíso and hardy. There are four to nine bright red flowers with greenish bases in the umbel, on stems 12 inches high in summer.

R. bifida (Herbert) Traub 1953. Argentina, Uruguay, southern Brazil. Two to six flowers, in shades of red, orange, purple, or pink, rarely white, before the leaves in late summer–early fall. In the South, *R. bifida* is the species likely to be cultivated, and no garden should be without it, as it is ruggedly persistent and free-flowering and can be grown in sun or shade, where winters are cold or mild and summers are wet or dry. The long-necked black-coated bulbs grow deeply, and if planted shallowly they will pull themselves down to their chosen level by contractile roots. They grow in sun or shade and can take the extremes of winter or summer in any kind of soil. The commonly cultivated dark-red-flowered forms are locally called "oxblood lilies" or "fall amaryllis" and are mostly sterile triploids. There is also a form with lighter red flowers that is widely distributed. Both increase easily by offsets and flower several weeks after the normal fertile diploid forms in late summer. Wild-collected diploid forms seldom make offsets and must be propagated by the generously produced seed, which will flower in about four years. All color forms should be intercrossed in order to obtain the widest color range from darkest red to pink. All are heat- and drought-resistant and reliably cold-hardy at least to zone 7.

Rhodophiala bifida

The triploid forms were imported and widely distributed before the end of the nineteenth century by P. H. Oberwetter, a resident of Austin, Texas, but it is not understood how he went about selecting sterile triploid forms from normal seed-bearing diploid forms. The triploid forms produce many offsets but no seed, contributing to their rapid distribution. The diploid seed-bearing forms, which are slightly smaller, could easily have naturalized across Texas and the rest of the South had they been given the opportunity. Aside from the fact that some diploid forms begin flowering several weeks earlier than the sterile forms, there is little to choose between them. When cross-pollinated, sterile forms may occasionally produce seed, but more often

Rhodophiala bifida (pink form)

nothing happens. Hybrids between various color forms are interesting and colorful, particularly if one parent is a pink-flowered form.

R. bifida has been hybridized with *Habranthus pedunculosus,* and the intermediate offspring (= × *Rhodobranthus*) are colorful, but sterile.

R. biflora (Philippi) Traub 1953. Chile: Valdivia, near San José. Flowers are rose at the tips, paler toward the base.

R. chilensis (L'Héritier) Traub. Sandy plains of southern Chile. Hardy. The leaves are contemporary with the flowers. One or two ascending flowers, colors variable: scarlet, pink, purple, or sulfur-yellow trumpets in spring or summer.

R. cipoana Ravenna 1970. Brazil, state of Minas Gerais. Two purple flowers.

R. colona (Philippi) Traub 1953. Chile, Araucanía region, from Ranaico to Temuco. Flowers in shades of fiery red, yellow near base, flowering in summer.

R. consolbrina (Philippi) Traub 1953. Chile, Santiago mountains. Three to five scarlet flowers.

R. elwesii (Wright) Traub 1953. Argentina. One or two yellow flowers with red throats. Considered to be a subspecies of *R. mendocina.*

R. flava (Philippi) Traub 1953. Chile. Synonym for *R. solisii.*

R. fulgens (J. D. Hooker) Traub 1953. Chile, Santiago mountains. Scarlet flowers with yellow tube. Said to be rare.

R. gladioloides (Hieronymus) Traub 1953. Argentina. Umbel with two to five red flowers.

R. jamesonii (Baker) Traub 1953. Argentina, in ravines near Jáchal. Two to four red or pink funnel-form flowers in late summer.

R. laeta Philippi 1860. Chile, Atacama Province and coastal Antofagasta Province in sandy or hard soils, on hilltops. Usually four flowers, pink, red, or purple, with narrow tepals. Late spring.

R. × 'LaJolla.' Traub 1958. *R. bifida* × *R. chilensis.* 2n = 18. The F-1 hybrids were fertile, with four to seven red or pink flowers in summer.

R. lineata (Philippi) Traub 1953. Chile, Metropolitana region. Two yellow flowers, lined red, in late summer. Said to be endangered.

R. mendocina (Philippi) Ravenna 1970. Argentina, Mendoza Province. Three to five erect yellow flowers, purple at the base, on 12-inch scapes in late summer.

R. modesta Philippi 1873. Andes of Chile. Flowers solitary, white with broad red keel. Now regarded as a synonym for *Traubia modesta* (Philippi) Ravenna 1974.

R. moelleri (Philippi) Traub 1953. Chile, Araucanía region. Three to six rose-red flowers.

R. montana (Philippi) Traub 1953. Chile, Talca Province. Two to four yellow flowers.

R. phycelloides (Baker) Traub 1953. Andes of Chile. Three to six bright red flowers with yellowish bases. Summer-flowering.

R. popetana (Philippi) Traub 1953. Chile. Solitary pink flowers.

R. pratensis (Poeppig) Traub 1952. Chile, on desert coast of Atacama Province. Two to five brilliant orange-red or violet-purple flowers, yellow at the base, on 12-inch stems, in summer or early fall, contemporary with the leaves. Sometimes found in cultivation.

R. purpurata (Philippi) Traub 1953. Chile, mountains of Linares Province. Solitary purple flowers.

R. rhodolirion (Baker) Traub 1953. Andean Argentina, Mendoza Province; Chile, in Colchagua, Aconcagua, and Santiago Provinces. Flowers solitary, rarely two-flowered, red or pink, rarely white, in early summer.

R. rosea (Sweet) Traub 1953. Chile, Chiloé Island. Solitary rose-pink flowers on stems a foot or more high in late summer or early fall. Hardy.

R. solisii (Philippi) Traub 1953. Chile, Maule Region of Chillán. Synonym for *R. flava*.

R. soratensis (Baker) Traub 1953. Now considered a synonym for *Chlidanthus soratensis*.

R. spathacea (Herbert) Traub 1953. Synonym for the pink-flowered form of *R. bifida*.

R. splendens (Renjifo) Traub 1953. Chile, Curicó Province. Polychrome flowers: yellow-green-orange-vermilion.

R. tenuiflora (Philippi) Traub 1953. Chile, Santiago Province, Valle Largo. Three to six tubular flowers.

R. tiltelensis (Traub & Moldenke) Traub 1953. Chile, Santiago Province, Til-Til. Many-flowered, scarlet. Said to be rare.

R. uniflora Philippi 1860. Chile, Atacama Province, Cachinal de la Costa. Solitary, erect red flowers, 2–4 inches high.

Scadoxus Rafinesque 1836

Scadoxus was formerly included in the genus *Haemanthus* but has recently (1976) been segregated as a separate genus by I. B. Friis and I. Nordal, on the basis of some *Scadoxus* species having rhizomatous rootstocks, several thin-textured leaves with distinct midribs on an ascending stem, and a 2n = 18 chromosome number. The inflorescence is a closely spaced, many-flowered umbel of globular or paintbrush form, often with prominent colorful bracts.

There are about ten species of *Scadoxus*. They are mainly from tropical Africa, but extend into South Africa to the Cape Province. Most of them are seldom cultivated. The popular blood lily, *S. multiflorus* subsp. *multiflorus*, is perhaps the best-known, hardiest, and best suited for shady out-of-door growing in the deep South. The following species are now recognized:

S. cinnabarinus (Decaisne) Friis & Nordal 1976.

S. longifolius (de Wildeman & T. Durand) Friis & Nordal 1976.

S. membranaceus. The flowers are composed of four greenish-wine spathe valves, turning green, filled with red flowers. The entire inflorescence looks like a single large flower. It can take deep shade.

Scadoxus multiflorus
PHOTO BY JO ANN TRIAL

S. multiflorus (Martyn) Rafinesque 1795.

Subsp. *multiflorus* (Martyn) Rafinesque. Tropical Africa. This form, with large *Allium*-like umbels of red flowers, is popular around the Gulf Coast. It prefers shade and is easy to grow under trees, flowering in early summer. It enjoys moisture in a well-drained situation, but slugs and snails can make holes in the foliage if not controlled, and root-knot nematodes may stunt the plant's growth. This form is winter-dormant and seems cold-hardy.

Subsp. *katherinae* (Baker) Friis & Nordal. Large, popular in Mediterranean climates such as California. It has dense multiflowered umbels with starry red flowers.

S. natalensis (Pappe) Hooker. Differs from *S. puniceus* in its color and time of flowering.

S. nutans (Friis & Bjornstadt) Friis & Nordal 1976.

S. pole-evansii (Obermejer) Friis & Nordal 1976. Zimbabwe. Like *S. multiflorus* but has fewer flowers, and they are salmon-colored.

S. pseudocaulus (Bjornstadt & Friis) Friis & Nordal 1976.

S. puniceus (Linnaeus) Friis & Nordal 1976. Natal. Occasionally grown, and excellent for pots, but too tender for the garden. The dark, petioled foliage is somewhat leathery, and the smallish umbels resemble small orange paintbrushes.

Sprekelia Heister 1753

Aztec lily, Jacobean lily, orchid amaryllis. The name honors J. H. von Sprekelsen, a lawyer in Hamburg, Germany, who sent a bulb to Linnaeus. Older texts say that there is a single species, *S. formosissima*, but there seem to be several. They are all somewhat similar, but each occupies its own niche and has its own characters which set it apart. The flowers are zygomorphic, in various shades of red, and orchid-shaped. The bulbs of *Sprekelia* should be planted deeply, and they are hardy at least to zone

Sprekelia glauca

8. The flowers last only a few days but some forms of *S. formosissima* can be counted on to flower several times between spring and fall.

S. clintiae Traub. A synonym for *S. glauca.*

S. formosissima (Linnaeus) Herbert is a variable species found in many sizes and shades of red over much of mountainous Mexico from Chihuahua, down the central slopes of the Sierra Madre, to the state of Oaxaca. The form known as 'Orient Red' is one of the best, as it flowers with the first summer rains, and in cultivation is apt to flower again in the fall. The species have been widely hybridized, and so there are many forms.

S. glauca Lindley (syn. *S. clintiae*). This species flowers later, with glaucous leaves and slightly different-shaped flowers in brick or pinkish red. It grows in southwestern Mexico in the states of Jalisco and Michoacán and normally flowers in early summer, after *S. formosissima.*

S. howardii Lehmiller 2000. A third, hysteranthous species is smaller and earlier, with narrow red segments and silvery green leaves, flowering with the first rains from a tiny bulb no larger than an ordinary *Zephyranthes.* It grows on the Pacific side at lower elevations in the Mexican states of Colima, Oaxaca, Guerrero, and Puebla. It is a somewhat difficult species to keep in cultivation.

Stenomesson Herbert 1821

Stenomesson represents the largest and most variable group of Andean pancratiod amaryllids, there being about 35–50 species. According to species, they are found from under 1,000 feet to 6,000 feet, and a few are true xerophytes. To date only 3 or 4 species have been reported outside of Peru. *Stenomesson* may have petiolate or sessile leaves, the petiolate group being the larger, but the sessile-leaved group having showier flowers. All grow in cool weather, and for this reason they are likely not suitable for widespread growing conditions in hot, dry climates.

Stenomesson incarnata
PHOTO BY MARCIA WILSON, COURTESY OF MRS. ALAN CLINT

S. incarnata (syn. *S. variegatum*). South American Andes of Ecuador, Peru, and Bolivia. Early summer. Variable in color, but mostly red.

Sternbergia Waldstein & Kitaibel 1805

Autumn daffodil, autumn crocus. A Mediterranean genus of at least eight species, extending north to Hungary and Romania and eastward to the Caucasus, northern Persia, and the mountains of Central Asia. Six species are autumnal and two are vernal. One species has white flowers, and the rest are yellow-flowered. They enjoy hot, dry summers, becoming active with the first late summer or early autumn rains. The flowers appear in advance of or contemporary with the leaves, depending on the species and cultural conditions. *S. lutea* and *S. sicula* are especially suited to the growing conditions of the deep South, thriving under neglect if planted where they receive no added summer irrigation.

Sternbergia candida

S. candida Mathew & Baytop 1979. Southwestern Turkey. Early-spring-flowering in its natural habitat; winter-flowering in cultivation. The handsome, sparkling white flowers open wide in full sun. The prettiest forms have wide tepals. The glaucous leaves appear in the spring. It is still very rare and must be kept very dry during dormancy lest it rot. Because of this, it may be best suited for pots in the Gulf states.

S. clusiana (Ker-Gawler) Sprengel 1825. Middle East. Late autumn. Wild-collected bulbs were formerly available from Turkey but have become scarce because of over-collecting. This is not the easiest species of this genus to maintain or flower freely in cultivation in our climate. The flowers are large, showy, and nearly stemless, making them look like squatty greenish yellow crocuses. However, only a percentage of them will flower in any given year, leaving the impression that they have not quite lived up to their full potential. The gray-green leaves appear after flowering. The bulbs must be kept dry while dormant lest they succumb to basal rot and perhaps are best suited for pots.

Sternbergia clusiana

S. colchiciflora Waldstein & Kitaibel 1803–1804. Yugoslavia, Iran, and the Caucasus. Autumn. Nearest to *S. lutea*, but smaller, requiring similar culture.

S. fischeriana (Herbert) Ruprecht 1868. Caucasus, Kashmir, Iran, Iraq, and Syria. A lovely yellow-flowered species blooming in late winter. It grows well here, but may fail to reappear the following year, perhaps due to basal rot. It must be kept dry during dormancy and thus is best suited for pots if you want to keep it. Apparently it is no longer commercially available and may be endangered.

S. greuteriana Kamari & Artelari 1990. Greek Aegean islands (Karpathos, Kasos,

Crete). This is a recently discovered miniature with small, stoloniferous bulbs, flowering in autumn. As with most *Sternbergia* species, the small flowers are yellow. They do not open wide, but form slightly tilted trumpets. While charming, this species is more interesting than beautiful and requires pot culture, as it is intolerant of frequent summer watering while dormant, quickly succumbing to basal rot.

Sternbergia lutea

S. lutea (Linnaeus) Ker-Gawler & Sprengel 1825. Widespread in Mediterranean regions. Autumn. This is easily the most popular and hardiest species and a favorite in zones 7–9, where it thrives in sun or part shade, flowering in the garden in late August and September along with *Rhodophiala bifida* and certain *Lycoris*. Var. *angustifolia* has narrower foliage (less narrow than that of *S. sicula*), but is otherwise similar.

S. sicula Gussone 1845. Italy, Sicily, and Greece. The leaves of this species are considerably narrower than those of *S. lutea*, but it is otherwise just as vigorous and free-flowering, while sharing the same flowering period. The flowers are starrier, with the same golden yellow color. Although still rare in cultivation in the South, it is highly recommended and belongs in any collection.

× *Sydneyara* (Traub) Howard 1990 (syn. × *Sydneya*)

Trigeneric rain lily hybrids, uniting *Zephyranthes*, *Cooperia*, and *Habranthus*. The spelling of × *Sydneyara* is in accord with the rules of the international code for trigeneric hybrids, according to which the suffix must end in -*ara*.

Tapeinanthus Herbert 1837

T. humilis (Cavanilles) Herbert. A primitive relative of *Narcissus* with one or two small yellow flowers with only a rudimentary dentate cup. Spain and Morocco. Now regarded as *Narcissus humilis* in some quarters. Rare in cultivation.

Urceolina Reichenbach 1828

Urceolina, from the Andes of Bolivia and Peru, consists of two species with umbels of showy pendulous flowers in spring. They are suitable for pots.

U. peruviana Presl (Macbride) (syn. *U. miniata*) has umbels of red or orange flowers on stout scapes about a foot high. Each pendant, urn-shaped flower is carried on a long pedicel. The petiolate leaves are hysteranthous.

Urceolina peruviana

Vagaria Herbert 1837

V. parviflora Herbert 1837. Syria and Asia Minor. *Vagaria* is similar to *Pancratium,* but the six to eight small white flowers have small staminal cups that are split to the base. It flowers in autumn, minus foliage, and combines well with *Lycoris* and other fall-flowering bulbs. The foliage follows the flowers. The bulb must be kept dry while dormant and given perfect drainage.

Vallota Herbert 1821

V. purpurea. Synonym for *Cyrtanthus elatus.*

Worsleya (Hooker) Traub & Moldenke 1943

W. rayneri. This is the so-called blue amaryllis from the Brazilian Serra dos Órgãos (Organ Mountains). A beautiful plant, its color is a lavender-blue (mauve). It is occasionally, if temporarily, found in cultivation. The culture is difficult to duplicate, as it grows on the sides of high, steep mountains. X = 21.

Vagaria parviflora

Zephyranthes Herbert 1821

A genus of 60 or more species from the southeastern United States, Texas, Mexico, the West Indies, and South America. *Zephyranthes* literally translates as "flower of the West Wind," but the plants are more commonly known as "rain lilies" or "fairy lilies." They resemble small lilies or crocuses and have the habit of flowering after rains during the warmer months. Their color range is impressive, and a field of them in bloom is a sight to behold. They fairly glow with vibrant colors that can light up any garden situation, especially during the oppressive heat of summer and early fall. They love a sunny situation and a good soil with regular moisture and good drainage. The vast majority will do well in ordinary garden conditions that suit other garden plants. By means of alternate soaking and drying, many of the hybrids can

Zephyranthes atamasco
PHOTO BY JOHN D. FELLERS

be flowered almost at will during warm weather, provided that they are not allowed to dry out too much between times. For instance, if well-grown hybrids are heavily watered, they will bloom about a week later. The species are more seasonal. Modern hybridization has created an array of new colors and color combinations. The original colors were mostly yellow, white, and pink, but intercrossing them has produced shades of cream, orange, and red, in bicolors, tricolors, and quadricolors. X = 6, 7.

Z. albiella Traub 1950. Colombia, Bogotá. A small white-flowered species from Colombia with slightly declinate flowers, somewhat approaching *Habranthus* in form.

Z. albolilacina. A synonym for *Pyrolirion albolilacinus.*

Z. americana. A synonym for *Haylockia pusilla.*

Z. arenicola Brandegee 1889. Mexico, Magdalena and Santa Margarita Islands, Baja California. White flowers with a short perianth tube. This is the most northwestern Mexican species, with high chromosome numbers (108–120).

Z. atamasco (Linnaeus) Herbert 1821. Southeastern United States. Atamasco lily, wild Easter lily. The most northeastern American species, from Alabama and northern Florida to Virginia, with white flowers up to 5 inches wide and narrow, glossy foliage. It blooms in the spring and goes dormant in early summer. 2n = 24.

Z. bakeriana Marong 1893. A synonym for *Z. mesochloa.*

Z. bella Howard & Ogden 1990. Mexico, confluence of states of Aguascalientes, Zacatecas, and San Luis Potosí. A tiny pink or white species from a dry region, with filiform leaves and crocus-like flowers. Difficult to flower in cultivation.

Z. bifolia (Aublet) M. Roemer. A synonym for *Habranthus cardinalis.*

Z. boliviensis Baker. A synonym for *Pyrolirion boliviensis.*

Z. candida (Lindley) Herbert 1826 (syn. *Argyropsis candida*). Argentina. A popular crocus-like species with rush-like leaves and white flowers, blooming in late summer and fall.

Z. capivarina Ravenna 1974. Brazil, state of Paraná. A yellow-flowered species from the banks of the Capivari and Jangada Rivers.

Z. chichimeca Howard & Ogden 1990. Mexico, states of Nuevo León, San Luis Potosí, and Zacatecas. A clumping desert species, with erect filiform leaves and pink or white crocus-shaped flowers. A somewhat difficult species, best for pot culture in full sun.

Z. chlorosolen Dietrich 1840. A synonym for *Cooperia drummondii.* There is still much controversy as to whether this belongs in *Cooperia* or *Zephyranthes.*

Z. citrina Baker 1882. Mexico, in the Yucatán peninsula. A popular species. It has small golden yellow flowers faintly streaked bronze from midsummer until fall. It is related to *Z. pulchella* but begins flowering earlier. Easily raised from seed. Full sun. 2n = 48.

Z. clintiae Traub 1952. Mexico, state of San Luis Potosí. A variable species in shades of pink or red. The lengths of pedicel and tube are nearly equal. Allied to *Z. lindleyana, Z. macrosiphon,* and *Z. erubescens.* 2n = 48.

Z. commersoniana Herbert. A synonym for *Z. mesochloa.*

Z. concolor (Lindley) Bentham & J. D. Hooker 1883. A synonym for *Habranthus concolor.*

Zephyranthes crociflora

Z. crociflora Howard & Ogden 1990. Mexico, on the southeast side of the city of Saltillo, Coahuila. It has erect filiform leaves and blunt-tipped white crocus-like flowers, tinged pink. The short pedicel, long floral tube, erect stamens clustered closely around the style, and light yellow pollen suggest that this is a natural apomictic × *Cooperanthes* hybrid. It grows naturally with a Mexican look-alike of *Cooperia traubii* and needs full sun in order to bloom.

Z. cutleri Cárdenas 1973. A synonym for *Pyrolirion cutleri.*

Z. dichromantha T. M. Howard 1996. Mexico, state of San Luis Potosí, in tropical valleys where sugarcane is grown. A light-yellow-flowered species streaked and tipped bright red. It flowers from July until fall.

Z. drummondii D. Don 1836. A synonym for *Cooperia pedunculata.* With some hesitation, I still follow the older nomenclature.

Z. erubescens S. Watson 1890. Mexico, San Luis Potosí. A desert species with leaves ¼ inch wide, a floral tube less than ¼ inch long, and large white flowers tinged red at the tips.

Z. filifolia Herbert ex Kraenslin 1913. Argentina, in the north of Patagonia, and several northern provinces in sandy places. The flowers are yellow and pedicellate.

Z. flavissima Ravenna 1967. Argentina, Entre Ríos, Misiones, and Corrientes Provinces, and Brazil, states of Rio Grande do Sul and Santa Catarina. A near-ever-

Zephyranthes grandiflora
PHOTO BY KATHERINE CLINT

green plant with orange-yellow flowers, needing plenty of water and a short summer rest.

Z. fosterii Traub 1941. Mexico, states of Jalisco and Michoacán. A species from southwestern Mexico in pink or red, rarely white, somewhat similar to *Z. verecunda*, but with sessile flowers that have narrow tepals. 2n = 48.

Z. grandiflora Lindley 1825. Guatemala, Honduras. A popular Central American species with large rose-pink flowers. It has glossy carinate leaves and flowers with large, spreading anthers with the stigma and style lolling to one side. Midsummer. Some think it to be of hybrid origin, but this is unlikely, as I found it growing wild in Central America. 2n = 46.

Z. guatemalensis L. B. Spencer 1986. Guatemala. A rare species from the Guatemalan highlands. It has bright green leaves and large white flowers with a greenish center. The flowers continue growing larger each day when in bloom. 2n = 36.

Z. insularum Hume 1952. West Indies. A white-flowered species with glossy carinate leaves and the flower tepals in two planes. Not known to set seed, and may need pollen from a different clone. 2n = 28.

Z. jonesii (Cory) Traub 1951. A synonym for *Cooperia jonesii*.

Z. katherinei L. B. Spencer 1986. Mexico, environs of Jacala, Hidalgo. Forms are known in pink, rose, red, and yellow. Hybrids between the yellow and red forms (var. *lutea* and var. *rubra*) occur and these have been named *Z. katherinei*. Because the parents are similar, save for color, they deserve the same nomenclatural treatment. 2n = 48.

Z. latissimafolia L. B. Spencer 1986. Mexico, states of Guanajuato and Jalisco.

Zephyranthes katherinei var. *rubra*

Zephyranthes katherinei var. *lutea*

Zephyranthes lindleyana
PHOTO BY KATHERINE CLINT

Zephyranthes longifolia

Zephyranthes macrosiphon
PHOTO BY JO ANN TRIAL

Zephyranthes mesochloa

Zephyranthes moctezumae

The pink or white flowers are like those of *Z. verecunda*, but the leaves are wider and flatter, and it has twice the chromosome numbers. 2n = 48.

Z. leucantha T. M. Howard 1993. Mexico: Hidalgo, in mountains south of Jacala. A large white-flowered species with narrow leaves.

Z. lindleyana Herbert 1837. Mexico, states of San Luis Potosí, Nuevo León, Querétaro, and Guanajuato. Including "Horsetail Falls" and *Z. clintiae*. This is a variable long-tubed form in shades of pink, rose, red, or rarely white. The large flowers are produced in the spring and occasionally thereafter on 10-inch stems. The rounded segments open nearly flat, with a style and stigma subtending the erect stamens. The pedicels and floral tubes are about an inch long. After the initial flowering season (March to May) it may throw occasional flowers throughout the rest of the year. It must be propagated from seed because it rarely makes offsets until it becomes very large and mature. In some cases the bulbs are as large as golf balls. The leaves are wide and glaucous. One of the best Mexican species. 2n = 24, 48, 96.

Z. longifolia Hemsley 1878. United States: west Texas, southern Arizona, and southern New Mexico. Mexico: states of Coahuila, Durango, San Luis Potosí, and Chihuahua. A desert species with filiform leaves and small, cup-shaped pale yellow flowers. Pretty but not showy in the better forms.

Z. longistyla Pax 1889. Argentina. A South American species with yellow flowers. Rare.

Z. macrosiphon Baker 1881. Mexico, states of Hidalgo and San Luis Potosí. The flowers are rose-pink, but lighter-colored forms are known. Rather like *Z. grandiflora*, and often confused with it, but slightly smaller, with shorter stamens, incurved anthers, and a much shorter style. 2n = 48.

Z. mesochloa Herbert 1830. Argentina, southern Brazil, Uruguay, Paraguay. A widespread species from central South America. Has somewhat the appearance of a white *Habranthus*. Somewhat tender.

Z. minima Herbert 1837. Argentina, Brazil, Uruguay. The flowers are produced in autumn and are small, pinkish or whitish, with three fertile stamens. Var. *hexandra*, from Entre Ríos Province, Argentina, has larger flowers with six fertile stamens. It grows in winter and is summer-dormant.

Z. miradorensis (Kranzlin) Flory & Flagg. Mexico, in pastures near Jalapa, Veracruz, and Tuxtla Gutiérrez, Chiapas. The flowers are pink or white above narrow 2-mm-wide leaves. It may be a form of *Z. nelsonii*. Not especially showy. 2n = 48.

Z. moctezumae T. M. Howard 1996. Mexico. Found along the tropical riverbanks of Río Moctezuma, Hidalgo. The small flowers have wavy tepals and are flesh-pink in color, turning paler with age. Somewhat tender.

Z. nelsonii Greenman 1898. Mexico, states of Chiapas, Oaxaca, Veracruz. A spe-

Zephyranthes nelsonii

Zephyranthes primulina

cies with pink or white flowers. Said to differ from *Z. miradorensis* in having an exerted stigma, shorter spathe, and shorter perianth tube, but since it is similar and occupies the same habitat, it may be the same species. If so, the name *Z. nelsonii* has precedent.

Z. nervosa (Humboldt, Bonpland, & Kunth) Herbert 1837. Venezuela. A little-known species that has ½-inch white flowers, with the style longer than the filaments. Said to be difficult. 2n = 24.

Z. nymphaea Howard & Ogden 1990. Mexico, southern Tamaulipas and San Luis Potosí in El Naranjo river valley. It has narrow leaves and greenish yellow flowers with narrow tepals from midsummer to fall.

Z. paranaensis Ravenna 1974. Brazil, state of Paraná. Yellow flowers. Similar to *Z. capivarina*, and perhaps a form of it.

Z. plumieri Hume 1939. Dominican Republic. This has erect broadly funnel-form rose-pink flowers with tubes ¾ inch long, long pedicels, and short, slender filaments, in two distinct sets. The stigma is three-cleft.

Z. primulina Howard & Ogden 1990. Mexico, near Valles, Tamaulipas. Tender. The leaves are glossy, flattish, and carinate, and the medium-sized flowers are light yellow with the exterior tinged reddish. 2n = 50, 52, or 53.

Z. puertoricensis Traub 1951. Puerto Rico, Jamaica. Similar to *Z. insularum*, but the white flowers are produced in midsummer with the segments all on one level. It is seed-fertile. 2n = 27.

Z. pulchella J. G. Smith 1893. United States, around the Texas coastal bend and inland, and Mexico, states of Tamaulipas and Coahuila. The leaves are linear and gray-green, and the flowers are small, but a bright golden yellow, and produced in late summer and fall. 2n = 48, 24.

Z. refugiensis F. B. Jones 1961. Texas, Refugio and Goliad Counties. It has glossy narrow leaves and showy bright yellow flowers with green tubes. Late summer and fall. Believed to have originated in nature as a hybrid between *Z. pulchella* and *Cooperia jonesii*.

Z. reginae Howard & Ogden 1990. Mexico, tropical valleys of eastern San Luis Potosí. Showy light yellow flowers with narrowish tepals, and with the exterior lightly flushed copper. Superficially it looks like *Z.* × 'Ajax' but has lax narrow leaves. Flowers throughout the summer. 2n = 48 + 1 B.

*Zephyranthes
pulchella*

*Zephyranthes
reginae*

Zephyranthes rosea
PHOTO BY JO ANN TRIAL

Z. robusta. J. G. Baker. A synonym for *Habranthus robustus.* But plants currently sold by this name are usually *Z. grandiflora.*

Z. rosalensis Ravenna 1974. Bolivia. An ally of *Z. mesochloa* but with serotine leaves and pinkish flowers.

Z. rosea Lindley 1824. Mountains of Cuba. Popular where hardy and common in Florida. Flowering in late summer (August–September) and fall, with small rose-pink flowers above flat glossy green leaves. Sometimes confused with *Z. grandiflora,* which is much larger and a very different plant. 2n = 24.

Z. simpsonii Chapman 1892. Peninsular Florida. A species with erect funnel-form white flowers, tinged pinkish on the outside. 2n = 48.

Z. smallii (Alexander) Traub 1951. Synonym for *Cooperia smallii.*

Z. stellaris Ravenna 1967. Paraguay, and Argentina in Entre Ríos, Misiones, and Santa Fe Provinces. A hysteranthous winter-growing species producing narrow-tepaled white flowers in late summer before the nearly filiform leaves.

Z. subflava L. B. Spencer 1986. Tropical Mexico, San Luis Potosí, near El Naranjo. A cream-white-flowered form, somewhat like *Z. pulchella* in habit, flowering mid- to late summer. 2n = 24.

Z. sulphurea. An unpublished synonym applied to *Z. citrina* and having no scientific merit.

Z. texana (Herbert) Baker 1888. A synonym for *Habranthus texanus.*

Z. treatiae S. Watson 1879. Northeastern Florida. This species is essentially similar to *Z. atamasco* and is considered to be a variant of it from the dry pine woods of Florida. 2n = 24.

Zephyranthes verecunda

Z. tubispatha Herbert. A synonym for a variety of *Habranthus tubispathus.*

Z. verecunda Herbert 1825. Mexico, states of Mexico, Michoacán, Puebla, San Luis Potosí. A variable dwarf species with (usually) sessile small flowers in white, pink, or rose, flowering in early summer. 2n = 24.

Z. wrightii Baker 1888. Cuba, Isle of Pines. A Cuban species with narrow erect leaves and pink flowers, similar to *Z. rosea,* but flowering earlier.

Hybrids

Through the years there have been many attempts to hybridize *Zephyranthes,* as well as × *Cooperanthes,* × *Zebranthus,* × *Coobranthus,* and × *Sydneyara.* These are the tip of the iceberg, and since there are so many species, the possibilities are endless.

Z. × 'Ajax' (*Z. candida* × *Z. citrina*). Straw-yellow hybrid. Erect, narrow leaves. Flowers in summer.

Z. × 'Capricorn.' T. M. Howard. A colorful hybrid, flowering freely and increasing rapidly. The color is orange-red.

Z. × *flaggii* R. Flagg (*Z. albiella* × *Z. rosea*). A hybrid from Panama, called the "Panama pink."

Z. × *floryii* (*Z. grandiflora* × 'Ajax'). Light pink hybrid.

Z. × 'Libra.' T. M. Howard. An early-flowering hybrid raised by me, and now widely spread. It is a cross between *Z. lindleyana* and Z. × 'Ruth Page,' setting apomictic seed freely and also making offsets. It has wide, flat leaves and flowers over a long time period with small rose-pink blossoms.

Z. × *ruthiae* T. M. Howard (*Z. rosea* × *Z. citrina*). Deep rose, pink, or bicolored pink-and-yellow hybrids. The best known of these were 'Ruth Page' and 'Ellen Korsakoff.'

Z. × T. M. Howard hybrids. Crosses involving many *Zephyranthes* and *Cooperia* species produced in the middle of the twentieth century. Some still exist.

Echeandia sp.

■ ANTHERICACEAE

Included in the Anthericaceae are about 90 species of plants with corm-like roots and lily-like habits, found in the Americas from Arizona, New Mexico, and Texas to Argentina and Chile. The small white or yellow flowers last only a day but are produced in succession on a branched peduncle. Recent molecular and anatomical studies indicate that this group (formerly part of the Liliaceae) merits familial status of its own.

Echeandia Ortega

The American plants formerly considered part of the genus *Anthericum* are placed in *Echeandia* by some modern authors. The plants grow from a cluster of fleshy-fibrous roots, with a rosette of linear leaves and flowers in simple or compound racemes. The anthers may be connate or free, according to the species.

E. chandleri Greenman & Thompson is from the Rio Grande Valley and coastal Texas. It grows in clay soil in chaparral, thickets, and prairies, flowering from May to November. The small yellow flowers open in a long panicle daily for several weeks. Although it can be attractive, especially in spring and fall, it is inclined to be invasive.

E. torreyi Baker. Torrey anthericum, clabellina. West Texas. Similar to the above species but with narrower leaves. Common in the grasslands of the Davis Mountains.

E. sp. Mexico. One of many Mexican *Echeandia* species. This one has small white flowers with recurved tepals and connate anthers. The flowers open late in the afternoon. They are produced on branched stems above a rosette of a dozen or so basal leaves and make a fine accent in the border in late summer. They are not invasive. This species persisted in my garden for years in dappled shade.

Sauromatum guttatum

■ A R A C E A E

There are about 2,000 species in the Araceae. The flowers are usually crowded on a spadix enclosed in a large colored sheath or hood (the spathe). The long-petioled leaves arise from corms or rhizomes. The family contains some of the more bizarre bulbous species, including some eerie, ghoulish plants as well as a few of the more colorful and beautiful ones. In some cases, the malodorous flowers, with the scent of feces or carrion, leave one with a sense of having been through the bowels of the Plant Kingdom, but other members of the family have sweetly scented flowers.

Alocasia

See Elephant's Ears.

Amorphophallus **Blume ex Decaisne**

Devil's tongue, snake palm, voodoo lily. A group of unusual aroids from Indonesia and Sumatra, some forming corms that can reach nearly 100 pounds in weight. There are about 90 species, only a few of which are cultivated. Some species are known for their unpleasant odor lasting through the first day. They attract flies, yet can be sensually beautiful. As a bad joke, you might care to celebrate their flowering with friends, but they should keep their distance the first few hours, or they may never forgive you. The flowers can smell potent when they are "high." After flowering, the plant produces a large, palm-like leaf, divided into three parts, which will last for several months into the summer. The leaf and stalk are exotic, but can be slow-developing, and often don't put in an appearance until midsummer, so one must be patient. If the leaf reaches the proper height and diameter, the plant may flower the following season.

A. bulbifer (Roxburgh) Blume. Northeast India, Afghanistan. This species differs from the others in having arum-like, odorless greenish or pinkish flowers with reddish centers that look like shell sculptures. For a dramatic effect, the flowers are long enough for cutting. The late spring flowers are followed by the foliage, which has stems mottled with blackish spots. By late summer each segmented leaf produces aerial cormels which can be removed and planted.

A. campanulatus (Roxburgh) Blume ex Decaisne. May be a synonym for *A. paeonifolius*. Northeast India to Vietnam, Philippines, and New Guinea. The corms are used for food.

A. koratensis. The dark, purplish flowers appear to be made of vinyl, and the attractive palmate leaf that follows has a dark, blackish stem.

Amorphophallus rivieri

A. paeonifolius (Dennstaedt) Nicolson (syn. *A. campanulatus*). Peony-leaved arum. The dark, ruffled flower has a spadix that looks squat and brain-shaped, or like a snake ready to strike, or perhaps like a large cow patty. Weird. It is followed by a minutely tuberculed black-and-green stalk supporting the beautiful, glossy, palm-like leaf. Often it may produce a second leaf later in the season. The developing process is well worth watching.

A. rivieri Durieu. Snake palm, leopard's tongue. Indochina. Produces a large, handsome mottled stem of palm-like form divided into three leaflets. When it gets quite large, there will be a flower the following spring. While busily attracting flies, the large, ruffled maroon flower looks somewhat ghoulish, and yet mysteriously handsome. Unfortunately the flower only lasts a couple of days. Cultivar 'Konjac' is listed.

A. titanum Beccari. Titan arum. Sumatra. The largest species. When mature, the corms may be up to 1½ feet across and weigh 100 pounds. The leaf stalk can be 10–15 feet tall with a spread of about 15 feet. It produces a large, ill-smelling flower of unreal proportions. The smell is like rotting fish and burnt sugar, but does not last long. If you can afford it, it's the world's largest flower, 4 feet tall and about 6 feet wide, and, though macabre, it is stunning. It is followed by an equally large mottled leaf. It may be hardier than previously thought, so if you can grow it, mulch it and give it much-needed space. For zones 9–10.

Arisaema Martius

More than 190 species. Most are from Asia, but 3 are native to North America.

A. dracontium (Linnaeus) Schott. Green dragon. Eastern United States to Texas and north-central Mexico. This early-summer-flowering woodland species has a green palmate leaf enclosing a green hood with an S-shaped spadix. There are clusters of red berries in late summer and fall. Although not showy, it makes a fine accent plant when planted under the canopy of trees where the leaves can be viewed to advantage.

A. quinatum (Nuttall) Schott. North America. The five-parted-leaf Jack-in-the-pulpit is similar to the more common three-parted Jack-in-the-pulpit. Rare.

Arisaema dracontium
PHOTO BY SCOOTER CHEATHAM

A. triphyllum (Linnaeus) Torrey. Jack-in-the-pulpit, Indian turnip. Eastern United States. A woodland herb with quaint, hooded flowers in early spring. The spathe, which is striped inside with purple, encloses the short spadix. It is modestly attractive for a few weeks in late spring. If necessary, give it enough water for maintenance until it becomes dormant.

Arisarum Targioni-Tozzetti

A. proboscideum (Linnaeus) Savi. Mouse plant. Italy. This rhizomatous plant is occasionally available. The quaint spring flower, which has a dark purple-brown spathe with a white base and a mouse-like tail, is 3 inches high. It is shortly followed by the arum-like foliage in early summer. Zones 7–9.

Arum Linnaeus

About 15 species from Europe and the Mediterranean, most of which are not grown here. Tuberous, stemless herbs, with oblong to ovate long-petioled leaves and unisexual flowers consisting of spadix and spathe.

A. palaestinum Boissier, with a spathe that is green-white on the outside and red-purple on the interior, and *A. italicum* Miller, with marbled green leaves and greenish cream flowers, are sometimes sold and planted in our climate. In the case of *Arum italicum,* the calla-like red-purple-spathed flowers are produced near the end of the season and are followed by orange berries in late summer. The plants normally come up early in the fall and grow through the winter, but as they are usually shipped in the spring, they may skip a flowering season. If they survive this treatment, they will adjust to a normal cycle. If possible, one should find a grower who will ship them at the proper time in late summer or early fall.

Caladium Ventenat

Elephant's ear, angel-wings. About 15 species of tropical American aroids that are grown for their gaudy summer foliage in shade or part shade. Their flowers are typically of *Arum* form, while their leaves are many-colored and useful in pots or in the garden. Refer to spring catalogs for lists of available varieties. In order to keep them, dig them up in the fall when they go dormant and store them over winter. Otherwise you take a chance that they will rot during winter and spring months because rains keep the soil so moist at that time.

Colocasia

See Elephant's Ears.

Dracunculus Adanson

The divided foliage is produced early, followed in later spring by a large flower, usually nurtured by flies. The first day the smell is atrocious, but later it is scarcely noticeable. Unfortunately, by the time the odor is gone, the flower is beginning to go too. Give it a sunny spot where water can be withheld after the growing season, and it will return year after year.

D. *canariensis* Kunth. Canary Islands and Madeira Islands. Spathe is white above, green beneath.

D. *vulgaris* (Linnaeus) Schott. Mediterranean Europe and Asia Minor. The common purple-flowered form.

Elephant's Ears

Several allied genera are known as "elephant's ears."

Alocasia (Schott) G. Don f. includes about 70 species of erect, mostly rhizomatous perennial herbs of tropical Asia. *A. macrorrhiza* is one of the better-known species, with tropical foliage and edible roots. Other related genera, *Colocasia* and *Xanthosoma,* are somewhat similar and are also called elephant's ears. Treatment is the same for all. Give them rich, humusy soil, and keep them damp until they go dormant.

Helicodiceros **Schott**

H. muscivorus (Linné) Engler. Twist arum. Corsica, Sardinia, Balearic Islands. Though a plant not frequently encountered, it is included here for those few who might seek it out to grow as a pot plant. The leaves are palmately cut, the lobes spirally rolled around the ribs. One of the fly-gatherers, it has large bent, spotted flowers with a "high" scent.

Sauromatum **Schott**

Four species with corm-tubers.

S. guttatum (Wallich) Schott (syn. *S. venosum*). Northwest India. Voodoo lily, monarch of the East. The flower arises in spring, pretty in a somber way, with chocolate brown markings on an olive background, nearly sitting on the ground on a short stem. A "high" stable-like scent emanates from the flower, which lasts only a couple of days and then withers. It is followed by a single large leaf of palm-like form, persisting until late summer. Although the flower is notable, it appears rather suddenly and does not remain long enough to make more than a fleeting impression. One can easily miss it in the busy days of spring. But the leaf remains for months afterward and fits into the tropical scheme of things.

Thompsonia

T. nepalensis Wallich. Nepal to Assam. A single-species aroid similar to *Amorphophallus* in appearance, but with the terminal part of the spadix covered with tuberculate rudimentary flowers. The inflorescence has a convoluted base, expanded above to 18 inches long, with the exterior bright green on the outside and paler inside. It is rarely seen, but may occasionally be found growing in southern California.

Zantedeschia **Sprengel**

Calla, calla lily. South Africa. There are five or six species of these more colorful members of the Araceae. Lately a number of new intermediate hybrids have greatly enlarged the choices. Like some other members of the Araceae, callas may need digging and storing after they become dormant. During the growing season, give them a sunny or partly shady spot. The pleasantly scented flowers open greenish before turning into the color that they are to be. They are then revealed in all their glory before turning green again. This process takes several weeks.

Z. aethiopica (Linnaeus) Sprengel 1826. White flowers and unspotted leaves. This is a semi-aquatic species and will grow in wet places not favored by the others. All the others thrive with better drainage.

Z. albomaculata (W. J. Hooker) Baillon 1860. Mainly a white-flowered species, but can vary from pink to cream, ivory, and yellow. Has white-spotted leaves.

Z. elliottiana (W. Watson) Engler 1915. Yellow flowers, with white-spotted foliage. Thought by some to be a hybrid, but this is still uncertain. In the right situation it can remain for years.

Z. jucunda Letty 1961. Yellow flowers, white-spotted foliage.

Z. pentlandii (P. Watson) Wittmack 1898. Yellow flowers and unspotted leaves.

Z. rehmannii Engler 1883. From white or pink to dark maroon flowers. Narrow, lanceolate unspotted leaves.

The hybrids bridge the gap between pink and yellow, giving rise to shades of lavender, purple, apricot, and red.

Calochortus purpureus

CALOCHORTACEAE

Calochortus Pursh

Calochortus is a genus of about 65 species of the western United States, British Columbia, and Mexico. It was formerly placed in the Liliaceae but is now in a family of its own. Although in older literature the plants were said to grow from corms, close examination will show that these are tunicated bulbs. Many of them are difficult in cultivation and for that reason will be only briefly mentioned. Some of them prefer scree conditions, and watering must be completely controlled. After flowering they should not receive any water until the next growing season. The Mexican species are less fussy about summer water, as they grow where they get water in the summer and are dry and dormant in the winter. They don't need scree conditions and will take considerable water while growing, as long as they are kept dry while winter-dormant. Still, they are best grown in pots. All *Calochortus* species grow from tunicated bulbs with fibrous reticulated coats, and many produce bulbils in the leaf axils. The following are two common species to be found in Mexico.

C. barbatus (Humboldt, Bonpland, & Kunth) Painter 1911 (syn. *Cyclobothra barbata*). Grasslands, meadows, pastures, and roadsides, in oak or oak-pine forests in much of mountainous Mexico. Has branched, flexuous stems and paired nodding, bright yellow flowers with fringes and beards and a lemon-candy-like scent. Small bulbils are produced in the leaf axils. This is the most frequently cultivated of the Mexican species.

C. purpureus (Humboldt, Bonpland, & Kunth) Baker 1874. Durango, Zacatecas, Guanajuato, Jalisco, Guerrero, Michoacán, México, Morelia, and Oaxaca. Grasslands, oak or pine forests. The flowers are campanulate and nod demurely, with outer tepals shorter and duller in color than the inner tepals. They have a purplish-brown-and-yellow exterior, an orange-yellow interior, and a strange scent. Small bulbils are produced in the leaf axils. Midsummer.

Canna x 'Tiger Moth'
PHOTO BY H. KELLY, JR.

CANNACEAE

Canna Linnaeus

The canna family consists of a single genus of tropical plants with showy flowers and foliage. A proposed revision will reduce the genus to about 25 species, about 18 in tropical and subtropical America and about 7 in Asia. The native species, having smaller, less conspicuous flowers, are rarely cultivated, whereas the common large-flowered garden forms of mixed ancestry are popular. Refer to summer garden catalogs for a listing of what is available in the modern hybrids. Cannas are called "bandera española" (Spanish flag) in much of Spanish America.

Cannas are tropical rhizomatous plants with terminal simple or branched inflorescences and often large and showy asymmetrical flowers. The sepals and petals are inconspicuous, but the showy staminodes more than make up for this. Cannas are of simplest culture in any moist, fertile soil. They have been popular for tropical landscapes in parks since Victorian days and can be used in modern gardens if carefully selected according to height. In warm climates they are troubled only by the canna leaf roller (an insect), too much shade, and dry conditions.

C. flaccida Salisbury. South Carolina to Florida. A yellow-flowered aquatic native.

C. glauca Linnaeus. Southwest Mexico and lowlands of northern and eastern South America in flood plains and marshes. Though not now in general cultivation, this is a particularly attractive canna with lanceolate leaves and medium-sized light yellow flowers. I found it to be an eye-catching roadside plant in the wet ditches of Pacific southwestern Mexico.

C. indica Linnaeus (syn. *C. coccinea*, *C. edulis*). Indian shot. Mexico, Central America, and South America. Found in moist, rocky ravines and on mountainsides and low hills in deep, well-drained soils and clearings. A plant with ovate leaves, usually green but sometimes bronze. The flowers are small and variable in color (yellow, orange-yellow, orange, or scarlet), as in the number and form of the staminodes.

C. iridiflora Ruiz & Pavón. Peru. To 10 feet, with green leaves and large, pendant, rose-colored flowers.

C. latifolia Miller. South America. The leaves are ovate, purple-margined when young, and the flowers are scarlet.

C. warszewiczii A. Dietrich. Central and South America. A tall bronze-leaved species with small scarlet flowers.

Canna indica
PHOTO BY MARCO BLEEKER

Gloriosa superba
PHOTO BY BOBBY WARD

■ COLCHICACEAE

These lily-like plants with inferior ovaries were previously placed in the Liliaceae but have since been split off. Their rootstock is a corm or stoloniferous corm. This group includes perennial bulbous herbs from Africa, western Asia, Australia, and New Zealand.

Gloriosa Linnaeus

G. superba Linnaeus. Africa and Asia. Gloriosa lily, climbing lily. The plants resemble lilies, but their rootstock is a stoloniferous corm and they climb by leaf tendrils. The bud at the tip of the corm annually produces a new plant, which can grow to a height of 6 feet. The flowers are large with fully reflexed tepals and may be red, yellow, or red and yellow. All parts of the plant are poisonous, so they are not for munching by pets or small children. According to Richard L. Doutt, author of *Cape Bulbs* (1994), it is currently believed that there is but a single species of *Gloriosa*, *G. superba*, with several distinct varieties. Some believe that there are two species, while still others believe that there are nine species with many cultivars. You pays your money and takes your choice.

Littonia W. J. Hooker

Tropical Africa and Arabia. A genus of about six perennial herbs with tuberous corms and orange-yellow campanulate flowers in the leaf axils. The 2- to 6-foot stems require support.

Sandersonia W. J. Hooker

S. aurantiaca W. J. Hooker. South Africa. A monotypic genus somewhat like *Gloriosa*, but the leaves lack tendrils. *S. aurantiaca* is shorter in stature than *Gloriosa* and has orange-yellow bells resembling small Chinese lanterns in the leaf axils. The flowers need some support. The rootstock is a stoloniferous corm and must be kept dry in winter.

Achimenes sp.
PHOTO BY HERBERT KELLY JR.

■ GESNERIACEAE

Achimenes P. Browne

Achimenes is a genus of about 26 species native from Mexico to Panama. They are small hairy perennials about a foot or two in height, related to gloxinias and African violets. The catkin-like scaly bulbs are shaped like caterpillars or small elongated pine cones. The solitary or clustered flowers are borne in the leaf axils and shaped like pansies or petunias. They are unusual in occurring in the primary colors of red, yellow, and blue, as well as white, violet, salmon, and pink. They do very well in warm climates and are frequently grown in the ground, planted under trees in leaf mold, or in hanging baskets. They need light shade and moist conditions to do well and are benefited by regular drenching with the garden hose to control thrips and red spider mites. The number of flowers diminishes with the advent of cool fall weather; the plants can then be divided and stored, and the process repeated the following spring.

One catalog lists *Achimenes* as "Stars of India," but "Stars of Guatemala," where they are native, would be closer to reality.

Sinningia Nees

There are about 70 species of *Sinningia* native to Mexico, Central America, and South America, but only one, *S. speciosa*, concerns us. It grows from a tuber and has large velvety leaves and colorful bell-shaped flowers produced in the leaf axils. Modern hybridizers have given us the wonderful flowers that we know today in red, purple, pink, violet, and white. In addition, miniature and double forms are known. As they are not hardy, they are regarded principally as houseplants.

Camassia scilloides

■ HYACINTHACEAE

The hyacinth family (Hyacinthaceae) is composed of plants formerly placed within the Liliaceae. They produce numerous flowers up and down the scape in a raceme and are well represented about the Mediterranean and in southwestern Asia, South Africa, North America, and to a lesser extent South America. Some garden ornamentals from North America are in the genera *Camassia, Schoenocaulon, Schoenolirion,* and *Zigadenus.* Old World representatives include *Albuca, Bellevalia, Boweiea, Chionodoxa, Drimia, Drimiopsis, Eucomis, Galtonia, Hyacinthella, Hyacinthoides, Hyacinthus, Lachenalia, Massonia, Muscari, Ornithogalum, Polyxena, Puschkinia, Scilla, Urginea,* and *Veltheimia.*

Albuca Linnaeus

Africa, especially South Africa, and Arabia. A genus of 75 or more species allied to *Ornithogalum,* but with three segments opening wide and three remaining somewhat closed. The inflorescence is a simple raceme of nodding or occasionally erect flowers, usually white or yellow, with a green stripe. The foliage is in a rosette. The winter-dormant, summer-growing species do best out of doors in warm climates. As a group, they are interesting and handsome accent plants, but not showy. One is left wishing that the three inner segments would open wide so that the flower could be fully appreciated. Apparently their remaining partly closed is a protective mechanism. A few species are fragrant.

A. aurea N. Jacquin. South Africa. Winter-growing with yellow flowers. Must be grown in a container and protected from summer moisture in our climate.

A. canadensis (Linnaeus) Leighton. South Africa. Winter-growing. Pale yellow flowers flushed green, with a green stripe along each tepal.

A. crinifolia Baker is about 3 feet tall and has white flowers with a green stripe. Summer-growing.

A. nelsonii N. E. Brown. South Africa. An evergreen crinum-like plant with tall scapes. The white flowers are striped with green.

Bowiea Harvey & J. D. Hooker

B. volubilis Harvey & J. D. Hooker. Climbing onion, Zulu potato. South Africa and eastern tropical Africa. A curiosity unlike any other bulb. Keep dormant from May to October. The large, succulent bulb rests on top of the ground and puts out a twining green shoot with one or two rudimentary leaves, growing to a height of several feet. It bears a leafless branched inflorescence with numerous small green flowers. Because of its green color, the inflorescence functions in photosynthesis in the absence of leaves. It will grow in sun or shade in sandy soil.

Camassia Lindley

C. scilloides (Rafinesque) Cory. Eastern camassia, wild hyacinth. Southeastern United States. The other species in the genus *Camassia* grow in the western half of the United States, but one, *C. scilloides,* is an easterner. It is smaller and less attractive than the others, but it persists under ordinary conditions if kept on the dry side while dormant, and if we ignore the facts that each flower lasts only a day or two and that the colors are mostly in grayish shades of lavender, tinged blue, we can enjoy it. Our southern camassias are making their last stand on the few remaining friendly sections of highway right-of-way, as they have been grazed out inside the fences. Fortunately, if left alone, they will easily grow from seed.

Camassia scilloides (left) and *Zigadenus nuttallii*

Drimia Willdenow

D. maritima (Linnaeus) Stearn. Sea squill. This is the new name for a plant once known as *Urginea maritima*. In a genus of many African species, only one, *D. maritima,* is grown to perfection in Mediterranean-like climates such as are found in California, where it thrives. In our own climate, it survives but never flowers, due in part to occasional freezes, from which it needs protection.

Drimiopsis **Lindley & Paxton**

D. maculata Lindley & Paxton. Little white soldier, small snake lily. Natal, Africa. *Drimiopsis* is a genus of African bulbous plants that were formerly classified as *Scilla*. This particular species has proved to be exceptionally easy as a pot plant and is hardy to frost out of doors in zones 8 and 9 because of being winter-deciduous. In its native habitat it is found in sheltered places in the bush, the bulbs often growing naturally partly exposed above ground; they may rot if deeply buried. In pots or in the garden, they are winter-dormant, sending up several broad, spotted petioled leaves contemporary with a spike of rounded *Muscari*-like green-and-white flowers in spring. The leaves are as handsome as the flowers, and the curious dark leaf spots are semi-transparent. *D. maculata* is modestly attractive in partial shade, and the bulbs seem to thrive under benign neglect, multiplying rapidly. They will need dividing after a few years.

There are other *Drimiopsis* species worthy of trial, including some that are native to Natal. *D. lachenalioides* (formerly called *Scilla lachenalioides*) is a small plant with pink *Muscari*-like flowers and two mauve-spotted, prostrate leaves.

Drimiopsis plants are still difficult to find, though available from a few collectors of rare bulbs. They have a good future as pot plants or, as in the case of *D. maculata*, out of doors in part shade in zones 9 and 10, if given winter protection.

Endymion **Dumortier**

A synonym for *Hyacinthoides*.

Eucomis **L'Héritier**

Pineapple lily. A genus of about ten species native to southern and central Africa, all but one of which are summer-growing and winter-dormant. The large bulbs of *Eucomis* produce a rosette of erect shiny leaves up to 24 inches long. The whitish, greenish, pinkish, or purplish flowers are produced in a terminal raceme crowned with a cluster of leaf bracts. The following species are sometimes grown: *E. autumnalis, E. bicolor, E. comosa, E. pole-evansii,* and *E. regia.* They succeed best in a raised sandy bed.

Galtonia **Decaisne**

South Africa. A small genus (3 species) of South African natives that have nodding white flowers in a tall, bracted raceme. The best known in this country is *Galtonia candicans.* Catalogs state that the flowers are fragrant, but I have tried them a number of times and have never found this to be so. I find them attractive, but scentless.

They usually will give a good account of themselves the first year but in our climate are less reliable after that, as they need a drying-out period.

Hyacinthoides Heister ex Fabricius

Wood hyacinths, Spanish bluebells. A small genus formerly placed in *Scilla* and then in *Endymion*, but now considered a separate genus. The Spanish bluebell, *H. hispanica*, from Spain, is the species that we are most concerned with. It comes as an afterthought plant, always nice to see again, but quickly forgotten with the advent of another summer. I refer to the blue form, which always does best here. Perhaps it is because I expect so little from it that it seldom disappoints me. If tucked away in some shaded spot, it may come back for years. The racemes of nodding blue flowers are hyacinth-like. Pink and white forms are also known.

Hyacinthus Linnaeus

Mediterranean region, Asia Minor, and Iran. The hyacinth takes its name from the tragic character in Greek mythology who was accidentally slain by Apollo and whose spilled blood turned into a trail of purple flowers that we know as hyacinths. It is a small genus with three species, and only one, *H. orientalis*, is commonly cultivated. Originally the species had blue, purple, or white flowers, but breeders have managed to develop flowers in pink, red, yellow, and apricot, all by selection, as no other species has been involved. Amazing. Near the end of the nineteenth century, hyacinths peaked in number with an incredible 1,700 listed varieties, and even now they are known for their wide range of colors and wonderful fragrance.

Hyacinth bulbs are unusual in that those with blue, purple, pink, or red flowers have wine-colored tunics, while those with white or yellow flowers have white tunics. These tunics are irritating and will cause an itchy sensation if rubbed on the skin, such as the back of the hands, so handle them carefully.

They do erratically well in our climate, some staying for years and others quickly passing on. If they are to remain, they must be planted where they will receive little or no water other than rain, in a raised sunny bed. I have a partly shaded place in my garden in which a pale blue hyacinth was planted twenty years ago, and it still persists and flowers from year to year with no attention, even though it gets occasional summer water. Some things just cannot be explained.

Lachenalia J. F. Jacquin ex J. Murray

A large genus of South African plants, of which as many as 110 species are now recorded. The flowers are in racemes or spikes, and may be tubular, bell-shaped, or urn-shaped, and in all the known colors. In our climate all are suitable for pots, and they can be impressive while in bloom. In frost-free areas, they make good rock garden plants, but water carefully, as too much moisture may cause them to rot. While actively growing they don't pose any problems, but while dormant they must be kept bone dry.

L. aloides (yellow), *L. bulbifera* (red), and *L. mutabilis* (pale blue with yellow tips) are a few of the commonly grown winter-flowering forms. *L. aloides* is longest-lasting here.

Massonia Thunberg ex Linné

Pincushions. A curiosity for collectors, and especially fit for pot culture, these South African bulbs do exceedingly well. There are about five species, all characteristically having two leaves that lie flat on the ground. Some species have hairy leaves and look like some sort of carnivorous plants when first emerging. All species are winter-growers. They naturally grow in flat, sandy areas in poor soil, hot and dry in summer. The flowers are in a sessile umbel that looks like a small, colored paintbrush, with the stamens longer than the pale perianth.

Muscari Miller

A genus of about 40 species from Europe and the Mediterranean and southwestern Asia. They have bottle-shaped flowers drooping or looking outward. The best one for warm areas is *M. neglectum*. The others may need to be treated as annuals, as they need a colder climate if they are to persist.

M. ambrosiacum Moench. Musk hyacinth. Asia Minor. The bottle-shaped flowers, opening purplish and aging yellowish, have a wonderful musk scent. They are not showy but more than make up for it with their delightful fragrance. They do well in a sandy, well-drained, sunny situation where they can bake during the dormant months.

Muscari neglectum

M. neglectum Gussone ex Tenore. Bluebottles, starch hyacinth, grape hyacinth. Mediterranean. A leafy plant with small racemes of pendant dark blue bottle-like flowers with white "teeth." It is at its best in the blacklands, where it increases rapidly. It also loves sandy land, but may succumb to root-knot nematodes there. A large colony in flower can stain the landscape purple in the manner of bluebonnets. If content, it may persist, making many small bulblets and seed. The scent is interesting.

There are other species which may do variously well, as we travel northward, but in the deep South none do nearly as well as *M. neglectum.*

Ornithogalum Linnaeus

About 100 species, from Africa, Europe, and western Asia. Most have white flowers with greenish stripes, produced in racemes.

O. arabicum Linnaeus is a pretty thing with creamy white flowers and blackish ovaries. But in our climate it behaves as an annual and we can forget it after the first year. It is just as well, as the leaves always turn an embarrassing shade of yellow as it begins blooming.

O. caudatum Aiton. Sea onion. South Africa. Tender, but as a pot plant it is nearly indestructible. Just set in any pot and watch it grow. The raceme of greenish white flowers will eventually appear, and the bulbs will multiply.

O. dubium Houttuyn. This is a lovely species with flowers in yellow, orange, or red, and otherwise similar to *O. thyrsoides.* Unfortunately, besides being tender to cold, it is said to be very sensitive to viruses.

O. narbonense Linnaeus, from the Mediterranean, is a handsome sort, looking like a white-flowered version of *Camassia* in late spring. There are three to five leaves, which persist at flowering time, and the racemes of flowers are a greenish white. They are borderline plants with us, often dying off in zone 9 but persisting in zones 7 and 8.

O. pyramidale Linnaeus. Southern Europe. This plant is often confused with *O. narbonense,* which is similar, yet distinctly different. There are five to eight leaves, and the flowers are greenish yellow. The leaves wither by flowering time.

O. saundersiae Baker. South Africa. This is a large species, with 3-foot leaves resembling those of crinums. Since the bulbs are summer-growing and winter-dormant, they pose no problems in zones 8–10. The long racemes of white flowers have blackish ovaries and are quite attractive. Given a sandy raised bed it will persist for years.

O. thyrsoides N. Jacquin. Chincherinchee. South Africa. Another South African oddity, with starry white flowers. It usually fails here in spite of the fact that it is summer-growing. It is often the victim of virus disease.

O. umbellatum Linnaeus. Europe. This plant is of interest to us because it is easy to grow and is showy for a few hours each day. It can be a permanent resident if well situated. In the spring, satiny starry white flowers open on a short scape in the afternoon. But beware, as it is sometimes invasive. As with most ornithogalums, there is the ubiquitous green band on the reverse of the flower, a theme repeated again in the foliage, where there is a green leaf with a central white band.

Polyxena Kunth

Recently introduced miniatures from South Africa.

P. ensifolia and *P. corymbosa* are winter-growing species. They are grown as much for their ease of culture as for their beauty. They are small, producing clusters of lavender flowers on stems often less than an inch tall in midwinter. But they abide from year to year with ordinary care, and for some of us, this is enough.

P. corymbosa (Linnaeus) Jessop has semi-erect to erect narrow leaves, with clusters of flowers that can vary from white to pale pink.

P. ensifolia has two leaves that are first prostrate and then semi-erect. The small clusters of flowers range from white to pink to mauve.

Schoenocaulon A. Gray

Bottlebrush lilies, foxtails, green lilies. A genus of about 25 species. One species is found in Florida, two in Texas, one in New Mexico, and one in South America. The remainder are Mexican. They are related to *Zigadenus*.

The pronunciation for *Schoenocaulon* has always posed difficulties. In Latin, the letters "ch" are given a "k" sound, and the "oe" is pronounced like "e": "skeen-o-ᴋᴀᴡ-lon."

The greenish sessile flowers have short clasping tepals and prominently exerted whitish stamens that look much like the slender bottlebrushes that are used to clean test tubes. "Green lily" hardly conveys the true image of this unusual plant.

While many bottlebrush lilies are pleasantly scented, one tall species (5–6 feet) from Chiapas, Mexico, has creamy flowers with the unpleasant scent of rancid butter.

S. drummondii A. Gray. Autumn bottlebrush, green lily. Texas coastal prairie and northeastern Mexico. This species flowers in late summer and fall, with whitish racemes (1½ feet tall) of tiny flowers smelling something like grated coconuts in the afternoon sun. The leaves have the coarse look and feel of grass and are nearly evergreen. Although the plants glory in hot, sunny spots and have true bulbs with papery skins, they must not dry out for long out of the ground. They resent being moved, and if not replanted within a few weeks, they will die.

S. texanum Scheele. Sabadilla, spring bottlebrush, Texas green lily. In limestone soil in slopes, canyons,

Schoenocaulon drummondii

outwashes, and flats from the northeastern Rio Grande plains to the hill country and Edwards Plateau of Texas. The advice for *S. drummondii* applies here as well. This species is similar, but blooms in late spring instead of late summer. The tiny greenish flowers have extruded pinkish stamens and a faint sweet scent. Not showy, but interesting. The grassy leaves remain in active growth for most of the year, and the plants are not invasive. They can be planted in a poor, dry spot, where they will persist.

Schoenolirion Torrey ex E. Durand

A small genus of perennial herbs growing from a corm-like rootstock, with narrow leaves in a basal tuft and yellow or whitish flowers in a raceme. They are not commonly cultivated.

The name is pronounced "SKEEN-o-lir-ion." The "ch" has the "k" sound, and the "oe" has an "e" sound.

S. croceum (Michaux) Alphonso Wood. East Texas to Florida and North Carolina. This small species has yellow flowers and blooms in wet situations in the spring.

S. wrightii H. Sherman (syn. *S. texanum*). Endemic to central Texas, in dry woods and meadows. A rare plant, with small racemes of whitish flowers on slender stems.

Scilla Linnaeus

Squills. There are about 80–90 species of this genus in Europe, Africa, and Asia. The flowers are produced in racemes of blue or white. Its a large genus, but only a few can grow in hot, dry climates.

S. hyacinthoides Linnaeus. Mediterranean. This squill is often grown in the mid-South. In late spring the tall scapes have small blue flowers with long pedicels, elongating into what look like foxtails. The rosette of leaves looks like a small crinum. At its best, this plant can add interest to the late spring garden. Zones 8 and 9.

S. natalensis Planchon. This resident of South Africa looks somewhat similar to *S. hyacinthoides,* with similar flowers, but differs in having wider, shorter leaves which survive into late summer and much larger exposed bulbs. It is probably less hardy than the other species.

S. peruviana Linnaeus. The name for this plant is a misnomer, as it is native to the Mediterranean. It first arrived in England many years ago on a boat named *Peru,* and that name stuck. But it is a fine plant in the warm climates of zones 8, 9, and 10, and should be planted more often. The bright green foliage scape is short, but there are many small blue flowers packed on a tight raceme. There is a rarer white form with the same habits. Good for pots anywhere and in the ground in zones 8–10.

Urginea Steinheil

U. maritima (Linnaeus) Baker is now called *Drimia maritima,* which see.

Veltheimia Gleditsche

South Africa. The two species of *Veltheimia, V. capensis* and *V. bracteata,* look something like pink dwarf "red hot pokers" (*Kniphofia* spp.). Being winter-growers, they are suitable only for frost-free areas, unless grown in pots. The large bulbs require a sandy, loamy mix, with half of the bulb above the soil line, and can be watered while in active growth. The basally produced leaves of *V. capensis* have wavy margins. Both species are shade-tolerant and have waxy pinkish tubular flowers that hang downward from the dense raceme in a graceful manner. During the dormant summer period, water should be withheld, and for this reason it is best to grow them in pots.

Zigadenus Michaux

A genus of about 15 species from North America and Asia. Several species are found in the eastern half of the United States, including *Z. densus, Z. elegans, Z. glaberrimus, Z. leimanthoides,* and *Z. nuttallii,* which are found in Texas and are suitable for the wild garden. More species are found in the western half of the country. Only *Z. nuttallii* will be discussed here.

Z. nuttallii A. Gray. Death camas. Prairies and open woodlands from Tennessee to Kansas and Texas. March to May. It is said to be poisonous, but this should be of little concern if we confine it to wild gardens, where it looks its best, if we can obtain it. It would probably never occur to most of us to snack on such a bitter ornamental anyway. The small creamy white flowers are on a raceme and combine well with *Camassia scilloides,* both flowering briefly within a week of one another. They flower in a short time span and are gone in a matter of a week or so. Do not water while dormant. As they are becoming scarce, the best advice is to leave them alone while we still can enjoy them in the wild.

Hypoxis decumbens PHOTO BY J. A. CASTILLO

HYPOXIDACEAE

Formerly classed with members of the Amaryllidaceae, but now a separate family. Most species have starry yellow flowers and inferior ovaries. They are found mainly in the Southern Hemisphere in South Africa, South America, and Australia, with a few North American representatives.

Hypoxis Linnaeus

The genus *Hypoxis* includes about 118 species growing from short corm-like rhizomes; most are not very interesting. The flowers may be white or yellow, on a scape that is one- to several-flowered, and plants may be deciduous or evergreen.

H. decumbens Linnaeus. Argentina. Clusters of large, starry yellow flowers lying on the ground around the base of the plant in early summer. One of the showy ones.

H. hirsuta (Linnaeus) Coville. Maine, south to Florida and Texas. The hairy leaves are up to a foot long, with one- to seven-flowered scapes. The perianths are yellow and star-like. One of the easier ones, and almost everblooming.

H. rooperi T. Moore. Gorilla's armpit. South Africa. A fanciful name for one of the showier members of the genus. Large, star-like yellow flowers. The bulbs are large, black, and shaggy, hence the name.

Dutch iris

▪ IRIDACEAE

Plants in the Iridaceae have three stamens, rather than the six of the Alliaceae, Liliaceae, and Amaryllidaceae, and inferior ovaries rather than the superior ovaries of the Liliaceae. This is a very large family that includes such familiar plants as *Crocus, Freesia, Gladiolus, Iris,* and *Tigridia,* to name but a few. Old World species are either bulbous, cormous, or rhizomatous, while the rootstocks of the New World species may consist of tunicated bulbs, rhizomes, or tuberous or fibrous roots. Although older literature erroneously described some New World bulbous irids as having corms, the fact is that in this group corms are conspicuous by their absence.

Old World irids, most of which are rhizomatous or cormous, include *Anomatheca, Babiana, Belamcanda, Crocosmia, Crocus, Dietes, Ferraria, Freesia, Geissorhiza, Gladiolus, Gynandriris, Hesperantha, Hermodactylus, Homeria, Iris, Ixia, Lapeirousia, Moraea, Pardanthopsis, Romulea, Sparaxis,* and *Tritonia.*

New World irids are mostly rhizomatous or bulbous, often with ephemeral flowers. The North American species include *Ainea, Alophia, Cipura, Cobana, Eleutherine, Fosteria, Gelasine, Iris, Nemastylis, Rigidella, Sessilanthera, Sphenostigma,* and *Tigridia.* South American species include *Calydorea, Cypella, Gelasine, Herbertia, Hesperoxiphion, Kelissa, Mastigostyla, Neomarica, Onira, Pseudotrimezia, Sympa,* and *Trimezia.*

In the Americas, the irids break down into several tribes. The first of these is the Irideae, of which the genus *Iris* is the best known, with many rhizomatous North American species. In Central and South America, these are replaced by the rhizomatous Mariceae, of which there are three genera, *Trimezia, Pseudotrimezia,* and *Neomarica.*

Another tribe, the Sisyrinchieae, is found in both North and South America. This group is widespread and includes many species. Their roots may be fibrous, tuberous, or rhizomatous, but not cormous or bulbous, and they are not included here.

The tribe Tigridieae is found in the United States, Mexico, and South America, and consists of about 20 genera, with ephemeral flowers, pleated leaves, and tunicated bulbs. An effort has been made to include many of these.

Acidanthera Hochstetter

The plants formerly classified as *Acidanthera* are now included in *Gladiolus. A. bicolor* is now considered a synonym for *Gladiolus callianthus.*

Ainea Ravenna 1979

A. conzattii (Foster) Ravenna 1979 (syn. *Sphenostigma conzattii*). Mexico, state of Oaxaca, endemic in mountainous wooded areas north of the city of Oaxaca. A monotypic genus of slender plants less than 10 inches high that have fugacious nodding, triangular white flowers with finely black-spotted inner tepals. They open at dawn and close by midmorning. Rare, endangered, and not in cultivation. The bulbs are tunicated.

Alophia Herbert 1840

A genus of several *Tigridia*-like irids with tunicated bulbs and ephemeral flowers in blue, white, or purple, with the cup dotted purplish and inner tepals marked white or yellow. Texas, Mexico, West Indies, and South America.

A. drummondiana (R. C. Graham) R. Foster 1940 (syn. *Eustylis purpurea*). Texas and Mexico in sandy soils. The *Tigridia*-like purple flowers normally appear in early summer and may bloom until fall if conditions are to their liking. They can make ideal garden plants if their environment is in tune with their needs. I have planted seed in rich, sandy soil in spring and flowered them by midsummer. They had made clumps by fall and were still flowering at first frost.

Alophia drummondiana

A. intermedia Ravenna 1964. Mexico, state of Sinaloa. Pendant lilac flowers with a yellow center. The genus placement is in doubt, as the type specimen has unfortunately not been available for study.

A. medusa (Baker) Goldblatt. South America. A listed form.

A. sylvestris (Loesener) Goldblatt. South America. A little-known species.

A. veracruzana Goldblatt & T. M. Howard 1992. Southeastern Mexico, state of Veracruz. The flowers are in white and shades of purple, with lavender-blue the predominant color. Does very well in the garden and will reseed in the South. It tolerates ordinary garden conditions very well. August–September.

Anomatheca Ker-Gawler

Southern Africa. A genus of about six cormous species. The foliage is usually lance-shaped with simple or branched inflorescences of long-tubed flowers in red, light blue, white, or green. At least one species, *A. laxa,* is occasionally grown in mild climates. Culture is like that of *Gladiolus,* but it is a much smaller plant and can tolerate light shade. In frost-free situations, it reseeds.

Babiana Ker-Gawler

Babiana is a large genus of about 63 cormous species mainly from the southwestern cape of South Africa. It is a deciduous genus, of summer-growing and winter-growing species which are hardy in frost-free climates but need protection elsewhere. They are susceptible to attacks of red spider mites and mosaic virus disease. Babianas have lance-shaped, hairy, pleated foliage and inflorescences in shades of red, pink, purple, mauve, blue, yellow, or white. Some species are strongly fragrant.

Belamcanda Adanson (syn. *Pardanthus*)

B. chinensis (Linnaeus) de Candolle. Blackberry lily, leopard flower. China, Japan. Although *B. chinensis* arguably belongs with perennials rather than bulbs, it is often placed with bulbs. The roots are stout rhizomes with broad, iris-like deciduous fans. The inflorescence is loosely corymbose. The six perianth segments, which are not united, are orange with red dots, or rarely yellow. The flowers are followed by glossy black seeds resembling a blackberry. This species does best in sandy loam and full sun with plenty of moisture. I planted one in a raised sandy bed, where it lived and bloomed for several years before disappearing. But then they are reputed to be short-lived.

Calydorea Herbert 1843 (syn. *Cardiostigma, Salpingostylis, Catila, Itysa*)

Ephemeral blue, purple, or white flowers from Florida, Mexico, or South America with tunicated bulbs. In cultivation they should probably be treated like other tig-

Calydorea sp.

ridioids, i.e., give moisture in a well-drained soil while growing and keep dry while dormant.

C. amabilis (Ravenna) Goldblatt & Henrich 1991 (syn. *Catila amabilis*). Argentina, Entre Ríos Province. A South American species with blue flowers. Easy from seed.

C. azurea Klatt. Argentina, Entre Ríos Province. Has star-shaped blue flowers, wiry stems, and narrow foliage.

C. coelestina (Bartram) Goldblatt & Henrich 1991 (syn. *Salpingostylis coelestina, Sphenostigma coelestina*). Florida. Once called "Bartram's Ixia," but this has fallen by the wayside in the name-changes that followed. The blue flowers appear after sunrise and last about three hours. It flowers well only after fires in April and May. It is the only member of this genus found in the United States and is rare in cultivation.

C. hintonii B. Foster 1945. Mexico, state of Michoacán, in grassy openings in oak-pine forests. Blue-flowered. July.

C. longispatha (Herbert) Baker 1876 (syn. *Gelasine longispatha*). Central Mexico, states of México, eastern Michoacán, and Jalisco. Flowers blue or purplish blue.

C. pallens. Northwest Argentina. A summer-growing species, growing in alkaline soil in areas of summer rains, this may do very well in cultivation in our climate if protected.

Other *Calydorea* species sometimes listed are *C. gardneri* (syn. *Itysa gardneri*), *C. venezolensis* (syn. *Itysa venezolensis*), and *C. mexicana* (syn. *Cardiostigma mexicanum*).

Cardiostigma Baker 1876

A synonym for *Calydorea*, which see.

Catila Ravenna 1983

A synonym for *Calydorea*, which see.

Cipura Aublet 1775

Cipura is a New World genus allied to *Cypella*, with tunicated bulbs and plicate leaves, growing from southern Mexico's coasts and inland, to Central America, the West Indies, Bolivia, southern Brazil, and Paraguay. The flowers may be white, yellow, or violet, and are fugacious, opening early in the morning and closing before noon. The segments may be of two different forms and sizes, or may be of similar form and size, according to the species.

C. campanulata Ravenna 1964 (syn. *C. inornata*). Yucatán. A tropical species. The white, bluish white, or pale blue flowers have subequal segments.

Cipura paludosa

C. formosa Ravenna. South America. Violet flowers.

C. paludosa Aublet 1775. A tropical species with white or bluish white flowers, larger than *C. campanulata*, and with segments that are not as noticeably unequal, making the flower look like a small gladiolus. The bulbs are yellow or orange if peeled, in contrast to *Eleutherine* bulbs, which are reddish.

C. rupicola Goldblatt & Henrich 1987. Venezuela. Erect yellow flowers with unequal segments.

C. xanthomelas Martius ex Klatt (syn. *C. flava*). Brazil, state of Goiás. Yellow flowers with unequal segments.

C. sp. #1. Brazil, states of Bahia, Goiás, and Mato Grosso. Violet flowers, rigid leaves, and large bulbs.

C. sp. #2. Venezuela and adjacent Colombia. Violet flowers. Taller than the preceding species.

Cobana Ravenna 1974

A monotypic genus consisting of *C. guatemalensis* (Standley) Ravenna 1974 (syn. *Eleutherine guatemalensis*). Guatemala, in the department of Alta Verapaz, near the city of Cobán, and east-central Honduras. It has slightly nodding white flowers with segments nearly equal, but the inner tepals slightly narrower and more acute. The bulb, leaves, stem, and spathe are similar to those of other American members of the Iridaceae with plaited leaves and tunicated bulbs. Flowers during the summer rainy season. Probably not in cultivation.

Crocosmia Planchon

Crocosmia comprises nine cormous species native to South Africa with spikes of small red or yellow flowers. They are popular in the South, but can be infested with red spider mites. There are a number of hybrids, but the best is still *C.* × *crocosmiflora* (*C. aurea* × *C. pottsii*). Culture as for *Gladiolus*, which they somewhat resemble.

Crocus Linnaeus

Most of the delightful crocuses are among the harbingers of spring for northern gardeners, but in the warmest climates they may do indifferently or poorly. If one cares to try them, the best bet is the one sometimes called "Dutch Yellow," which can sometimes manage to give an initial account of itself. Crocuses are available everywhere, but few ever bloom in zones 9 and 10. Sometimes they fail to even come up. Often they may flower the first year and then fail to reappear the next year. Perhaps they fall victims to various soil-borne pathogens. There are also fall-flowering kinds, and some of these do somewhat better initially. Cormous.

Cypella Herbert

Mexico and South America. *Cypella* is a genus of at least 20 subtropical or tropical spring- or early-summer-flowering species growing from tunicated bulbs, with narrow pleated leaves and showy ephemeral flowers like those of *Tigridia* or *Neomarica*. Although most of them are not hardy, cultivation is easy if they are grown in light, sandy acid soils in raised beds, or as potted plants. They can be propagated by offsets or by seeds, flowering in two to three years from seed. A few are occasionally available from collectors. *C. herbertii* is the hardiest, and will take considerable frost.

C. armosa Ravenna. Argentina, Corrientes and Misiones Provinces. A rare species with lemon or orange flowers.

C. fucata. Southern Brazil, Uruguay. An orange-yellow species somewhat similar to *C. herbertii,* and flowering in spring with similar cultural needs.

C. gracilis. Paraguay. This is like *C. herbertii,* but is smaller, with narrower leaves.

C. hauthali subsp. *opalina.* Argentina, Corrientes Province. Winter-growing and summer-dormant under very hot conditions. It has white flowers in autumn and spring. It can take summer rains, so may be a candidate for our climate if soils are acid.

Cypella herbertii
PHOTO BY J. A. CASTILLO

C. herbertii (Lindley) Herbert. Argentina, Brazil, and Paraguay. The most popular species, having fugacious flowers of mustard-yellow with wine-brown markings, produced in a series, and somewhat like *Tigridia* in form. Reasonably winter-hardy in warm climates if kept protected and dry when dormant. It sometimes reseeds itself and does well in a sheltered sunny border if kept moist, but not wet.

C. herbertii subsp. *brevicristata.* Argentina, Uruguay. Similar to the above, but with canary-yellow flowers on smaller, more slender plants.

C. lapidosa Ravenna. Argentina, Corrientes Province. A lemon-yellow species dotted maroon-brown and flowering twice a year. A winter-grower in frost-free situations. Needs an acid soil.

C. linearis. Colombia, Bolivia, and Venezuela. The purplish flowers are spotted and are about an inch wide.

C. mexicana Morton & Foster 1950. Mexico, in Pacific lowlands and foothills of Jalisco, Michoacán, and Guerrero. In marshes, poorly drained savannahs, sandy soils, and grassy hillsides, at 1,000–2,300 feet. July–September. The flowers are more spreading, smaller, and darker than those of *C. rosei.*

C. osteniana Beauverd. Uruguay. A rare winter-growing white-flowered species, with wine-and-yellow inner tepals, it flowers in late spring. It is of easy culture out of doors and is also fine for pots. It can take light frosts with no harm. Unfortunately, it is becoming endangered through overgrazing.

Cypella rosei

C. plumbea Lindley. Northern Argentina, southern Brazil, and Paraguay. A robust species with 3-inch dull blue flowers, yellow at the base. It is robust but tender to frost and is best wintered in pots, as it is deciduous.

C. rosei Foster 1945. Mexico, in coastal southern Sinaloa and Nayarit. It is found on sandy, grassy flats and at woodland openings, at edges of seasonally wet spots, in full sun, at elevations of 350 feet or less in the lowlands of Nayarit and Sinaloa in June–August. The little spotted globular flowers may be white, blue, or purple.

Dietes Salisbury ex Klatt

Dietes is similar to *Moraea* but has rhizomes instead of corms. The danger for *Dietes* plants is low temperature rather than disease. If it gets too cold, they are damaged or killed outright. They are grown in zones 9 and 10 with protection. The flower stems are perennial and will produce flowers year after year if not cut off to the last node. Each flower lasts only a single day, but they can bloom over a long period of time.

Two species are grown, *D. iridoides* (syn. *D. vegeta*), with white or lavender flowers, and *D. bicolor*, with yellow flowers. Also occasionally seen are 'Lemon Drops' and 'Orange Drops,' which are hybrids between the two species.

Eleutherine Herbert 1843

A small genus of afternoon-flowering plants with plicate leaves, reddish tunicated bulbs, and regularly shaped white flowers. Some have an interesting odor.

E. bulbosa (Miller) Urban. West Indies. Considered by some as a synonym for *E. latifolia.*

E. latifolia Standley & B. S. Williams. Mexico, state of San Luis Potosí, on the banks of Río Moctezuma. Not a showy plant. From June until fall the small flowers open in the afternoon and remain open until evening. They are creamy white with

Eleutherine plicata
PHOTO BY JO ANN TRIAL

yellowish midribs and are permanent in southern gardens, where they may bloom for months. The segments are rotate, with no glandular surface. They resemble *Nemastylis* on a slightly smaller scale. The flowers have a strange, musky scent. The bulbs do not form offsets, but the plants reseed themselves and can easily invade a lawn. The foliage is robust and plicate, and these plants can take a lot of water, even when dormant. Although tropical, they are amazingly enduring where winters are not severe. Rare in cultivation, but once established they remain as garden plants and have no problems.

E. plicata (Swartz) Klatt. West Indies. Plants that I received by this name were similar to *E. latifolia*, but larger in all parts, with erect plicate leaves and wine-red bulbs increasing by division and forming clumps. *E. latifolia* does not form clumps.

Ferraria Burman ex Miller

There are ten cormous *Ferraria* species from Africa, but only one (*F. glutinosa*) is summer-growing. Of the remaining species, *F. densipunctulata*, from the southwestern Cape Coast, is currently apt to be encountered. Growing from flattened corms, it flowers from winter to spring, with several flowers opening a few at a time over several weeks; each one remains open for two days. The perianth segments are wavy and grayish with purple spots. It is an easy plant to maintain in pots and for this reason is recommended.

The African cormous *Ferraria* are often confused with *Tigridia*, which are true bulbous plants from Mexico.

Ferraria densipunctulata

Fosteria Molseed 1968

Southern Mexico. A monotypic genus.

F. oaxacana Molseed 1968. Mexico, state of Oaxaca, dry grassy, often rocky areas in company with oaks and palms. This nodding little irid is interesting but not showy, as the small triangular flowers are an odd shade of tawny yellow, with tiny purplish spots near the base of the tepals. The anthers are tongue-like and comparatively large for the size of the flower. The six to ten ephemeral flowers are produced singly in succession, opening each morning throughout the summer. The foliage is narrowly plicate, above a small tunicated bulb. Very rare, and may not be in cultivation. The culture is like that of most *Tigridia* species.

Freesia Ecklon ex Klatt

South Africa. Originally there were 19 species of *Freesia*, which were widely intercrossed as they became a major part of the world's floriculture. In addition to the variously colored single sorts, there are now "double" types, which are really semi-doubles. But all of this was at the expense of the wonderful fragrance, which was originally quite fine and strong. Freesias are quite tender and if grown outside will need protection from frosts, but they can be greenhoused in pots in zones 8 and 9 with no major problems. Cormous.

Geissorhiza Ker-Gawler

Wine cups, blue sequins, or red sequins. A genus of up to 60 cormous species from the Cape Province of South Africa. The flowers are somewhat like *Hesperantha* but with shorter style branches; like *Ixia* but larger and with green spathes. They are still mostly unknown in this country, except in California. They need to be planted in large numbers to be effective. Unlike other bulbs from South Africa, they are found in moist, marshy soils in frost-free areas. Some species produce one or two large, variable flowers, while others produce four or five smaller flowers. They are fine for pots in a sandy-peaty mix. Available in this country from seed.

Gelasine Herbert 1840

Uruguay and southern Brazil. Allied to *Cipura* and *Nemastylis*. Tunicated bulbs, pleated leaves, and two or three fugacious flowers in a terminal cluster, emerging from two green spathe valves. Flowers have a cup-shaped perianth, a very short cup-shaped tube, and nearly equal segments with the filaments united at the base.

G. azurea Herbert. Flowers bright blue, with small basal white blotches.

G. uruguaiensis Ravenna. Uruguay. Blue flowers in spring. Easy from seed.

Gladiolus Linnaeus

Aside from the modern hybrid gladioli, there are more than 180 cormous species widely distributed through much of Africa, the European Mediterranean, and the Middle East. The current concept of the genus now includes the species formerly classified as *Acidanthera*. *Gladiolus* species fall into three main groups, the summer-flowering species of tropical and subtropical Africa, the winter-growing species from the Cape Province, and the spring-flowering species of Europe, North Africa, and the Middle East. The flowers of most species are irregular in form, but a few have symmetrical blossoms. The majority of modern hybrids are descended from about a dozen South African species. The flowers are usually held on one side of the stem. A sunny, well-drained situation suits the spring- and summer-flowering ones well.

Gynandriris Parlatore

Africa, the Mediterranean, and central Asia. There are about nine species of cormous plants. The fugacious iris-like blue, white, or mauve flowers are produced in succession in clusters. At times they can be infested with red spider mites. Culture as for *Gladiolus*.

 G. sisyrinchium (Linnaeus) Parlatore is sometimes listed and is hardy in zones 9 and 10 with slight protection.

Herbertia Sweet 1827

A small genus from southern Texas, the southeastern United States, and South America. The plants have tunicated bulbs and purplish *Tigridia*-like ephemeral flowers opening in the morning and closing in the afternoon. Sometimes confused with *Alophia*. They are of easy culture in a garden or in pots and are hardy to zone 8.

 H. guareimana (syn. *H. amatorum*). Brazil, in Rio Grande do Sul Province; Uruguay; and northeastern Argentina. A deep-purplish-blue-flowered species with a white cup and violet spots. Easy from seed. Spring.

 H. lahue (Molina) Goldblatt, from Texas, and *H. lahue* subsp. *amoena* (Grisebach) Goldblatt, from South America. This is one of several bulb oddities found in South America and Texas, but there is some question whether the Texas form is identical and the same species as the South American form. The Texas form has larger flowers. Both are lovely subtropical spring-flowering plants of easy

Herbertia lahue

culture when given adequate moisture. The flowers are violet, with white cups spotted violet. Easily propagated from seed.

H. pulchella Sweet. Uruguay and southern Brazil. A lovely spring-flowering species from Rio Grande do Sul, Brazil. The purple flowers have white markings in the cup.

H. tigridioides (Hick.) Goldblatt. Bolivia and northwestern Argentina. This species grows in alkaline soils in full sun in summer and has spotted purple flowers. It takes light frost while dormant and is easy to grow and flower in mild climates. Easy from seed.

Hermodactylus Miller

H. tuberosus (Linnaeus) Miller (syn. *Iris tuberosa*). Snake's head iris. Mediterranean region. *Hermodactylus tuberosus* is now the preferred name for the plant formerly known as *Iris tuberosa*. In our climate it gives the impression of trying to please, growing well, but often failing to flower after the first season. The small, beardless-iris-like flowers are a dark velvety plum purple. Initially they are attractive in spite of their somber coloring, but getting them to flower after the first year is problematical. They always give the false impression that they are awaiting another, better year. They have odd corm-like rhizomes.

Hesperantha Ker-Gawler

A genus of about 30 species growing naturally from corms in the mountainous areas of South Africa. They have grass-like foliage, up to a foot tall in some species, and fragrant flowers. The flowers open late in the afternoons, hence the name.

H. stanfordiae L. Bolus is a charming little thing with bright yellow tepals opening in the afternoon. It has small, hard-coated corms and sets many seeds. It flowers out of doors in the spring in zones 8 and 9.

Hesperoxiphion

Peru. A small genus sometimes included with *Cypella*, consisting of high-elevation (12,000 feet) Andean species from near Cuzco, failing in a hot climate unless given alpine culture (as in a cooled greenhouse), yet considered too tender for outside cultivation. The bulbs are tunicated.

H. herrerae. Peru. The outer three tepals are deep blue, and the smaller inner blue tepals have spotted yellow signals, minutely spotted at the base, white in the center. Easily propagated from stem bulbils.

H. peruvianum. Peru. Has deep yellow flowers with pubescent inner segments. Can be obtained from seed.

Homeria comptonii

Homeria Ventenat

While there are about 30 South African cormous species, only a handful are commonly cultivated. Many of these are regarded as toxic weeds in Australia, where they have become a serious problem. The inflorescence has paired, few- to many-flowered scapes in yellow, pink, orange, or rarely white. They are cultivated like *Gladiolus,* but subject to attacks of spider mites. In areas where they are less inclined to spread, they are quite charming spring flowers. *H. flaccida* (syn. *H. collina*) comes in both salmon and yellow varieties, while *H. comptonii* is salmon, and *H. ochroleuca* is yellow. They produce offsets and in time will form clumps.

Iris Linnaeus

A genus of about 200 species. Who is not familiar with the irises? These are ubiquitous perennials of the New and Old Worlds with triangular flowers that have standards and falls in many colors. Thus the name, for Iris, the goddess of the rainbow.

Iris albicans J. Lange. While it is not my intention to discuss the many old rhizomatous garden forms, I would like to mention the rugged *I. albicans* as a reliable

Iris albicans

old plant worth growing even if you can't grow anything else. Little wonder that it is widespread, since year after year it returns with white or blue flowers even when given complete neglect and isolation. It was originally brought from the Arabian peninsula and planted everywhere the Spaniards went in the New World. There are two color forms of this species, blue and white, with the blue form the less common of the two. I have observed plantings of the blue form, sometimes called 'Madonna,' gradually switch from blue to white over a period of a few years, often producing flowers half white and half blue, and in time becoming all white. Perhaps the change is due to a mu tation or a virus. In any event they seem not to revert to blue again. Planted in a sunny spot, they last forever, flowering in the spring and occasionally in the fall. Other than being given a sunny, dryish situation, they need little or no care. These and other irises that were formerly in vogue in gardens can often be found in old cemeteries. The fact that they remain without care after many long years is to their credit.

Series *Hexagonae* (Diels) Lawrence. Louisiana irises. No discussion of irises is complete without mentioning the water irises from the Mississippi River delta. The series *Hexagonae* is composed of *Iris fulva, I. brevicaulis, I. hexagona, I. giganticaerulea,* and *I. nelsonii.* Even though only a few basic species are involved, the variety in these plants is nothing short of amazing, and intercrossing them has produced a myriad of colors and forms. These species and their hybrids can do very well under normal garden conditions, but the slender rhizomes have a tendency to "run" across a flower bed. In a short time they will be in areas other than where they were originally planted. To curb this, I plant mine in large washtubs with rich soil and water added, and they then tend to grow in circles and stay contained. Since the list of cultivars available is continuously changing, you will need to order an up-to-date list to make selections. If in doubt, some of the finest forms can be selected from winners of the Mary Swords DeBaillon Award, an annual award for the best new Louisiana iris.

I. japonica Thunberg × *nada.* Tender subtropical hybrid irises from the late James Giridlian of Arcadia, California. They are for zones 9 and 10, and require winter protection. They form slender rhizomes and evergreen fan-like foliage and produce ruffled white flowers speckled lemon or orange in the late winter and spring. Where climate permits, they are ideal plants in part shade.

I. pseudacorus Linnaeus. A European water iris often seen as a companion for Louisiana irises in gardens. There are variegated and double-flowering forms. The yellow flowers are produced in the spring, and the plant can be quite tall (to 5 feet).

I. spuria Linnaeus. Europe and Asia. Spuria irises are widespread, flowering here in late spring or early summer. They are nearly 3 feet tall and like full sun. They produce flowers in yellow, white, blue, and bronze. After flowering they become dormant for the rest of the year. Although they don't like being disturbed, this is the time to divide and reset them.

Bulbous Irises

The bulbous irises are both exciting and vexing. The vexing ones are the Junos and the Reticulatas, which do poorly in the South. Apparently it is neither cold enough in winter nor dry enough in summer to meet their needs. On the other hand, many members of the *I. xiphium* group, with the exception of the English iris, are cheap and plentiful, and no warm winter garden should be without them. The English iris, *I. latifolia* (syn. *I. xiphioides*) needs a cool, damp climate such as is found in the Pacific Northwest. The Dutch and Spanish irises, on the other hand, love warmer, drier conditions and do well in the Southwest. The Dutch irises are hybrids between varieties of *I. xiphium*, *I. tingitana*, and to a lesser extent, *I. filifolia*. The smaller and later-flowering Spanish irises are hybrids within *I. xiphium*. The choices in either group are extensive but continue to change over the years, as new varieties make older ones obsolete. The old Dutch iris cultivar 'Wedgewood' is an early-flowering blue member of this group that has yet to be improved upon. There is also a pure white version of it, as well as several darker blue ones. Practically all of the *I. tingitana* hybrids excel in our climate, blooming several weeks ahead of the others. Since they are relatively inexpensive, they can be planted in large numbers.

Itysa Ravenna 1986

Two species from northern South America were formerly in this genus, now considered as a synonym for *Calydorea*, which see.

Ixia Linnaeus

The genus *Ixia* is comprised of about 50 South African species. They are hardy only in the mildest areas (zone 10) and must be grown in pots elsewhere. Their inflorescence is a spike of star-like flowers in shades of red, green, purple, blue, orange, yellow, white, or cream. Flowers may remain closed on cold days. The genus is very sensitive to watering and susceptible to mealybugs and aphids, and for these reasons it is not the best candidate for a long life even in hot climates.

Kelissa Ravenna

Brazil, state of Rio Grande do Sul. The spring-flowering *K. brasiliensis* has pleated foliage and flowers on stems about 10 inches tall. The flowers are upfacing, with three large lilac segments each partly divided to give the appearance of six segments, and are attractively spotted purple on a white background. Though very lovely, they are still scarce in collections. Tunicated bulbs.

Kelissa brasiliensis

Lapeirousia Pourret

A genus of about 35 cormous sub-Saharan African species. Although formerly listed with *Anomatheca*, they are now listed separately. Compared to *Anomatheca*, *Lapeirousia* has dwarfer plants with longer perianth tubes. They do very well under greenhouse culture or out of doors with protection.

Mastigostyla

A little-known genus from Peru. The spotted mauve or violet flowers last only a few hours, and the three outer segments are larger than the three inner segments. Tunicated bulbs.

Moraea Miller

A genus of about 120 cormous South African iris-like plants, monographed by Peter Goldblatt in 1986. They require Mediterranean conditions.

Moraeas can be grown from seed. In zones 9 and 10, they should be grown in pots if one is to enjoy their great diversity.

M. polystachya (Thunberg) Ker-Gawler. A common irid in southern California, this is a fall-winter bloomer with iris-like blue-violet flowers. In its native South Africa, it is considered poisonous to cattle.

Nemastylis Nuttall 1835

Southeastern United States and Mexico. Except for one notable exception, the yellow-flowered *N. convoluta*, this is a genus of violet or blue (rarely white) flowers. Initially only about five species were known, but there are probably more. Among other things, they differ from one another in that the flowers of some species open in the morning while others open in the afternoon. All grow from tunicated bulbs.

N. convoluta Ravenna 1968. Mexico, state of Colima. The large yellow flowers have three large tepals and three small tepals. The leaves differ from those of the other species in being broadly pleated. These grew well for me, flowering briefly, and then abruptly dying. This is the only known yellow species, and it probably should be in a genus by itself.

N. floridana Small 1931. Swamps and low flatwoods of east-central Florida. This one flowers in August–October with dark blue flowers in the afternoon.

N. geminiflora Nuttall 1836 (syn. *N. acuta*). Celestial lily. Widespread in the central Texas blackland prairie and adjacent hill country in the spring. The flowers are in shades of blue, with an occasional white one. As in most *Nemastylis*, the tepals are all the same size. This species wants a sunny spot where the narrow, pleated leaves

Nemastylis convoluta   Nemastylis floridana   Nemastylis sp., Durango

receive occasional water in spring and then can dry off as they go dormant. Seed can be gathered at this time and planted in fall or winter.

N. nuttallii Pickering ex R. C. Foster 1945. An evening-flowering *Nemastylis* from the Ozarks of Arkansas, Missouri, and Oklahoma. It has pale bluish flowers from early to midsummer.

N. tenuis (Herbert) S. Watson 1883 subsp. *pringlei* (S. Watson) Goldblatt. West Texas, Arizona, and Mexico in June, July, and August. The leaves are narrowly pleated. The flowers are pale blue or violet and open in the afternoon.

In Mexico there are other *Nemastylis* species, some morning-flowering and others afternoon-flowering, with violet, blue, or white flowers. There are still additional unpublished species, so the list is by no means complete.

Neomarica T. Sprague (syn. *Marica*)

Walking iris. South America. About 15 species of tropical evergreen rhizomatous iris-like perennials with fugacious flowers in blue, white, or yellow, reminiscent of *Cypella* and hardy only where winters are mild, as in Florida. They are best given protection from frost by winter mulching or grown as container plants where they can be wintered indoors. Like the rhizomatous irises, they are really lovely and worthy of cultivation, but are not true bulbs, although often listed as such for convenience. They flower in the spring. Be sure to give half-shade and abundant moisture, never letting them dry out. Propagation is simple: after flowering they form plantlets at the end of the flowering stems, which bend over, allowing them to root and "walk" away from the mother plant. Since they take shade well, they make good houseplants, enjoying a mixture of peat, sphagnum, and leaf mold to which is added a bit of sand or sandy loam. They are fine plants for sharing with fellow gardeners, and the species are easily hybridized, yielding many lovely, robust clones.

N. caerulea (Ker-Gawler) T. Sprague. Walking iris. Large plants with 4-inch flowers, pale blue or lilac, with transverse bars of yellow, brown, or white.

N. gracilis (Herbert ex W. J. Hooker) T. Sprague. Medium-sized plants with fugitive 2-inch white flowers with yellow-and-brown markings and blue inner tepals.

N. longifolia (Link & Otto) T. Sprague. Yellow walking iris. Medium-sized plants with 2-inch yellow flowers, marked brown.

N. northiana (Schneevoogt) T. Sprague. Apostle plant. Medium-sized plants with fragrant 4-inch white flowers, the inner tepals marked violet.

Neomarica caerulea
PHOTO BY MARCIA WILSON,
COURTESY OF MRS. ALAN CLINT

Onira Ravenna 1983

A monotypic genus allied to *Herbertia* from Rio Grande do Sul, Brazil, with large *Cypella*-like flowers on short stems. They are smoky light blue and flower in spring from tunicated bulbs. *O. unguiculata* Ravenna is sometimes in cultivation.

Pardanthopsis Lenz

P. dichotoma (Pallas) Lenz. Vesper iris, an Asian relative of *Belamcanda* with fan-like leaves. The flowers open in the evening and are bluish lavender with an iris-like form. They are somewhat short-lived. They cross-breed easily with *Belamcanda* to produce plants known as × *Pardancanda* and have given rise to a variety of new colors and forms. The culture is the same as for *Belamcanda*.

Pseudotrimezia

A Brazilian perennial irid growing from slender rhizomes and an ally of *Trimezia*, with somewhat similar habits, but with smaller yellow flowers opening in the afternoon.

Rigidella Lindley 1840

A genus of about five Mexican and Guatemalan *Tigridia*-like species with large tunicated bulbs and showy scarlet flowers of Turk's-cap form, erect, suberect, or pendant. The flowers open early in the morning, remaining open until late afternoon, or open in the afternoon and close at night. Hummingbird-pollinated. Closely allied to *Tigridia* and can be hybridized with *T. pavonia*. The bigeneric hybrids are vigorous, showy, and infertile. They thrive in cultivation where summers are

Rigidella flammea

cool enough for *T. pavonia* to succeed, but likely would fail where summers are hot and dry.

R. flammea Lindley 1840. Mexico, state of Michoacán, near Morelia, on cliffs and ledges. A robust species with pendulous scarlet flowers opening in the afternoon and closing before sunset. The interior of the flowers is spotted purplish against a yellow background. The basal leaves are produced after flowering. This is another high-elevation plant that needs cool alpine conditions and thus is not recommended for hot summers.

R. immaculata Herbert 1841. Guatemala and Mexico, state of Oaxaca. This is similar to *R. flammea*, but has smaller, unspotted pendulous flowers. The basal and cauline leaves are well developed at flowering time. A high-elevation species suited only for alpine culture in cool greenhouses in hot climates.

R. inusitata Cruden. Mexico, state of Guerrero in cloud forest, Cerro Teotepec, west of Chilpancingo. July and August. The erect scarlet flowers are irregular in form, unique for the genus. This is another rare high-elevation plant suited only for alpine culture.

R. orthantha Lemaire 1845. Mexico, states of Chiapas and Oaxaca, and Guatemala, near Huehuetenango, in cloud forests of higher mountains. The largest and showiest species, dazzling in scarlet and yellow, but since it is a high-elevation plant, it needs alpine culture. It wastes away in a hot climate. Not recommended where summers are hot and dry.

R. sp. #92-1. Mexico, state of Hidalgo, at lower, near-tropical elevations, growing on the rocky face of cliffs. Flowers in early summer on arching stems 2 feet long or more. The pendant flowers are 2 inches wide, with outer tepals 1 inch long x 1¼ inches wide. The outer tepals are vermilion, with darker red markings in the throat. The inner tepals are yellow, spotted and streaked with red, inrolled at the margins, and pointed. The cauline leaves (stem-leaves) are broadly plicate, to 2½ inches wide, produced at the time of flowering, followed by basal leaves after flowering. This species is much like *R. flammea* save that the flowers open early in the morning and close in the afternoon. This cliff dweller has the most northerly and most tropical known range for the genus, thriving in the hottest weather in part shade. Though the known population is very rare, it is deserving of cultivation as the species best known to succeed in hot weather.

Romulea Maratti

A genus of about 90 species of small South African and Mediterranean cormous irids, of which only a few are grown in this country as pot plants. As a group they are quite diverse and colorful, with scentless funnel-shaped flowers. The Mediterranean sorts are winter-hardy, but the South African forms will need protection in zone 9.

Sessilanthera Molseed & Cruden 1969

An allopatric genus of three known species restricted to the Mexican states of Guerrero and Chiapas and, in one case, Alta Verapaz, Guatemala. All have showy yellow or white rotate flowers with saffron-yellow centers, and the two yellow-flowered species have purple spots at the tepal bases. All grow from tunicated bulbs and have plicate foliage. They are easily cultivated, in pots or in the ground, if lifted at the end of the growing season and stored while winter-dormant. Easily propagated from seed.

S. citrina Cruden 1975. Mexico, state of Guerrero, in mixed pine-oak woodlands. The flowers are lemon-yellow with purple spots at the bases of the inner tepals.

Sessilanthera latifolia

S. heliantha (Ravenna) Cruden 1969. Mexico, central Guerrero south of the Río Balsas and one locality in the state of Chiapas, at Fenia, in dry habitats in oak woodlands. The golden yellow perianth is circular and nonglandular and opens at sunrise, closing before noon. The tepals are 2½ inches wide, with small purple spots near the saffron-spotted center. This species is distinguished from *S. citrina* in the deeper golden yellow color and in the placement of the spots at the center of the flower. The plicate foliage differs from *S. latifolia* in that the leaves and stems are pigmented purplish near their bases.

S. latifolia (Weatherby) Molseed & Cruden 1969. Mexico, state of Guerrero north of the Río Balsas, and in Alta Verapaz, Guatemala. White flowers, with segments of equal size and shape, golden yellow at the base, on stems 1–2 feet tall. The stems and leaf bases are unpigmented, and the flowers are slightly smaller than those of the yellow-flowered species.

Sparaxis Ker-Gawler

A colorful spring-flowering genus of six cormous species and their hybrids native to the Cape Province of South Africa. They are not hardy outside of zone 10. The inflorescence is a short spike in white, cream, purple, yellow, or orange, and they are grown like *Gladiolus*. Fine for pots.

Sphenostigma Baker

This name is now regarded as a synonym for the genus *Calydorea*, which see.

Sympa Ravenna

This is a little-known monotypic genus from southern Brazil with tunicated bulbs and appearance and habit very much like *Herbertia*. Lilac-blue flowers in the spring. Culture is the same as for *Herbertia*.

    S. riograndensis Ravenna. Brazil, state of Rio Grande do Sul. Cultivated in South America.

Tigridia Jussieu 1789

A genus of mostly Mexican irids of more than three dozen species and subspecies having colorful triangular ephemeral flowers with a spotted cup-like center and more or less abbreviated tepals. Like many New World tigridioids, they have erect pleated leaves and grow from tunicated bulbs, not corms, as older literature erroneously stated. One may wonder what kind of "tiger" early plantsmen had in mind when they named spotted flowers (e.g., the tiger lily and the tiger flower) for the great striped cat, especially when truly spotted, not striped, cats (cheetah, leopard, jaguar, ocelot, etc.) were available for that honor.

    Most species of *Tigridia* have upfacing flowers, but a few are gracefully pendulous. They are perfectly hardy in warm-climate gardens and also make fine pot plants, needing only to be kept on the dry side during winter dormancy. As one might expect from such a large genus ranging from central Mexico to Guatemala, different species have a variety of requirements for habitat, soil, temperature, and water. In hot climates the greatest problem is keeping them cool and moist but free from nematodes and red spider mites. Part of the problem is solved by planting them in part shade and spraying the leaves regularly with miticides.

Tigridia species are classified according to the placement of the nectaries. In subgenus *Tigridia* the nectaries are borne in a groove near the edge of the tepal: *T. catarinensis, T. chiapensis, T. chrysantha, T. dugesii, T. durangense, T. hintonii, T. lutea, T. mexicana, T. mortonii, T. pavonia, T. philippiana, T. seleriana, T. tepoztlana,* and *T. violacea*. In subgenus *Hydrotaenia* the nectaries are borne superficially and exposed on the tepals: *T. alpestris, T. bicolor, T. ehrenbergii, T. galanthoides, T. hallbergii, T. huajuapanensis, T. illecebrosa, T. matudae, T. meleagris, T. molseediana, T. multiflora, T. pulchella, T. purpusii, T. vanhouttei,* and *T. venusta*.

T. alpestris Molseed 1970.

Subsp. *alpestris*. Mexico, state of Hidalgo at high elevations. Erect, chocolate-purple flowers. The three inner tepals are nearly as large as the three outer tepals.

Subsp. *obtusa* Molseed. The flowers are erect, with purple segments and white frosted cups with purple veins.

T. bicolor Molseed 1970. Mexico, state of Oaxaca. The flowers are small, with the cup, inner tepals, and inner half of the outer tepals colored maroon and the outer half of the outer tepals a muddy yellow. This species is xerophytic, growing on limestone hills, and thus can take more heat and drought than most species. However it must be kept dry when dormant.

T. catarinensis Cruden 1975. Mexico, state of San Luis Potosí. Has maroon flowers with yellowish cups, spotted maroon, opening in the afternoon. Found in oak woods with palms.

T. chiapensis Molseed ex Cruden 1968. Mexico, state of Chiapas, in wet pastures south of San Cristóbal de las Casas. White flowers with yellow cups spotted wine-brown. This species grows in muddy, grassy fields and needs to be kept wet while in growth and dry while dormant.

T. chrysantha Cruden & S. J. Walker 1989. Mexico, state of Jalisco, foothills in pine-oak forest. Showy lemon-yellow flowers with wine-red spots, at 2,300–4,000 feet.

T. dugesii S. Watson 1885. Mexico, mountains of Durango, Guanajuato, and Jalisco, in dry oak and pine woods. The showy flowers are golden yellow lightly dotted with red-brown spots. Unlike most tigridias, the flowers open in the afternoon rather than in the morning.

T. durangense Molseed ex Cruden 1968. Mexico, in state of Durango in wet mountain meadows and often standing in water. This small plant has pretty lilac flowers with white cups spotted lilac. It needs wet culture with the pot set in a saucer of water. Keep dry when dormant.

T. ehrenbergii (Schlechtendal) Molseed 1966. Mexico, widespread in transvolcanic regions of Jalisco, Guerrero, Veracruz, Morelos, and Puebla in dryish tropical habi-

Tigridia ehrenbergii

tats, at elevations of 1,000–5,000 feet. The smallish nodding flowers are pale green-ish yellow, somewhat like a snowdrop in form, lightly spotted in wine-purple. They bloom July to September. A true perennial, this is the largest species of *Tigridia*, and the most enduring. The pendant flowers are graceful and modestly pretty, but the muted colors prevent them from being showy, which is a shame, since those in my small collection faithfully return each summer to flower in a partly shaded spot in a mixture of sand and alkaline clay soil. They seem not to object to winter moisture while dormant. This species has the potential for hybridizing with other species, as it is one of the most permanent. My plants never make offsets, so propagation must be by seed.

Subsp. *ehrenbergii* is the usual form, while subsp. *flaviglandifera*, a more recent discovery from San Luis Potosí, is more robust and grows at lower elevations, which accounts for its unusual heat-tolerance. As for cold-hardiness, my plants have survived a number of near-zero cold spells with impunity in the past two decades. Rare, but recommended.

T. galanthoides Molseed 1970. Mexico, states of Guerrero, Oaxaca, and Veracruz. When I first encountered this plant, my impression was that it looked like a purplish snowdrop, so when Elwood Molseed named it *galanthoides*, I agreed that the name was appropriate. The flowers are similar in form to those of *T. ehrenbergii*, but smaller, on slender branched stems. The coloring is quite interesting: the flowers are essentially pale mauve, with purple veins and a blackish purple blotch at the tepal bases. They are said to be ill-smelling, but I failed to notice this. Since they grow at higher elevations, they are best suited for the cooler growing conditions of alpine culture.

T. hallbergii Molseed 1970. Mexico, state of Chiapas and adjacent areas. Tall fall-flowering plants with attractively spotted brown flowers. There are two forms: subsp.

Tigridia meleagris
PHOTO BY JAMES A. BAUML

Tigridia mexicana subsp.
mexicana

Tigridia mexicana subsp.
passiflora PHOTO BY JAMES A. BAUML

hallbergii, from Chiapas, Guerrero, Oaxaca, and Guatemala, has dull maroon-purple flowers; subsp. *lloydii* has yellow flowers with maroon spotting and is known only from the state of México.

T. hintonii Molseed 1970. Mexico, state of Guerrero in pine forests. A small fall-flowering white *Tigridia* known only from the type location.

T. huajuapanensis Molseed ex Cruden 1968. Mexico, in state of Oaxaca, from semi-arid hills surrounding Huajuapan. This little *Tigridia* has erect purple-brown flowers of small size in July. In cultivation, water carefully.

T. illecebrosa Cruden 1975. Mexico, state of Oaxaca, steep rocky open areas in oak woods. A fall-flowering species that has pendant tan flowers with maroon streaks.

T. lutea. A South American species widespread in the Andes of Chile and Peru. The flowers are yellow, speckled blackish, and sweetly scented.

T. matudae Molseed 1970. Mexico, state of México. Known only from the type location, *T. matudae* grows in shady woodlands. The flowers are blue-violet.

T. meleagris (Lindley) Nicolson. Widespread in southern Mexico, on steep slopes and in ravines, in heavy, well-drained soils in pine forest, open oak woodland, or deciduous forest. The beautiful nodding flowers resemble fritillarias, with all three segments of similar size. The mauve exterior is pretty enough, but looking at the interior is like opening a spotted jewel box. There is an unspotted triangular glandular zone toward the center, usually followed by more spots and the reproductive organs, giving the flower a surreal appearance.

T. mexicana Molseed 1970. At present there are three subspecies: subsp. *lilacina,* from Jalisco, with lilac flowers; subsp. *mexicana,* from the state of México, with yellow flowers; and subsp. *passiflora,* from Nayarit, with white flowers. They differ in color and habitat, but are of similar triangular form.

T. molseediana Ravenna 1968. Mexico, state of Oaxaca, in pine forests at higher elevations. The flowers are inconspicuous and fetid, with deep purple-maroon spots on a yellowish background.

T. mortonii Molseed 1970. State of México, on cliffs of Nanchitla, state of México at Temascaltepec. Known only from the type location. The flowers are small, and unusual for *Tigridia* in being red in color.

T. multiflora (Baker) Ravenna 1964. Much of central Mexico, in grassy hills, rocky openings, and ledges, in margins of dry oak or oak-pine woodland, at 6,500–10,000 feet on isolated edges of western sierras, July to September. Flowers are purplish and said to be ill-smelling.

T. pavonia (Linné) de Candolle in Redouté 1802. Tiger flower. Much of Mexico to Guatemala. Widely cultivated. This is the best-known species, with large, bright-colored flowers in shades of scarlet, rose, white, lilac, or yellow, with spotted or un-spotted cups. Each flower lasts but a day, but the plants flower for several weeks. They do well in zones 5–7 (if dug and stored in winter) and where summers are cooler, not so well in the southern parts of zones 8–10, where they are much bothered by red spider mites. They must have a good deal of shade and moisture to prosper. The bulbs should be planted in early spring; otherwise they will soon dry up.

T. philippiana. An unusual species from the Atacama coast of Chile. It is one of the *Tigridia* stragglers that venture into South America. Unfortunately it is not in cultivation, and little else is known about it at this time.

T. pulchella Robbins 1892. Mexico. Hillsides and openings in rocky or deep soils in pine forests at 5,000–8,000 feet in September.

T. purpusii Molseed 1970. Mexico. A rare violet species from the Tehuacan area of Puebla and known only from the type location.

T. seleriana (Loesener) Ravenna 1964. Mexico and Guatemala. A lavender-blue flower found in wet alpine meadows, at 9,800 feet or more. At about 4 inches, this is the smallest species.

T. tepoztlana Ravenna 1964. Mexico. From the thin soils of the tops of knobs of the Sierra de Tepoztlán, south of Mexico City. Known only from the type collection. The plant and flowers are small and thought to be violet in color.

T. vanhouttei Roezl ex Van Houtte 1875. Mountains of central Mexico. There are two subspecies, subsp. *roldanii* and subsp. *vanhouttei.* The plants are large, but the flowers are small, upfacing, and brownish. Elevations of 7,000–8,000 feet. Allied to *T. ehrenbergii.*

T. venusta Cruden 1975. Mexico, state of Michoacán, in the mountains east of Morelia. This species has erect or suberect flowers with white centers and purple tips. Known only from the type location.

Trimezia martinicensis
PHOTO BY MARCIA WILSON, COURTESY OF
MRS. ALAN CLINT

T. violacea Schlechtendal 1838. Mexico. Grasslands and moist depressions 6,000–10,000 feet on Central Plateau and in Sierra Volcánica Transversal in July and August. Flowers are light rose-purple-violet with darker-colored cup rims. Needs plenty of moisture to grow well.

Trimezia Herbert

About nine species of tropical rhizomatous American irids with unpleated linear or linear-lanceolate, fan-like leaves. They have *Cypella*-like flowers in blue or yellow, with strikingly marked inner tepals. They are tender, doing well out of doors in tropical and subtropical climates, and are well worth growing as container plants to be wintered inside where winters are very cold.

T. martinicensis (N. Jacquin) Herbert. West Indies. Small yellow *Cypella*-like flowers with purple-brown spots. The foliage is rush-like and produced in a fan. Tender.

Tritonia Ker-Gawler

A genus of about 28 cormous species, hardy only in zone 10, and subject to *Botrytis* infection. They are colorful, with simple or branched spikes and flowers in pink, orange, reddish orange, cream, or yellow, cultivated like *Gladiolus*.

Erythronium albidum var. *coloratum*

■ LILIACEAE

Formerly the Liliaceae consisted of a large group of bulbous plants having six stamens and a superior ovary. More recently the family has been subdivided into new families such as the Alliaceae, Calochortaceae, Colchicaceae, Hyacinthaceae, and Liliaceae. As always when major taxonomic nomenclatural revisions are made, it takes time for people to adjust to the new nomenclature. The now much-abbreviated Liliaceae list is cut to genera such as *Erythronium, Fritillaria, Lilium,* and *Tulipa.*

Erythronium Linnaeus

Dog's-tooth violet, fawn lily, trout lily. There are about 25 species, mostly in western North America, with members in Europe and Asia. In spite of what has been written in the literature, all species in the genus grow from true tunicated bulbs, not corms. Only a handful, all midwestern or eastern species, will be of interest to us. Unfortunately, the western species fail in warm southern climates.

E. albidum Nuttall. White dog's-tooth violet. From Ontario and Minnesota south to Georgia, Kentucky, Missouri, and northeast Texas, in moist dense woods, especially along slopes or banks overlooking creeks, lakes, and rivers. Each plant has two mottled leaves and a whitish perianth that recurves when open. The plant propagates by long stolons.

E. albidum var. *coloratum* has solitary pale lilac flowers with recurving tepals in early spring.

E. mesochoreum Knerr (syn. *E. albidum* var. *coloratum*). In prairies and dry open woods, mostly in north-central Texas. There are two leaves, glaucous on both sides, often mottled, the flowers spreading or at most half-reflexed in full bloom, opening with white segments tinged purple. This is the best species for the South, flowering year after year from the same bulb. It must be grown from seed if there is to be an increase, since the bulbs do not make offsets.

E. × 'Pagoda.' This is a total failure here, but is included for those who may garden north of zone 8. It is very lovely, with foot-high clusters of yellow flowers above mottled foliage. It is a pity that we can't grow it, but if you live far enough north, it may be for you.

E. rostratum W. Wolf (syn. *E. americanum*). Yellow dog's-tooth violet, trout lily. Common from the Big Thicket of east Texas to the Appalachian Mountains. Growing along creeks and river banks in rich moist woods, this has small yellow flowers above two mottled leaves. Although collected plants are often offered for sale, they fail in dryish alkaline soils.

Fritillaria Linnaeus

Fritillarias are a fascinating group, mostly unsuited to our climate. If you insist on growing them, select from them carefully, as they will have to be grown in pots. Most need scree conditions and careful watering while growing, and no water while dormant. In this respect their culture is not unlike that for many *Calochortus* species. They don't like hot, dry conditions.

F. affinis Schultes (Sealy) (syn. *F. lanceolata*). British Columbia south to California. The flowers are greenish or purplish. It can be grown in equal parts of sand, soil, and humus. It produces numerous "rice-grain" offsets. Plants vary from only 6 inches to 3 feet high. For part shade.

F. recurva Bentham. Oregon and California. The plants can grow to 2 feet tall. There are many scarlet flowers in May with orange and red-flecked interiors and recurved tepals. The bulb forms "rice-grain" offsets. Difficult.

Lilium Linnaeus

The genus *Lilium* is a strange lot. There are about 100 species scattered around the northern hemisphere, and about a fifth of these have been used to produce today's modern hybrids. In general, they are somewhat unpredictable in the South, unless careful consideration is given to their needs. Many lilies will grow only in an acid or neutral soil, but a few are lime-tolerant. None like hot, dry situations or waterlogged soils. Lilies like a sunny situation, but many are shade-tolerant. There was a time when Easter lilies and *Lilium regale* were about all that Southerners could grow, but this has changed, and we now realize that many others can do very well, at least during the first season, if we can keep them virus-free. Keeping them beyond a year is a challenge. The grubs of June bugs will attack and eat the bulbs during dormancy—another reason they may not last long.

L. candidum Linnaeus. Madonna lily. The Balkans. Our spring climate is often too dry for the Madonna lily, and when it blooms, the flowers are often on the small side. Plant shallowly in the fall so it can make its fall rosette of leaves. In spring it will put up a stem topped by waxy white funnels. Does best in zone 7 and northward in limy soils.

L. formosanum A. R. Wallace. Taiwan (formerly called Formosa). The late-flowering white trumpets of this lily may do well if it can be kept virus-free, but it is one of the most susceptible species and is sometimes grown as a detector plant for this reason. The flowers are similar to Easter lilies, but the bulbs are smaller and the blooms come later in the summer on taller plants with more slender leaves. Lime-tolerant.

L. henryi Baker. China. A late-blooming orange lily of Turk's-cap form and easy culture, tolerant of alkaline soils. It will grow in shade but tends to be spindly there. To make the stems more erect, stake them and give them maximum light.

L. lancifolium Thunberg (syn. *L. tigrinum*). Tiger lily. China. In the acid or neutral soils of the middle and upper South, the tiger lily grows well, but it may be good for only one season in the limy soils in zones 9 or 10, west of central Texas. Still we plant it occasionally if only to enjoy the showy orange-red spotted flowers. In all honesty, the color is a harsh one that doesn't combine with many things. Reputed to be of hybrid origin, but this is doubtful, as there are several forms, including yellow and double kinds and a diploid form that sets fertile seeds. The most popular form is the common triploid.

L. longiflorum Thunberg. Easter lily, white trumpet lily. Taiwan. The familiar white trumpets are one of the longer-lasting lilies for outdoor culture in the lower South, if given a warm, sunny or partly shady spot and adequate moisture. Any of the several forms will work in a garden situation. In the marginal areas of zones 8 and 9 they are tender and will need protection. They delight in an acid soil but are lime-tolerant.

L. michauxii Poiret (syn. *L. carolinianum*). The name is pronounced mee-SHOH-zee-eye. Gardeners in the lower South who have acid sandy soils, such as are found in east Texas, may try *L. michauxii,* which is a low-growing native lily with small, scaly, rhizomatous bulbs. It has clusters of one to five nodding, recurved orange-red Turk's-cap flowers spotted purple-brown with yellow centers. It is shade- and moisture-loving and intolerant of lime. It is hard to find a source for it. Since the bulbs are too rare to be collected from the wild, it should be grown from seed or obtained from a specialist who grows it from seed.

L. regale E. H. Wilson 1905. Often planted, as this Chinese lily tolerates both alkaline soils and warm climates. It likes a sunny spot where its umbel-like inflor-escences of white trumpets with yellowish centers and purplish exteriors can flower in midsummer. Unfortunately it has a tendency for the growing point and buds to "go blind" before it should flower, leaving only an unflowered plant. Still it is worth trying for its wonderful fragrance.

Hybrids

The genes of several Chinese trumpet lilies were combined with one another and with the related *L. henryi* to form the "Sunburst Strain" and other similar strains. These are intermediate between the trumpet forms and Turk's cap forms, with fra-grant blooms in yellow, orange, pink, and white. They are lime-tolerant and will persist in a sunny spot. Recommended.

Asiatic hybrids: Developed by crossing about a dozen Asian species with one another, Asiatic hybrids come in a large variety of colors, generally outward- or upward-facing in posture and of chalice form. One must experiment with them in order to find varieties that will tolerate heat and dry, limy conditions.

Oriental hybrids: These are crosses made from *L. speciosum* and *L. auratum,* and, to a lesser extent, the pink trumpets of *L. japonicum* and *L. rubellum* and their crosses with *L. henryi.* If planted in a container in a mixture containing sand and peat moss plus perlite and vermiculite, they will do well.

The oriental hybrids sometimes do well in the garden and can sometimes toler-ate lime, even though they are not reputed to do so. Be lavish in incorporating sand, peat moss, and a mixture of vermiculite and perlite beneath and around the bulbs when planting them.

L. longiflorum × Asiatic hybrids: One of the most interesting modern miracles was achieved by using *L. longiflorum,* through embryo culture, with Asiatic forms to achieve early colored forms. Some fertility was achieved through second-generation crosses, and this was a breakthrough. Early reports show that these hybrids are far-ing well in the lower South, and that they seem to be as easy as *L. longiflorum,* unit-ing the trumpet forms with those that have upright, wide open flowers. Since they appear extremely early in the year, the young plants may need some protection. Southern gardeners may wish to try a few of the hybrids recently introduced, such as 'Yellow Gold,' with yellow flowers flushed red. 'Royal Fantasy' is lovely in honey tones of soft yellow to cream, while the large rose-pink flowers of 'My Fair Lady' and especially the warm mauve-pink trumpets of 'Casa Rosa' are equally compel-ling. 'Casa Rosa' does not have large-flowered scapes, but what is there is choice.

Lilium × 'Gold Eagle'

'Gold Eagle' is a free-flowering yellow hybrid that does very well in the South. All of these are lime-tolerant and are the lily wave of the future for the South.

Tulipa Linnaeus

Tulips. Europe, Mediterranean, Asia Minor. What would spring be like without tulips, even in the South? The concept of spring-flowering bulbs is epitomized in the genus *Tulipa*. Tulips hybridize easily, propagate readily, and many varieties are wonderful for forcing. They are easy to grow and can be combined with both early- and late-flowering spring bulbs of other sorts. As they originated mostly in cold climates, cold-hardiness is their forte, but this fact is of little value if you live in zones 9 or 10, where they are short-lived and are best regarded as annuals. Fortunately their special cold-weather needs can be artificially reproduced in warm climates. For those who insist on growing them, even as annuals, refrigeration is the answer. Most tulips need distinctly cold winters in which the ground freezes with some regularity and spring moisture needs are reinforced by melting snows. Winter should be followed by a long hot, dry dormant period in which they can bake. In warm climates, the cold period can be supplied in autumn by six to eight weeks of refrigeration in the vegetable compartment of the refrigerator. Warning! Do not put them in the freezing compartment or they will quickly freeze hard and perish.

In southern California and the deep South the most reliable garden tulips, at least in the first year, are the Darwin Hybrids, a series of crosses made between the May-flowering Darwin tulips and *T. fosteriana*. Even these will need digging at the end of the growing season as explained below. Given this treatment, certain other varieties will also succeed, such as the Triumph tulip 'Kees Nelis,' the Lily-flowered 'Queen of Sheba,' and 'Louis XIV,' a now-obsolete Breeder tulip. Because our autumn weather can be very warm, they should not be planted until winter starts to settle in, usually in early December. Our weather will remain at its coldest through January and early February, when the tulips will be coming up.

Gardeners are traditionally advised to plant tulips deeply (to 10 inches) in order to keep the bulbs at a cooler depth for more permanent plantings. This works fine where winters are cold, but in hot climates the opposite is true. Our winter freezes won't hurt them, so they should be planted only a few inches deep, which will facilitate the necessary digging at the end of the growing season. In any case, they must not be left in the ground if they are intended to be used for another season. Otherwise, even though a few bulbs may survive dormancy, they won't perform well without being refrigerated again the following autumn.

By mid-February, bulbs will be well-rooted and showing signs of activity. If well-grown, they can be harvested after flowering when they complete their ripening cycle and the leaves begin to yellow. Certain varieties will regularly perform better than others, and there may be a generous harvest as they go dormant. The important thing is not to leave them in the ground where they will receive summer precipitation while dormant. Autumn refrigeration is essential to their success once again or they will perform poorly. But don't keep them refrigerated during the summer! They must have that long, dry summer dormancy in which to develop. They should be kept in a cool shady spot for a few days until they fully ripen, as they easily sun-scald when freshly dug. They can be conveniently stored in mesh bags while dormant and hung in a cool dry place, out of reach of rodents and insect pests.

Luckily, sometimes a very few tulip species will grow as perennials in warm climates, seemingly oblivious to summer moisture and not needing refrigeration. If we are to believe the glowing catalog descriptions and the writings of enthusiastic tulipophiles, most tulip species should thrive here, but unfortunately this is not so. Our tulip garden success seems restricted to a small handful of species.

T. chrysantha (A. D. Hall) Sealy, from Afghanistan, Kashmir, and the slopes of the Himalayas into Tibet, and *T. stellata*, from Afghanistan and northwest India, are closely related and considered as subspecies of *T. clusiana* by some authorities. *T. chrysantha*, with yellow flowers stained red on the outside, endures if given good drainage and kept dry during dormancy. Probably the same can be said of *T. stellata*, which I have yet to test because of its scarcity and higher prices. It is said to be white with outer segments backed with light red and a dark purple center. On the other hand, *T.* × 'Cynthia' (syn. *T.* × 'Sulphide'), a later-flowering hybrid between *T. clusiana* and *T. chrysantha*, with sulfur-yellow flowers flushed with a dark rosy exterior, has proved inexpensive and enduring.

T. clusiana de Candolle. Lady tulip. Iran to Afghanistan; southern Europe. The

Tulipa clusiana

"Lady tulip" is the most enduring, with white flowers banded with cherry red on the exterior and a small purple basal blotch within. The stoloniferous form will persist forever. Probably because it is easier to harvest commercially, the non-stoloniferous form is usually the only form available, although less permanent. *T. clusiana* can be grown from seed if one has the patience.

T. linifolia Regel, from Uzbekistan, and *T. eichleri* Regel, from Turkestan, each with showy scarlet flowers, perform well as annuals (without refrigeration) but fail to reappear the following year. *T. linifolia* has smaller flowers and shorter stems than *T. eichleri*.

T. montana Lindley (syn. *T. wilsoniana*) has long, narrow leaves and bears large, cup-shaped cherry-red flowers on short stems. It has recently been reported as a welcome addition to the species tulips that repeat in the South.

T. orphanidea Boissier ex Heldreich, from the eastern Mediterranean, especially Greece, Crete, Bulgaria, and western Turkey, has bronzy star-shaped flowers and is reported to persist as far south as Dallas, in the upper part of zone 8. I have not yet tested it in zone 9, but hope springs eternal.

T. saxatilis Sieber ex Sprengel (syn. *T. bakeri*). Crete. The species and the variety 'Lilac Wonder' are somewhat permanent in the lower part of zone 7 and upper part of zone 8 and marginally into zone 9, where a few may return to flower a second or third season. They bloom on short stems and open into lovely large lilac flowers with yellow centers.

T. sylvestris Linnaeus. Europe, western Anatolia, North Africa, Central Asia, and Siberia. Another enduring stoloniferous species, in yellow, which rarely does more than produce a few "blind" leaves after the first year in the lower part of zone 8 or in zone 9. Because of this it is guardedly recommended. Common sense suggests that precious garden space could be occupied by more reliable ornamental tulips such as *T. chrysantha, T. clusiana, T. stellata,* or cv. 'Cynthia.'

T. wilsoniana Hoog. Synonym for *T. montana.*

One of the ironies of growing tulips: I once planted 'Louis XIV,' one of the May-flowering "Breeder tulips," a group which has become obsolete. This late-flowering tulip not only thrived in our heat but produced large bronzy-purple flowers, edged brownish gold, on stems fully 3 feet tall. These were the first tulips that fully lived up to catalogue measurements in height and size. After flowering they ripened nice clusters of large bulbs for the following year. As good as the modern Darwin Hybrids are, I wonder if we have not gone overboard in relegating such stalwarts as the once-beloved Breeder tulips to obsolescence. The colors of this group were "arty," harmonious and subdued, but they had their place in gardens as a welcome relief from the gaudy Cottage and Darwin tulips, illustrating how tastes in garden tulips have changed through the years.

■ ORCHIDACEAE

Orchid family. This is a very large family of 20,000 to 25,000 species in about 725 genera. Only one terrestrial form is dealt with here. Though many terrestrial forms are very beautiful and rare, they mostly belong in the woods, as they don't take to cultivation.

Bletilla striata (Thunberg) H. Gustav Reichenbach (syn. *B. hyacinthina*)

Chinese ground orchid. China, Japan. This is a very tough spring-flowering orchid with clusters of small Cattleya-like flowers in rosy purple or near-white, not opening very wide. The purple form is a stronger grower and the most commonly grown version, but the flowers last only a short time. As it is precocious, flowering before spring frosts are over, it may require some early spring protection. The pleated leaves follow the flowers and last until fall. The plants do very well in a shady nook and occasionally make a powdery mass of seed, but I have yet to see seedlings emerge.

Oxalis regnellii PHOTO BY JO ANN TRIAL

■ OXALIDACEAE

Oxalis Linnaeus

Wood sorrel. About 850 species. The bulbous members of the oxalis family comprise a large group of plants and are found on nearly every continent. Although they are dicots, some of them have true scaly bulbs or rhizomes. All have five-petaled flowers which open in the sun, and many have beautiful foliage. One can select oxalis for nearly every season of the year.

Oxalis foliage is attractive even when the plants are not in bloom. Some species are clover-like, with leaflets in threes or fours, while others have even more leaflets, making them look like miniature palms. Often they are marked purple underneath. When ripe, the seedpods explode, scattering the seeds everywhere. Each flower lasts but a day, but there are many of them, singly or in a cluster, produced in succession. The juice is mildly acid and somewhat pleasant, but consuming them can cause serious toxic problems. It's a matter of how much oxalic acid one can tolerate before getting sick. Most bulbous *Oxalis* species come from the United States, Mexico, South America, and South Africa. Listed below are a few species that may be found in cultivation.

O. adenophylla Gillies. Chile and Argentina. Mentioned here only because it is frequently listed in catalogs. I have tried it repeatedly over many years, but the bulbs always turn out to be dead, whether ordered by mail or bought locally. Apparently dealers have trouble getting them alive or keeping them alive, as they have a very short lifespan when out of the ground. The flowers are said to be pink with white centers on 2- to 4-inch stems, and the bulbs are planted in the fall for late spring–early summer flowering.

O. bowiei Lindley (syn. *O. purpurata*). South Africa. A popular species for fall planting and winter flowering. It has large bulbs, leaves consisting of three unmarked leaflets, and umbels of large rosy pink flowers. Needs winter protection.

O. brasiliensis Loddiges ex Westcott & Knowles. Brazil. Has three leaflets, purplish beneath, with rosy purple flowers, on one- to three-flowered peduncles.

O. corymbosa de Candolle. Tropical America. Has three leaflets and many-flowered cymes of violet flowers.

O. crassipes Urban. Brazil. Nearly stemless mounds of plants with three leaflets, with pink or white flowers. Nearly evergreen and a popular perennial.

O. deppei Loddiges ex Sweet. Good-luck plant, lucky clover. Southern Mexico. A widely cultivated plant with four leaflets and 5- to 12-flowered umbels in red, rose, or violet. The form known as 'Iron Cross' is now very popular.

O. drummondii A. Gray. Texas. A fall-flowering, winter-growing stoloniferous herb with three leaflets and violet flowers in four- to eight-flowered umbels. Recommended.

O. hirta Linnaeus. South Africa. A leafy, branched, decumbent plant with solitary flowers on axillary pedicels, to 1 foot. It requires winter pot culture, as it is tender.

O. lasiandra Zuccarini. Southern Mexico. This one blooms in summer with five to ten palm-like leaflets and flowers in red, pink, or violet, in many-flowered umbels.

O. latifolia Humboldt, Bonpland, & Kunth. Mexico. This has three leaflets and 6- to 13-flowered umbels of pink to violet flowers.

O. nelsonii (Small) R. Knuth. Mexico. Has four or five leaflets and deep purple flowers.

O. pes-caprae Linnaeus. Bermuda buttercup. South Africa. A tender yellow-flowered form with 3–20 umbellate cymes. Lovely, but it tends to become a weed where conditions are right. In our climate it does not usually last too long. There is a double-flowered form that is very attractive.

O. regnellii Miquel. South America. A popular plant with scaly rhizomes and three leaflets, purplish beneath and sometimes on top as well, with white or pink flowers, in three- to seven-flowered umbels.

O. tetraphylla Cavanilles. Mexico. It has three to six leaflets, usually four, with four- to nine-flowered umbels in lilac or rose.

O. vespertilionis Zuccarini. Mexico. Has three V-shaped leaflets and lavender flowers in three- to ten-flowered umbels. There is considerable confusion about the name for this plant.

Anemone heterophylla

RANUNCULACEAE

Crowfoot or buttercup family. There are about 50 genera, including medicinal and ornamental plants.

Anemone Linnaeus

Windflowers. Our native anemones are among the most charming of spring flowers and rival *A. blanda* and *A. apennina* of the flower catalogs. They do the same thing in approximately the same way, but with more permanence in the lower South, where the other two don't do well. The tiny tubers are oddly shaped and don't look like much until they have been plumped by a good soaking.

A. caroliniana T. Walter. Eastern United States. This species is smaller and daintier, and reproduces by stolons, but is otherwise similar to *A. heterophylla*, which it replaces in the acid sandy soils of the Southeast. Flowers may be blue, pink, or white.

A. coronaria Linnaeus. Mediterranean region. These familiar poppy-like flowers are produced in red, blue, and white, in single- and double-flowered forms. They seldom last long, but they are easy and inexpensive, and a few should always be planted for early color.

A. edwardsiana Tharp. Texas, in Edwards Plateau. The hill country of central Texas is home to the smaller *A. edwardsiana*, which has two flowers to the stem and the same color range as *A. heterophylla*. As in that species, the white ones predominate. Rare.

A. heterophylla Nuttall (syn. *A. decapetala*). Calcareous soils of central Texas. Blooms with the first warm days of January or February, continuing through March or April in our climate. From dull, colorless buds open small daisy-like flowers in white, pink, or blue. At this time we are starved for a few flowers, and they are most welcome. Anemones have colored, petal-like sepals, as there are no true petals. They begin opening when only a few inches above ground, each day expanding into taller and larger flowers until the segments finally fall off. At that time the flowers are replaced by the ripening fruits, which are less presentable, but we must leave them to ripen if they are to complete their cycle.

On cold or cloudy days the flowers remain closed. It can be amusing to watch them close on a cloudy day and reopen when the sun breaks through.

For some unknown reason, the white forms of *A. heterophylla* are the most common, and one must really search in order to find the intensely colored blue ones, followed in order of increasing scarcity by purple, pink, and red. The pink and red ones are wonderful if you can find them. I once found a rare double pink form and then promptly lost it.

Of the garden forms, *A. coronaria* and *A. fulgens* are fine as annuals. Occasionally a few of them will repeat, but they are not permanent. Still, they grow well, adding a lot of color, if only temporarily. The tubers are inexpensive and expendable, but they can be dug and stored for another season.

Delphinium Linnaeus

Often overlooked as bulbous plants, the native delphiniums belong here. The stick-like tubers of *D. carolinianum* will survive if collected at the end of their growing cycle, and can either be transplanted then or replanted in the fall. They will produce tall stems of lovely white, purple, or deep blue flowers the following spring. Each small flower has an amusing "face" reminding one of a rabbit. They will take sun or shade and are best planted where they can be left undisturbed.

Ranunculus Linnaeus

R. asiaticus Linnaeus. Asia Minor. The Asian ranunculus is useful for bedding, but not long-lived if allowed to remain in the ground without lifting after one season. The strange "claws" are planted in cool weather, around December here, with the pointed ends down. If planted too early they may leaf out and be cut down by early freezes. Planting later prevents this, as they don't have time to make much top growth before the colder January weather sets in. If wanted for another year, they can be lifted and stored. A secret not usually divulged is that they can be kept up to five years without planting, but this is certainly not recommended. The plants are bushy and produce a large number of flowers from the largest tubers. Novices will want to get them into the ground early in order to appreciate their precocious early growth, but experience teaches us that it is better to wait for cold to set in.

R. macranthus Scheele. Western half of Texas. Although the familiar *R. asiaticus* is short-lived with us, the native *R. macranthus* is not. It will remain for years, often colonizing into lawns and elsewhere, and flowering each spring with brilliant clusters of golden yellow flowers. They are showy but are invasive if not carefully watched, as they produce large quantities of seed.

■ TECOPHILAEACEAE

These are herbs with corms or tubers and actinomorphic flowers in simple racemes or panicles, with ovaries more or less inferior. Mostly from Chile and South Africa, they are in the genera *Conathera, Cyanella, Tecophilaea,* and *Zephyra. Tecophilaea cyanocrocus* is occasionally cultivated.

Tecophilaea Bertero ex Colla

T. cyanocrocus Leybold. Chile. Chilean crocus. Solitary fragrant blue flowers in spring are only a few inches high, with low, grassy foliage. The flowers are somewhat like crocuses and the truest blue imaginable. They are now said to be nearly extinct in their natural environment. Best for pots.

Bessera elegans (purple)

THEMIDACEAE

A family recently erected. The *Brodiaea* section consists of *Androstephium, Bloomeria, Brodiaea, Dichelostemma, Muilla, Triteleia,* and *Triteleiopsis.* The *Milla* section contains *Behria, Bessera, Dandya, Diphalangium, Milla,* and *Petronymphe.* All were formerly placed in the Alliaceae, and before that in the Liliaceae. They have membranous or fibrous coated corms and flowers in *Allium*-like umbels on leafless stems but lack alliaceous chemistry. They are now recognized as being most closely allied to the Hyacinthaceae. There are six functional stamens, or three functional stamens and three staminodes. The leaves are linear. All but *Androstephium* are native to the western United States, Mexico, and Guatemala.

Androstephium Torrey 1858

There are two species, one being the easternmost representative of this group and the other a western species. Both produce corms with fibrous-reticulated tunics. The spring flowers are whitish or bluish, with six stamens united into a narrow funnel. Rare in cultivation.

A. breviflorum Watson. Eastern California to western Colorado. This species, with pale purplish to whitish flowers, is not as attractive as the next one. It must be watered carefully and kept dry while dormant. Mostly suitable for a scree or in pots. Not generally in cultivation.

A. caeruleum (Scheele) E. Greene. Prairie lily, funnel lily. A rare plant of undisturbed prairies from South Dakota to central Texas with few-flowered fragrant umbels of bluish, lavender, or

Androstephium caeruleum

white flowers on short stems in early spring. The scent is like chocolate candy. The individual flowers have the succulent, icy texture of hyacinths. This species succeeds in a sunny raised bed in alkaline soil when left undisturbed. It is worthy of cultivation, but should be protected from doubtful "progress," as it has become rare over much of its range.

Bloomeria Kellogg 1863

One or possibly two species. The plants have corms with fibrous tunics and yellow flowers with cup-like filaments at their bases. Baja California and southern California.

    B. crocea (Torrey) Coville. Golden stars. California. Often confused with *Triteleia crocea* and *T. ixioides.* The showy *Bloomeria* requires dry summer-dormant conditions and full sun. Outside of Mediterranean climates (as in southern California) it is best grown as a pot plant. The large umbels are loose and airy with many starry, narrow-tepaled golden yellow flowers held on long, delicate pedicels. There is a single linear basal leaf which ripens by flowering time.

Brodiaea J. E. Smith 1939

About ten species of cormous plants with fibrous tunics. In the true *Brodiaea* and *Dichelostemma* there are only three fertile stamens, plus three flattish, antherless staminodes. The leaves begin yellowing as the flowers come into bloom, which can be disconcerting. The flowers are held in loose umbels and are useful for cutting.

    A problem shared by most members of *Brodiaea* (as well as *Dichelostemma* and *Triteleia*) is that some species will tolerate summer moisture but others need to be kept reasonably dry. European gardeners deal with this routinely, but some Americans seem to believe that gardening is a question of the survival of the fittest: if it dies, it dies. Supplies of these plants are no longer inexhaustible. We must learn to rely on seed sources instead of collected corms, and we may have to go out of our way in order to maintain our stocks.

    A second minor flaw in growing this group is that they (like some *Allium* species) have the annoying habit of flowering just as the leaves are becoming dormant. One must accept the fact that it is perfectly normal for them to be in full bloom as the leaves turn yellow. They are not sick or dying from lack of water; for them this is the happy culmination of a long growing season. After flowering, the bulbs ripen seed and aestivate until the next growing season.

    B. californica Lindley 1896. California brodiaea. Northern California. The airy umbels have large pink to violet flowers, closing at night and opening in the mornings, with prominent whitish or pale lavender staminodes. They like good drainage and sun, and will tolerate some summer moisture while dormant. *B. californica* subsp. *leptandra* is similar, but the dark violet flowers are slightly smaller on shorter stems. All *B. californica* forms are recommended.

B. coronaria (Salisbury) Engler (syn. *B. grandiflora*). California north to British Columbia. The few-flowered umbels bear bell-shaped flowers ranging from pale to dark purple in late spring. Subsp. *rosea* has pink flowers. The stems are stocky and vary from short stems to some nearly a foot high. This species is of proven endurance in sunny raised beds in alkaline soil in the South and is recommended.

B. filifolia. A rare species in California, allied to *B. kinkiensis* and *B. orcuttii.* April–May. All have smallish flowers with the staminodes acutely pointed at the apex or completely lacking. *B. filifolia* usually has shorter pedicels and smaller 1-inch satiny purple flowers on rather lax stems a foot or more high. A group of these in flower can be attractive, and they may remain in flower for weeks. The flowers close at night, reopening the following morning. I have grown this species out of doors for over a decade in a sunny raised bed, where it has increased and flowered faithfully in spite of erratic summer irrigation. Under these conditions it is a permanent resident in zones 8–10 in the deep South or on the Pacific Coast, given a sunny, well-drained exposure.

B. jolonensis. Jolon brodiaea. Coastal California. Allied to *B. terrestris* but taller, with starry violet flowers on 8-inch stems, this species shows the promise of permanency in our area and is therefore recommended.

B. minor (Bentham) S. Watson. One of the short-stemmed species with purple flowers that look their best in a rock garden. Given the right conditions, i.e., good drainage in a raised bed in full sun, it endures surprisingly well in southern gardens.

B. purdyi Eastwood. Native to the Sierra Madre foothills. Allied to *B. minor.* A delicate, low-growing species with airy umbels of narrow-tepaled lilac flowers in late spring. The blossoms are surprisingly large and showy, considering their short stature, and are worthy of cultivation, especially in a rock garden. Finding a source may be difficult, as this is one of the less common species and may be available only from specialists. It tolerates summer watering if given a well-drained sunny situation.

B. stellaris S. Watson. Star brodiaea. Rocky hillsides of northern California. Umbels of small, delicate violet flowers on stems 5–9 inches tall. Likes full sun and flowers in late spring.

B. terrestris Kellogg (syn. *B. coronaria* var. *macropoda*). California and Oregon. A very dwarf species, often with no visible stem, making the umbels appear to sit on the ground. The flowers are lilac or violet colored with the segments about twice the length of the tube. The umbels are few-flowered, and the pedicels are quite long, giving the head a loose appearance. The flowers close at night and open on sunny days. Reputedly does best where it gets some relief from summer's heat.

Dichelostemma Kunth 1843

Washington, Oregon, California, and Baja California. Six species having corms with fibrous tunics, three fertile anthers and three staminodes, and a three-lobed stigma. The leaves are strongly carinate rather than concave-convex, and the corms increase well by offsets.

D. congestum (J. E. Smith) Kunth (syn. *Brodiaea pulchella*). Blue dicks, ookow. Similar to *D. pulchellum* and perhaps a form of it.

D. ida-maia (Wood) Greene 1870 (syn. *Brodiaea coccinea, Brevoortia ida-maia*). California firecracker, firecracker flower. Oregon to northern California. This is one of the more bizarre members of the Themidaceae, rivaling *Bessera elegans, Dandya hannibalii,* and *Behria tenuiflora* in its astonishing coloring. In this case, the nodding tubular flowers are a startling carmine-red with short recurving perianth segments of a cream-and-green combination, suggesting the colors of Christmas, and are perhaps the most impressionably colorful of the loosely connected *Brodiaea* clan and its relatives. The umbels are loose, with one or two flowers opening at a time on tall, slender scapes. The plants are said to enjoy heat, but appreciate a little shade in the afternoons. They will need good drainage if grown out of doors and are best grown in pots, as the corms must be kept dry while dormant. This is indeed a late-spring-flowering treasure and is worth growing, although scarce and subject to chlorosis. It needs an acid soil and increases by offsets.

D. multiflorum (Bentham) A. Heller. Similar to *D. congestum* but differing in that the pedicels are not joined toward the base, as well as in the staminode details.

D. pulchellum (Salisbury) A. Heller 1871 (syn. *Brodiaea capitata*). Ookow, wild hyacinth. Widespread in the western United States. I first collected it in southern Arizona, and it later became a permanent fixture in my south-central Texas garden. The flowers are lilac-blue in dense umbels similar to those of *D. congestum,* with which this species is often confused. This should be one of the first choices for the *Dichelostemma* beginner, as it usually succeeds and becomes enduring.

D. × *venustum* Greene 1892. A natural hybrid intermediate between its putative parents, *D. multiflorum* and *D. ida-maia,* and rare in cultivation. The flowers are fertile and resemble the California firecracker (*D. ida-maia*) in form but differ in color, as they are pink. Hybrid vigor should make for easy culture.

D. volubile (Kellogg) Heller 1874 (syn. *Brodiaea volubilis*). A California native that grows in gritty, heavy soils. This is a most unusual species with clambering, twining flower stems. The umbels are densely flowered with pinkish mauve flowers in late spring. The corms should be planted next to something the plants can lean against (such as a small shrub or a chain-link fence) so the stems can twine freely. A large number of corms can produce twining stems forming cables. Accidentally detached stems will usually continue flowering. Perfect drainage is important.

Muilla S. Watson 1879

Southern California to northwest Mexico in rocky, dryish, grassy places. The name *Muilla* is *Allium* spelled backward. There are three to five species, but only *M. maritima* is apt to be cultivated. These are all cormous plants with very narrow leaves and umbels of small flowers, whitish or yellowish, with greenish midribs, resembling an *Allium*, but lacking an alliaceous odor or flavor. Not showy, but regarded as curiosities for the collector.

Triteleia Douglas ex Lindley 1830

Sixteen or more cormous species with reticulate-fibrous tunics, ranging from Baja California to Arizona, California, Nevada, Idaho, Utah, Oregon, Washington, and British Columbia. The flowers have six functional stamens, and the pedicels are articulated.

T. bridgesii (S. Watson) Greene. Oregon to central California. The umbels are loose, with pink to lavender and purple flowers with whitish centers. It is not known whether this species can survive rainfall during its summer dormancy in the deep South.

T. crocea (A. Wood) Greene. California and Oregon. This is a distinct plant from *Bloomeria crocea*. The many-flowered rounded umbels have yellow flowers. Its performance in the deep South is unknown.

T. grandiflora Lindley. Widespread in the western United States. The umbel is rounded and has bell-shaped flowers in various shades of blue, rarely white.

T. guadalupensis Lenz 1970. A robust species from Guadalupe Island, Mexico, off the coast of Baja California. Rock crevices and slopes and cliffs of El Picacho. The flowers are golden yellow, and the foliage is 1¼ inches wide, broad for this group. This rare species makes a fine pot plant but has not been garden tested in the South. Its habitat suggests a very well drained situation in a garden. April–May. Allied to *T. lugens*.

T. hendersonii Howell ex Greene. Oregon. Has narrow leaves and a scape about a foot high, with umbels of flowers that have yellow perianths.

T. hyacinthina (Lindley) Greene 1833 (syn. *Brodiaea lactea*). Wild hyacinth. British Columbia to Idaho, south to southern California and Nevada. Umbels of white or bluish flowers on stems 1–2 feet tall. Enjoys water until midsummer. This has endured for a few years in a sunny situation in a raised bed where it received no water other than rainfall. A dwarf form is sometimes listed.

T. ixioides (Aiton f.) Greene 1831. Pretty face. Valleys, foothills, and higher elevations of the Sierra and Cascade mountains. There are several subspecies. They are unusual in that the starry flowers are in shades of yellow with a contrasting greenish or brownish keel. Durability in southern gardens is still being tested. They are fine in pots if kept dry during dormancy.

T. laxa Bentham 1832 (syn. *Brodiaea laxa*). Ithuriel's spear. This is one of the easiest and most adaptable of this group and will tolerate some summer water. The umbels are composed of blue-violet funnel-shaped flowers on stems 1–2 feet high. There are several forms, varying in color from white to pale blue, lavender, or dark violet. Cv. 'Queen Fabiola' is a selection of *T. laxa* from the Dutch bulb firm of Van Tubergen that has darker flowers and thrives with ordinary garden care and thus is highly recommended for the deep South as well as the Pacific Coast.

T. lugens Greene. California, Baja California. Scape to 1½ feet tall. Perianth dull yellow or brownish purple.

T. peduncularis Lindley 1896. Long-rayed hyacinth. Large umbels of long-pediceled funnel-shaped white flowers flushed bluish, on stems 30 inches tall. This one is reported to tolerate water through midsummer, but I have not personally garden-tested it. It is reported as being one of the hardiest species in this group.

T. × *tubergenii* is an intermediate fertile hybrid between *T. laxa* and *T. peduncularis* circa 1950, from the Dutch bulb firm of Van Tubergen. Although the name is established in the commercial trade, it is apparently of no scientific significance, as no formal description of this plant was published. The plant is robust, and the flowers are a rich blue-lilac, similar to forms of *T. laxa*. The corms of *T.* × *tubergenii* are inexpensive, of easy culture in full sun, and recommended.

Triteleiopsis Hoover 1941

Baja California, Mexico, to Yuma County, Arizona. The one species, *T. palmeri*, is apparently not in cultivation. There are three to eight leaves which bear cormels in the axils. The umbel is many-flowered with jointed pedicels topped by bluish or whitish flowers with six stamens.

The Millinae Traub 1963

The Millinae are cormous members of the Themidaceae from Mexico which have membranous coats of minutely parallel fibers and in which the ovary is produced on a gynophore, the gynophore and base of the ovary being united with the perianth, or generally adnate to it by lateral flanges opposite the segments. The group is composed of the following genera: *Behria, Bessera, Dandya, Diphalangium, Milla,* and *Petronymphe.* It is a colorful group containing red, purple, blue, lavender, pink, white, greenish, and yellowish flowers. Many are rare in cultivation, and a few are still unknown outside of herbariums. Successful culture requires that they be kept dry while dormant, as in pots, or they can be dug and stored over winter if grown in the garden. They are propagated by seed, basal offsets, or rhizomatous stolons.

Behria Greene 1886

B. tenuiflora Greene 1886. Baja California Sur, Cape region. The monotypic genus *Behria* has been transferred from *Behria* to *Bessera* and back to *Behria* again. I inadvertently played a small part in helping Dr. Lee Lenz restore *Behria* to its rightful position by discovering two new members of the genus *Dandya.* Until then *Behria* had been placed with the genus *Bessera* because of the basal union of the filaments, forming a tiny shallow cup no more than 1 mm high. In this respect *Behria* resembles members of the genus *Dandya.* In effect, the discovery of new *Dandya* species freed *Behria* from an unhappy union with *Bessera,* with which taxonomists had joined it for the sake of convenience.

The nodding tubular flowers of *Behria tenuiflora* have small tepals with the exterior a lively vermilion. The interior of each flower is yellow. Such a flashy color combination attracts hummingbirds and easily makes the flowers rivals of their *Bessera* cousins. *Behria tenuiflora* may be found in flower from September through February in Baja California. Being a cool-weather grower and somewhat cold-tender, it is not suitable for garden use in most of this country, which is just as well, as it is too scarce to withstand the predations of commercial bulb collectors. It is certainly lovely enough to make a fine plant for the greenhouse in autumn or winter. Unfortunately, like many members of the Millinae, it has a frustrating habit of refusing to grow in cultivation; the corms will stubbornly sulk without breaking dormancy until they eventually die. This can take a year or two, and it certainly takes the fun out of acquiring them. Perhaps it is better to leave this species to the enjoyment of the hummingbirds of Baja California.

Bessera Schultes 1829

B. elegans Schultes 1829. Lady's eardrops. A showy cormous plant from southwestern Mexico, growing on wiry stems to 2 feet high with umbels of exquisite pendant parasol-shaped flowers in scarlet, crimson, pink, lavender, violet, or purple. The interior white markings are always interestingly patterned and striped, and sometimes these markings are found on the exterior as well. A rare pure white form is also known.

Bessera elegans (red)

The filaments are usually purple and connected by a membrane to form a small trumpet. Often the tips of the tepals and the pollen are blue, creating fantastic red-white-and-blue flowers, augmented by the purple filaments.

As one might expect from such colorful flowers, the dazzling *Bessera* are scentless and hummingbird-pollinated. Their parasol form protects their pollen from the frequent afternoon showers of central and southern Mexico, so that they can remain open day and night. To fully appreciate their intricate beauty, one must look up into the umbel.

Unlike many members of the Millinae, most forms of *B. elegans* are fairly easy in cultivation and will do well as garden plants or in pots. The little corms can take a surprising amount of frost, but need to be kept dry while winter-dormant. Since *B. elegans* is found over a wide geographic range in Mexico, it is quite variable. In Guerrero, mature corms may produce one or two fistulous leaves, but in Nayarit they may have six to eight narrow, grassy leaves. In the limestone hills of central Colima may be found what is arguably the most majestic and robust *Bessera* of all, with the flowers in fuchsia or purple, striped white and with unusually long pedicels. The foliage is long and of a dark blue-green color. Unfortunately the corms of this form may refuse to break their dormancy the second year in cultivation and will then waste away. Were it not for this strange quirk, this might be one of the most popular of Mexican bulbs for cultivation. No one seems to keep it for more than two or three years, and thus it is not recommended except for the most dedicated collector and scientist.

B. tuitensis R. Delgadillo 1992. A newly discovered pink-flowered species from coastal Jalisco with the staminal cup reduced to a connate ring.

Dandya H. E. Moore 1953

Dandya is a little-known genus of cormous plants spread widely across northern and southwestern Mexico, usually in dry areas. They occur in white, lavender-blue, and mauve colors, and remind one somewhat of *Allium.*

D. hannibalii (Lenz) 1971. Mexico, state of Michoacán. I first discovered this delightful species in 1967 on a lightly shaded grassy hillside grazed by livestock in the "Tierra Caliente" of Michoacán. The umbels of up-facing flowers are lilac-blue on 10-inch stems, and the tepals are slightly recurved below the horizontal line in the manner of *D. thadhowardii.* In summer this species can be grown out of doors in a well-drained, sunny situation, but it won't tolerate winter dampness or cold when dormant. Unfortunately, it is rare and no longer in cultivation.

Dandya hannibalii

D. purpusii (Brandegee) H. E. Moore. Mexico, state of Coahuila. This is similar to *D. hannibalii,* but blooms in autumn, and the flowers are reported to be blue in color. Until now it has not been re-collected since the original collection was made in 1911, and has been un-known to cultivation. Because it is so remote from civi-lization, there is reason to hope that it still exists in the wild. Chris Peres and I collected this plant or a close relative of it in the state of Nuevo León in August 1999 when we were looking for *Jaimehintonia gypsophila,* thought to be a monotypic species. This may prove to be the long-lost *Dandya purpusii.* It is pink- or lilac-flowered and nearly as tall as *Bessera elegans,* which it somewhat resembles. Perhaps not suited to cultivation because of its affinity to chalky gypsum.

Dandya thadhowardii

D. thadhowardii (Lenz) 1971. Mexico, state of Guerrero. Fortunately for garden-ers, this little gem is fairly common on dry hillsides in full sun or shade and is not yet endangered. I discovered it among thorny trees and shrubs in Guerrero and mistook it for a *Muilla,* but it proved to be of a different genus. The umbels of small pendant flowers are white, keeled with a green line, and have recurved tepals; they look very much like "shooting stars" (*Dodecatheon* spp.) in form. More interesting than showy, the flowers close each night and reopen each morning and seem to beg the viewer to pause and study their intricate architecture. The slender extruded filaments are bowed to form a tiny cage surrounding a small bright green ovary and long delicate style, with the yellow anthers nearly touching at the center. There is a small bright green "star" around the ovary containing a "cup" not much higher than a hair, and the tepals sparkle with a crystalline sheen. This little *Dandya* is easy to grow in a pot, needing only to be kept dry during dormancy. With the first rains of summer it breaks dormancy like a rain lily, with an overnight rush, and the grassy leaves and scape seem to race one another to see which will be taller when it flowers the following week. While it will quickly form clumps if left undisturbed, it is easily propagated from the few large black seeds. These germinate shortly after ripening, so that a new generation can be started the first season. Although rare in cultivation, it is worth having.

Diphalangium Schauer 1847

D. graminifolium Schauer. The type specimen for this plant was in Germany, and the herbarium in which it resided was destroyed in an air raid in the Second World War. Unfortunately the plant has never been re-collected as such, and its Mexican habitat remains unknown. It was said to be *Milla*-like, with white flowers on very short stems, but the original description left much to be desired. It may be synonymous with one of several short-stemmed *Milla* species now known from Mexico. The consensus is that it was a *Milla* species, but without a type specimen to study we may never know for sure. Pity. (Included here because of the possibility that it may be rediscovered at any time.)

Jaimehintonia gypsophila Billie Turner

Likely a synonym for *Dandya purpusii.*

Milla Cavanilles 1793

The genus *Milla* consists of cormous plants found principally in Mexico, with *M. biflora* ranging northward to the southern borders of Arizona, New Mexico, and west Texas. One species is found in northern Guatemala. There are still several unpublished species known in this genus. All are characterized by having white flowers, keeled green on their backside. Often the green keels are flushed purplish, brownish, or reddish. The flowers of some species have jointed pedicels, but a few, such as *M. biflora,* may lack pedicels or have pseudopedicels. About half of the known species are nocturnal, expanding widely at night and closing the next morning. The remaining species are open both day and night. Most *Milla* species have fragrant flowers, and the corms of the various species may form basal offsets or stoloniferous rhizomes. Foliage varies from rosettes of several slender grassy leaves to long and hollow foliage like that of an onion. The chromosome numbers were supplied by Dr. Lee Lenz.

M. biflora Cavanilles 1793. Central Mexico, north to the southern borders of Arizona, New Mexico, and the Big Bend of west Texas. The most widespread *Milla*. In Mexico, it is found at middle and upper elevations growing south to the northern limits of Oaxaca and Guerrero. In central Oaxaca it is replaced by a nocturnal-flowering species, *M. oaxacana*, and also an undescribed stoloniferous species ranging from central Chiapas to Guatemala.

Milla biflora

This is the most common and most variable *Milla* species in Mexico, and while the name *biflora* suggests that it is two-flowered, the umbels can have from as few as one to as many as a dozen flowers, depending on the variety, soil, cultural conditions, and corm size. The flowers are typically white with green keels, sometimes flushed greenish, purplish, or brownish, and usually fragrant, with the scent of jasmines. *M. biflora* is easily distinguished from other species in that the flowers have sessile or near-sessile anthers less than 1 mm long and remain open both night and day until withered. (Many *Milla* species have flowers that open only in the evening and close before dawn.) Also the perianth segments of *M. biflora* narrow abruptly in their lower portion, creating the illusion of a small triangular "window" between segments.

The chromosome number for *M. biflora* is 2n = 14, but 2n = 28 numbers are also known.

M. biflora is easy to grow and can take some winter cold during dormancy. Occasional giant forms of this species may have stems 2 feet tall with several flowers 3 inches in diameter. At the other extreme may be found Lilliputian forms with tiny corms and 1-inch flowers on stems less than a foot tall. Mature corm size is always in proportion to the size of the plant. The once-plentiful *M. biflora*, like other *Milla* species, is becoming endangered around large cities because children pick the flowering stems daily in hopes of selling them to tourists in the summer evenings as the flowers expand and give off their heavenly fragrance.

M. bryanii I. M. Johnston 1943. A rare fall-flowering species from the state of Coahuila in northern Mexico. It is generally similar to *M. biflora* and *M. rosea* in appearance and habits, and like them the flowers remain open day and night. The chromosome number for *M. bryanii* is 2n = 18. The smallish flowers are white with the obligatory lime-green keels. The real distinction between *M. bryanii* and *M. rosea* is less clearcut than originally reported, since the lengths of the tubes and pedicels are more variable than first thought. *M. bryanii* is not in cultivation, and it is one of the more difficult *Milla* species to grow, since the corms may stubbornly pout and refuse to root out when their growing season arrives.

M. delicata H. E. Moore 1953. Mina District in the Mexican state of Guerrero. A little-known, rare fall-flowering species with pink flowers resembling *Bessera elegans,* determined in H. E. Moore's monograph as belonging to *Milla,* but which may belong in the genus *Dandya.* I have vainly made several attempts to reach its habitat, but there are no good roads to that area. Unfortunately it flowers in autumn, a season that has never been convenient for me to collect bulbs in Mexico. Perhaps someone someday may be able to find live material if a good all-weather road is built leading to it. But since this is a sparsely populated mountainous area, this seems unlikely.

M. filifolia T. M. Howard 2000. Mexico, states of Morelos and Guerrero. A rare species endemic to an area south and southwest of Mexico City. *M. filifolia* is like a more delicate version of *M. biflora,* but with thread-like leaves never more than 1 mm wide, and with smaller flowers. The only difference between the leaves of the young plants and mature ones is in the number of leaves produced. The stems and floral tubes are purplish at the base, minutely pubescent, and the filaments are longer than those of *M. biflora.* Mature corms are tiny, not exceeding 1⅛ inches in diameter. The chromosome number is 18. Miniature forms of *M. biflora* are known, but they differ from *M. filifolia* in the chromosome numbers and in the other characters mentioned. Although *M. filifolia* grows well in gardens, it is apt to be more permanent if dug and stored during dormancy, or kept dry in a pot.

M. magnifica H. E. Moore 1953. Mexico, state of Guerrero, in limestone hills around Taxco and Iguala. At last we have a *Milla* for Everyman. It is large, showy, and easy to grow in sun or shade. It has consistently survived excesses in rain, drought, and occasional near-zero cold spells in San Antonio for more than thirty-five years. When given the opportunity, it has reseeded itself in my garden. In a reasonably well-drained situation, it tolerates moisture while winter-dormant. Well-grown plants can have 20–40 flowers in the umbel on scapes 2–3 feet tall. The flowers are large (2–3 inches) and usually fragrant. Mature corms can be as large as those of hybrid gladioli. The chromosome number for *M. magnifica* is 2n = 18. The flowers are nocturnal, especially in hot weather, remaining closed until evening. In cooler weather, especially if the days are overcast, they may remain open during the day. As with most *Milla* species, the flowers usually open one or two at a time, and each will last two to three days. There are rarely more than six flowers open at any one time. On

Milla magnifica
PHOTO BY JO ANN TRIAL

Milla mexicana

the plus side, a scape can remain in flower for several weeks. *M. magnifica* is easily propagated by seed and by offsets. It also develops basally attached cormels, which may sometimes occur at the ends of stubby stolons. The 3- to 4-foot-long dark blue-green leaves are a half-inch or more wide, hollow and onion-like. As with onions, at first they are erect, becoming recumbent with the advent of the flowers in late summer and fall. At this time they may need protection from frost if one wishes ripened seed. *M. magnifica* is aptly named and is deserving of cultivation once commercial stocks can be propagated. This will be an easy task for anyone dedicated to that goal. A taller form with scabrous, darker foliage and with long, slender stolons is known, but it is not clear whether it is a variant or a different taxon.

M. mexicana T. M. Howard 2000. Mexico, states of Guerrero and Puebla. This is a night-blooming species, allied to *M. magnifica,* but with only a few flowers held above narrowly scabrous terete leaves. The chromosome number for *M. mexicanus* is 2n = 16, and 54. The corms are stoloniferous. The fragrant white flowers, keeled green and flushed wine-brown, are produced in late summer or fall. This species succeeds in our climate in alkaline soil with good drainage and full sun.

M. mortoniana H. E. Moore 1953. This is another rare fall-flowering species from the Mina District in the Mexican state of Guerrero. The flowers are reported to be blue, an unusual color for this genus. As with the pink-flowered *M. delicata,* it is little known and not in cultivation, and it too might prove to be a *Dandya.* Aside from the unique bluish color, the line drawing in H. E. Moore's monograph, made from a dried specimen, shows it to be of typical *Dandya* form and appearance. Nothing is known about its culture, or whether the flowers are fragrant. Certainly it would be worth trying, if it is ever available. There is no record of its ever having been in cultivation.

M. oaxacana Ravenna 1971. This *Milla* replaces *M. biflora* in the state of Oaxaca. Indeed it was once taken to be that species. *M. oaxacana* looks much like *M. biflora* but is nocturnal in habit and has a fragrance that is decidedly minty. The green keels are heavily flushed purplish blue. The foliage is dark green. It is apparently the same as forms of *M. biflora* that were originally collected by Smith (1895) and Conzatti (1896–1897) in Oaxaca and later cited by Dr. H. E. Moore (1953) as having longer stamen filaments and five to seven nerves in the keel, instead of the usual three. Moore decided that these plants were simply variations of *M. biflora*. There are one to five flowers in the umbel, and the plant has a chromosome number of 2n = 16. The small corms increase by basally attached offsets. In the evenings, children may be seen holding fistfuls of freshly picked *M. oaxacana* along the roadsides and in the city of Oaxaca, offering them for sale to tourists. It is little wonder that this once common species is rapidly disappearing from the landscape.

M. potosina T. M. Howard 2000. Mexico, state of San Luis Potosí, on rocky hillsides and pastures of the central plateau. It is generally similar to *M. oaxacana,* though geographically remote from it, and with different sets of chromosome numbers (2n = 18, 32, and 42). It is fairly abundant and replaces *M. biflora* at mid-elevations in central Mexico. The foliage is blue-green. The green-striped flowers remain closed until evening, when they expand to snowy white flowers exuding an anise-like perfume. By the next morning they are closed once more. Corms produce basally attached offsets, but culture for these is frustrating, as they may grow well one year and refuse to grow the next.

M. rosea H. E. Moore 1953. State of Nuevo León, on hills and flats north and northwest of the city of Monterrey. This is a xerophytic autumn-flowering species. Like those of *M. biflora,* its flowers remain open day and night in the month of October. The filaments are longer than those of *M. biflora,* and the pedicels are sometimes shorter, depending on the colony. Initially the type was reported to have pedicels and tubes shorter than the other species, based on a colony on a hill on the northwest outskirts of Monterrey, but colonies about 50 miles north of the city have longer tubes and pedicels, so that the condition must now be considered as variable. The flowers have white interiors, but the keels are wine-red or green, suffused pinkish or reddish. The keel color sometimes shines through the tepals, giving the illusion of blush pink flowers and making them somewhat colorful. The chromosome number for *M. rosea* is 2n = 20. Unfortunately, this is one of the difficult species to cultivate because the corms usually sulk and refuse to strike roots following late

August or early September rains. Because of their northern habitat, they should be able to withstand some cold weather. They grow in alkaline soil in full sun in Mexico, and respond to the first autumn rains there, following a good summer baking. I once soaked the corms in a rooting hormone at planting time, and this seemed to help awaken them into growth. When this method was repeated a year later, it was a failure. *M. rosea* is an endangered plant because of habitat destruction. Because of inherent cultural difficulties, it is not recommended for general use.

M. sp. #1 T. M. Howard. A species from Chiapas and adjacent Guatemala near Huehuetenango, with new corms formed at the ends of 6- to 8-inch stolons. It is somewhat similar to *M. oaxacana* but is a larger plant and has a higher chromosome number (2n = 32). It may be found growing at lower elevations.

Petronymphe H. E. Moore 1951

P. decora H. E. Moore 1951. Mexico, state of Guerrero. Called "rock nymphs," this is one of the more bizarre members of this family, with lax, wiry stems and umbels of greenish yellow flowers on long, slender pedicels resembling exploding skyrockets. It is graceful and lovely but not showy, due to the greenish color of the flowers. The attractive glossy leaves are three-sided, and the flowers are scentless. Rock nymphs are easy to grow and propagate, but unfortunately they have been intensively collected to near-extinction by greedy foreign commercial collectors. This is unnecessary, as they were never well-known or popular. Their disappearance is not an easy feat when one considers that they are endemic to out-of-the-way rocky outcroppings and seemingly inaccessible cliffs in a remote part of Mexico. Once locally abundant, they are all but gone from their former habitat.

Trillium pusillum
PHOTO BY BOBBY WARD

■ TRILLIACEAE

The genus *Trillium* was formerly included with the Liliaceae, but is now in the family Trilliaceae. Generally all parts of the plant are in threes or multiples of threes.

Trillium Linnaeus

Wake-robin. A genus of rhizomatous woodland plants. There are about 40 species, found in wooded areas of North America and eastern Asia. Most do poorly in the lower South. A few exceptions, though less showy, thrive in zones 8 and 9.

T. gracile J. D. Freeman. Wake-robin. This *Trillium* grows in east Texas and adjacent Louisiana and is appreciated more for its mottled leaves than its flowers. The sessile, erect flowers are dark purple, rarely yellow, and have a strange odor. Although not showy, the plants are interesting and are easy to grow and maintain in a shady, sandy spot rich in leaf mold.

T. nivale Riddell. A small form with unmottled leaves and snowy white flowers, native to the southeastern United States, in open limestone situations. Given enough moisture, it might do well in more western situations.

T. pusillum Michaux. Piney woods of southeastern U.S. Has green leaves and white flowers tinged pink.

T. recurvatum L. Beck. East Texas. Has obscurely mottled leaves with sessile or subsessile erect purplish or purplish-green flowers.

T. texanum Buckley. Texas trillium. This one has pedicellate white flowers turning reddish with age. Very rare, in low, moist woods, bogs, and stream banks. Probably not for cultivation.

T. viridescens Nuttall. Obscurely mottled, with erect greenish or greenish-purple flowers with a musty-spicy odor.

Zingiber zerumbet

ZINGIBERACEAE

The ginger family (Zingiberaceae) has about 40 genera and includes a wide spectrum of monocots with bilaterally symmetrical flowers that have inferior ovaries, a single fertile stamen with two pollen sacs, and sepals more or less fused at the base. The stems are often erect and cane-like, forming clumps. They are a diverse group of mostly shade-loving rhizomatous plants of tropical and subtropical regions. The hardier sorts do especially well in warmer climates of zones 8, 9, and 10, thriving in the summer heat if given enough water. While many gingers have lovely inflorescences, many also have equally ornamental foliage. The painted leaves of many *Kaempferia* species rival tapestries, and when viewed closely, the flowers of *K. rotunda* are orchid-like. The genus *Hedychium* has perfumed butterfly-like flowers rivaling honeysuckles and jasmines.

Gingers grow from rhizomes, typified by the familiar ginger root (*Zingiber officinale*) widely used in cooking. Fresh ginger root, with its peppery, slightly sweet taste and pungent aroma, adds wonderful flavor to many dishes, while ginger powder has certain medicinal uses. The "eyes" along the rhizome give rise to new growth in late spring, when all danger of frost is past. In climates cold enough to freeze the soil, the rhizomes can be dug and stored and kept in a cool, dry place until the following spring. The flowering time varies, with some species flowering in advance of the leaves and others not blooming until late summer or early fall. The rhizomes should be divided in spring or early summer, while growing, rather than in autumn when they are about to go dormant, lest cut surfaces rot. Containerized plants with good root systems can be planted anytime from spring to fall. Gingers prefer rich, slightly acid soil, but will tolerate alkaline soils if humus-enriched. They revel in an evenly moist soil, and some, like certain alpinias, tolerate "wet feet." Organic fertilizers are appreciated, but slow-release, balanced chemical fertilizers will also give good results in the landscape.

Alpinia Roxburgh

Alpinia is a large genus of more than 250 tropical Asian species. The "shell gingers" can vary from plants of reasonable height to giants of 12 feet or so. They are grown for their showy flowers and ornamental foliage. The flowers are terminally produced in their second year of growth, and for this reason they should be protected from frost.

A. formosana Schumann is 3–6 feet tall with wide green variegated leaves "pin-striped" in white. It is a striking landscape plant with requirements similar to those of *A. zerumbet* save that it is reported to be hardy to 28° F.

A. galanga (Linnaeus) Willdenow is medium in size (3–6 feet) and has small pink flowers. The leaves are bright green in color and have the spicy odor of cardamom when bruised.

A. luteocarpa is called the "bamboo ginger" and has clumping, grassy green leaves with red undersides. A tender plant with low light requirements, it can be grown out of doors in the summer, but must be wintered indoors.

A. purpurata (Vieillard) Schumann. This "red ginger" is 5–6 feet or more, with showy terminal bracts in red or pink, from which emerge small white flowers. It prefers a high humidity and adequate moisture, and since it is less hardy than other gingers, it is best wintered in a greenhouse.

A. sanderae hort. (Sander) is a tropical plant with showy variegated leaves 2–5 feet tall, requiring wintering in a greenhouse.

A. zerumbet (Persoon) B. L. Burtt & R. M. Smith (syn. *A. speciosa*). This is the classic "shell ginger" and occurs in green and variegated leaf forms. The added beauty of variegation makes the latter a valuable landscape plant even when not in bloom.

Alpinia zerumbet
PHOTO BY JO ANN TRIAL

"Shell gingers" are best wintered in the greenhouse, as they require a year of uninterrupted growth before flowering. Here they flower annually in the ground in a corner of my greenhouse. The pendant clusters of pleasantly scented waxy white flowers, somewhat orchid-like with red and yellow lips, are produced at the tips of 10-foot canes that reach the ceiling.

Amomum **Roxburgh**

A. cardamon. Tropical Asia. This species is important in the spice trade and is commonly known as "cardamom," used for the commercial production of cardamom seeds. It requires rich soil and abundant moisture. Grown as a foliage plant in warm climates.

Curcuma **Roxburgh**

These are "hidden lilies" because the colorful multi-bracted flowers are usually borne on short stems arising from the ground between the stalks of broad, *Canna*-like leaves. There are more than 65 Asian species. The inflorescence lasts for several weeks and makes fine cut-flower material. Like many gingers, curcumas prefer light shade but will tolerate a few hours of morning sun if kept moist. The leaves are thin and may burn in full sun if kept too dry. Species listed here are hardy to zone 8, except *C. roscoena*, which is hardy to zone 9.

    C. domestica has white flowers, *C. petiolata* has lavender flowers, and both are about 4 feet tall. *C. angustifolia, C. elata, C. latifolia,* and *C. zeodaria* are a foot taller and have colorful bracts that are greenish, whitish, pinkish, or purplish. Most of these inflorescences are produced on short stems hidden beneath the foliage, but *C. domestica* (turmeric), *C. petiolata,* and *C. roscoena* produce terminal flower spikes. *C.* × 'Olena' has dark rose flowers.

Curcuma roscoena
PHOTO BY JO ANN TRIAL

Curcuma elata   PHOTO BY JO ANN TRIAL

C. roscoena Wallich. Jewel of Burma. India. Dark green leaves to 3 feet and yellow flowers produced within a spike of showy orange bracts. It is marginally hardy out of doors in zone 8, and should be wintered reasonably dry (as in a pot), as it is sensitive to moisture while dormant.

Globba Linnaeus

Fancifully called "dancing ladies," the genus *Globba* consists of more than 70 Asian species. These are elegant gingers with erect or gracefully pendant flower heads, blooming from midsummer until frost. They emerge rather late in spring or in early summer, apparently awaiting the reassurance of warm weather before making an appearance. Their 2-foot foliage grows best in shade, and they enjoy shady, woodsy conditions with plenty of humus and constant moisture. Their terminal inflorescences arch gracefully, and they are ideal subjects for pots. While some fancy them as dancing ladies, others see the flowers as shaped like the head of an elephant, complete with ears and trunk. Perhaps they are living testimony for the fable of the blind men and the elephant.

G. bulbifera Roxburgh (syn. *G. schomburgkii*). Thailand, Vietnam. This is probably the best known of this group and is delightfully winsome with a succession of airy yellow terminal flowers until frost. *G. marantina*, a similar form with red-spotted yellow flowers, is also listed. The flowers of *G. bulbifera* are followed by solid aerial "bulbils" which will develop into new plants if they fall onto a suitable growing medium. Since these are solid structures, they are not technically bulbils, but apparently there is no accurately equivalent name for aerial corms and tubers.

G. globulifera. The "purple globe" is the rarest of this cultivated trio, with showy magenta terminal cones from which emerge small golden yellow flowers. It is easily propagated by small aerial "bulbils" formed in the leaf axils as well as in the mature

Globba globulifera
PHOTO BY JO ANN TRIAL

Globba winitii
PHOTO BY JO ANN TRIAL

flower heads. It can also be propagated by rooting severed stalks of the entire plant in water, as if to underscore its desire for moist cultural conditions. The purple globe is a welcome addition for dampish shady spots under trees.

G. winitii C. H. Wright. Thailand. A showy garden species with arching stems terminating in pendant rose-purple bracts from which emerge panicles of gracefully quaint, elephant-head-shaped orange-yellow flowers. It is becoming increasingly popular as it becomes more generally available. For sheer drama, a pot of this in bloom is sure to draw enthusiastic comments.

Hedychium Koenig

A genus of about 50 tropical or subtropical Asian species confined to India and Malaya, the popular "butterfly gingers" typify the ginger family with their showy flowers, jasmine-like fragrance, and kaleidoscope of colors. *Hedychium* flowers are embellished with long, upcurved filaments resembling butterfly antennae that often form a cylinder or crown a foot or so in length atop the narrow-leaved canes. Unlike many gingers, they enjoy several hours of sun each day, short of full sun, which may burn the leaves and shorten the lifespan of the flowers. All of the following species and hybrids are winter-hardy to zone 8, and may grow 3–6 feet tall, flowering from midsummer until fall.

H. aurantiacum Wallich ex Roscoe. Hardy ginger lily. This has soft salmon flowers with a darker throat. At 7 feet or more, it is one of the taller species.

H. coccineum Buchanan-Hamilton. The red ginger lily has wondrously colored flowers in shades of orange, brick, rust-red, salmon-pink, or bright red with pink filaments creating a bottle-brush effect, from a cone of green bracts atop 6-foot blue-green canes. As a garden plant, it has received fairly good reviews in zones 8 and 9 in south-central Texas, flowering most years if given a rich, moist, sunny situation and some winter protection.

H. coronarium Koenig. Tropical Asia. The white butterfly ginger or garland flower has large pure white flowers with greenish "eyes" and an intense jasmine-like fragrance on canes 5–6 feet high. It is extensively naturalized in tropical America, so it came as no surprise to find it in Guatemala, covering seepy hillsides at mid-elevations. It is the most popular species and is relatively inexpensive, needing only a soil rich in humus and abundant moisture while growing, as it hates being dried out.

H. coronarium var. *chrysoleucum* W. Carey. Another popular form with white flowers, the greenish "eyes" exchanged for yellow ones.

H. flavescens Roscoe is rather similar but has larger yellow flowers with darker yellow "eyes."

Hedychium x 'Fiesta'
PHOTO BY JO ANN TRIAL

Hedychium x 'Pumpkin'
PHOTO BY JO ANN TRIAL

H. gahlii has peach flowers.

H. gardnerianum Roscoe. Northern India. The "Kahili ginger" has bottle-brush yellow flowers with red filaments. These can grow to 8 feet and flower in late summer.

H. greenei W. W. Smith 1909. Bhutan. This has brilliant red-orange flowers with dark red lips and filaments in late summer, and has been much used in the creation of gorgeously colored hybrids.

Hybrids

Since some *Hedychium* flowers are produced at eye level, the simple structure of the flowers and the colorful diversity of other species and hybrids invite amateur pollinations, and they are easily hybridized.

'Gold Flame' has whitish flowers with an orange "eye" and blooms rather late, so may need protection. 'Fiesta,' 'Kewensis,' 'Pink V,' and 'Samsheri' have flowers in various shades of peach or salmon with contrasting "eyes" and stamens, while 'Pradhani' has cream-colored flowers with coral stamens. 'Pumpkin' is spectacular with deep orange flowers, while 'Peach Delight' is said to be one of the earliest to flower, with creamy-peach flowers until frost. All hybrids share the wonderful scent that typifies the genus.

Kaempferia Linnaeus

A genus of about 50 subtropical and tropical Asian and African species. The leaves of some kaempferias rival *Calathea* and *Maranta* species for their intricately beautiful patterns and colors. They are shade-lovers whose delicate leaves cannot tolerate more than several hours of morning sun, and they require a damp situation. Kaempferias are ideal accent or border plants when placed in front of taller plants. They are winter-hardy at least to zone 8, and many will flower continuously during the summer months. Although they are principally grown for their lovely foliage, the glistening rounded lavender flowers, often with contrasting white "eyes," which are produced in succession and last but a day, perfectly complement the low-growing leaves. Some species have aromatic, edible tubers.

K. galanga Linnaeus. India. The bright green oval leaves lie flat on the ground and have depressed veins. The sparkling crystal white flowers are a cut apart from the other species, with a striking purple spot on the lip.

K. involucrata. The light green oval leaves are prominently ribbed. Lilac flowers in summer.

K. mukeonden. A lovely low-growing species whose large leaves have peacock-like markings in alternating bands of purple and pale olive green, remaining even when fully mature. The flowers are sparkling mauve with a white center.

K. pulchra. Ridley. This is commonly called "peacock plant" because the leaves have bands of bronze and light green shining with an amazing iridescence on the wide leaf surface, held flat just 3 inches above ground level. *K. mansonii* (syn. *K. elegans, K. pulchra* var. *mansonii*) is similar to *K. pulchra* but darker, smaller, and with more erect leaves; *K. pulchra* var. *roscoeana* is similar but with white spots on the large-banded leaves.

K. rotunda Linnaeus. India. This edible-tubered species is commonly known as "resurrection lily" or "tropical crocus." Among a genus of typically low-growing species, *K. rotunda* is the tallest, growing to 2 feet. The showy, pleasantly scented, leafless flowers are produced at ground level in late spring. They more closely resemble orchids than lilies or crocuses, with their white tepals contrasting sharply against two large lavender and purple "lips" with white netting. The petioled foliage soon follows and is silver-green with a contrasting darker central "flame" pattern, blushed purplish on the undersides. It is hard to say whether the flowers are more beautiful than the foliage, but the leaves last a whole lot longer. They retain these pleasing colors until cut down by frost.

Kaempferia rotunda

Siphonochilus decorus   PHOTO BY JO ANN TRIAL   *Siphonochilus kirkii*   PHOTO BY JO ANN TRIAL

Siphonochilus J. M. Wood & Franks

S. decorus (syn. *Kaempferia decora*). Africa. A rare species with broad, pleated dark green leaves growing to 18 inches high. The large, crepe-like fragrant yellow flowers are formed on a separate stalk from the leaves, opening one or two at a time over a period of several weeks.

S. kirkii (J. D. Hooker) B. L. Burtt, a similar species with flowers of an intense rose color, is very rare in the trade.

Because of their exquisite jewel-like qualities, one will usually want to give *Siphonochilus* plants preferential treatment in a pot.

Zingiber Boehmer

A genus of about 85 species from tropical Asia. The flowers of some are commonly called "pine cones" because of the cone-like inflorescence. One of these is the tropical culinary ginger root, which is too tender to concern us here. The most popular hardy ornamental from this group is *Z. zerumbet*, the "red pine cone ginger," a thoroughly intriguing plant with gracefully arching dark green foliage 4–5 feet tall resembling giant fern fronds in the landscape. The inflorescence, with its club-like stem and tightly overlapping bracts, is produced separately from the base of the plant and is tall enough for cutting. The 1-inch yellowish flowers have crepe-textured tepals and are orchid-like. They open a few at a time each morning and close in the late afternoon. The cones are initially a glossy emerald green, turning pink or rosy red when the flowering is completed, making the inflorescence attractive at all stages. The variegated 'Darceyi' is a lovely form, slightly smaller in size than the type, and even more ornamental, with similar flowers and cones, and green and cream-white leaves.

Costus **Linnaeus**

Spiral ginger, spiral flag. Tropical America, Africa, East Indies. Although technically no longer regarded as true gingers, the genera *Costus* and *Monocostus* are still traditionally and sentimentally grouped with them. Unlike true gingers, *Costus* has each of its leaves offset by an eighth of a turn from the one beneath, giving a helix-like effect of a spiraled staircase; hence the common names. The flowers may be white, red, orange, or yellow. The leaves vary from 2 to 6 inches wide and can be smooth or velvety in texture. Most *Costus* species enjoy partial shade, but *C. spiralis* will tolerate sun for half the day. All bloom in spring or summer with colorful bracts terminating at the tips of each cane. The flowers open a few at a time, between the bracts. Most species are winter-hardy to zone 8.

C. igneus N. E. Brown (syn. *C. cuspidatus*). Fiery costus. Brazil. The leaves grow to 6 inches long on canes less than a foot high. The cone-like bracts have showy 2½-inch crepe-like flowers, deep orange in color.

C. malortieanus H. A. Wendland. Central America. This "stepladder plant" is tender to cold but well worth growing as a pot plant because of the showy yellow flowers terminating the broad hairy leaves on 3-foot stems.

C. pictus D. Don has red-spotted stems growing 5–8 feet tall and terminating in showy yellow flowers.

C. speciosus (Koenig) J. E. Smith. Crepe ginger. East Indies. Funnel-formed crepe-like white flowers emerge from dark red bracts above narrow leaves and dark red canes 6 feet tall.

C. spiralis Roscoe. Scarlet spiral flag. Bright green spiraling leaves provide an interesting contrast with smaller- or darker-leaved plants. The winter-hardy plants soon form clumps to 4 feet in height, terminating in showy scarlet bracts and flowers.

Costus igneus PHOTO BY JO ANN TRIAL

Costus speciosus PHOTO BY JO ANN TRIAL

Monocostus

Monocostus is a monotypic African genus related to *Costus. M. uniflorus* is a delightful clumping dwarf with reed-like stems only 6 inches tall, supporting 2-inch leaves
and a surprisingly large crepe-like yellow flower. Although tender, if kept in a humid greenhouse it will bloom almost continuously in summer and fall. In winter it
becomes nearly dormant while retaining some of its foliage.

SOCIETIES AND JOURNALS

American Daffodil Society
4126 Winfield Rd.
Columbus, OH 43220-4606
Website: http://www.mc.edu/~adswww

American Iris Society
13358 Sagle Rd.
Purcellville, VA 20132-1827
Telephone 540/668-9004
Website: http://www.irises.org
Quarterly bulletin

American Rock Garden Society
P.O. Box 67
Millwood, NY 10546
Website: http://www.nargs.org
Quarterly bulletin, seed exchange

Botanical Society of South Africa
Kirstenbosch Branch
P.O. Box 195
Newlands 7725, Cape Town
Republic of South Africa
Telephone 27-021-762-1621;
    fax 27-021-762-0923
E-mail: botbkshp@iafrica.com
Website: www.botsocsa@org.za

Indigenous Bulb Association of South Africa
P.O. Box 12265
N 1 City 7463
Republic of South Africa
Telephone/fax 27-21-558-1690;
    fax available only 21:00–6:00 GMT
Annual bulletin; forum for exchange of
    information and, where possible, bulbs
    and seeds

International Bulb Society
P.O. Box 92136
Pasadena, CA 91109-2136
E-mail: membership@bulbsociety.org
Website: http://www.bulbsociety.org
Annual bulb journal *Herbertia*, newsletter,
    seed list, e-mail bulb forum, bulb exchange

North American Lily Society
c/o Dr. Robert Gilman
P.O. Box 272
Owatonna, MN 55060
Telephone 507/451-2170
Website: http://www.lilies.com/nalshome.html
Quarterly bulletin, yearbook, seed exchange

SUPPLIERS

Australia

Bruce Knight
The Botanist Nursery
16 Victor Close
Green Point, N.S.W. 2251
Australia
Zephyranthes, diploid *Hippeastrum,*
    Lachenalia, Romulea

Pine Heights Nursery
Pepper St., Everton Hills
Queensland 4053
Australia
Telephone (07) 3353-2761;
    fax (07) 3353-5022
Bulb list $3 (U.S. bills OK; no checks)

Canada

Cruickshank's
780 Birchmount Road
Scarborough, Ontario M1K 5H4
Canada
Telephone 416/750-9249 or 800/665-5605;
    fax 416/750-8522
E-mail: info@cruickshanks.com
Website: www.cruickshanks.com or
    www.indigo.ca
Catalog $3.00 Canadian

Chile

Luis D. Arriagada Gamboa
Casilla 8261
Viña del Mar, Chile
Telephone 56-32-341244;
    fax 56-32-280802
E-mail: Jardinativo@hotmail.com
Chilean bulbs; catalog $10 (U.S.)

South Africa

Cape Flora Nursery
P.O. Box 10556
Linton Grange
Port Elizabeth 6015
Republic of South Africa
Telephone 27-41-73-2096; fax 27-41-73-3188
E-mail: capeflor@iafrica.com
Website: http://ftp.iafrica.com/c/ca/capeflor

Cape Seeds and Bulb
P.O. Box 6363
Uniedal 7612
Republic of South Africa
Telephone 2721-887-9418; fax 2721-887-0823
E-mail: capeseed@iafrica.com
Quarterly brochure $10.00 per year

Lowlands Nurseries
P.O. Box 9
Kei Road 4920
Republic of South Africa
Telephone 27-043-7820-731;
    fax 27-043-7820-731
Free catalog

Rust-En-Vrede
P.O. Box 753
Brackenfell 7561
Republic of South Africa
Telephone 27-21-9814515; fax 27-21-9810050

Rust En Vrede
P.O. Box 231
Constantia 7848
Republic of South Africa

Silverhill Seeds
P.O. Box 53108
Kenilworth
Republic of South Africa 7745
Telephone 27-21-762-4245;
    fax 27-21-797-6609
E-mail: silverhill@yebo.co.za
Website: www.silverhillseeds.co.za
Seeds only; catalog $2

Sunburst Bulbs
P.O. Box 183
Howard Place 7450
Cape Town
Republic of South Africa

Witkoppen Wild Flower Nursery
P.O. Box 67036
2021 Bryanston
Republic of South Africa

United Kingdom

Cambridge Bulbs
40 Whittlesford Rd.
Newton, Cambridge CB2 5PH
United Kingdom

Paul Christian
Rare Plants
P.O. Box 468
Wrexham LL13 9XR
United Kingdom
Telephone 44-(0)1978-366399;
    fax 44-(0)1978-266466
E-mail: paul@rareplants.co.uk
Website: http://rareplants.co.uk
Catalog £2/$3 (U.S. bills OK;
    no U.S. checks)
On-line catalog and newsletter

Brian Duncan Novelty and Exhibition
    Daffodils
Knowehead
15 Ballynahatty Rd.
Omagh, C. Tyrone, Northern Ireland
    BT78 1PN

United Kingdom
Telephone/fax 44-2882-242931
Website: http://ourworld.compuserve.com/
    homepages/europium/duncan.htm
Catalog $2

Monocot Nursery
St. Michaels
Littleton, Somerton
Somerset TA11 6NT
United Kingdom
Telephone 44-(0)1458-272356;
    fax 44-(0)1458-272065
Catalog $3

Nerine Nursery
Welland Worcestershire WR13 6LN
United Kingdom

R. A. Scamp
18 Bosmeor Close
Falmouth, Cornwall TR11 4PX
United Kingdom
Modern standard narcissi; excellent list for
    tazetta and *Jonquilla* hybrids, species

United States

Brent and Becky's Bulbs
7463 Heath Trail
Gloucester, VA 23061
Telephone 804/693-3966; fax 804/693-9436
Website: www.brentandbeckysbulbs.com
Free catalog

Brudy's Exotics
P.O. Box 820874
Houston, TX 77282-0874
Gingers

The Bulb Crate
2560 Deerfield Rd.
Riverwoods, IL 60015
Telephone 847/317-1414; fax 847/317-1417
Lilies, irises, etc.; free catalog

Davids & Royston Bulb Co.
550 West 135th St.
Gardena, CA 90248
Wholesale to nurseries only

Glasshouse Works
Plants Traditional & Unusual
Church St., P.O. Box 97
Stewart, OH 45778-0097
Telephone 740/662-2142; fax 740/662-2120
E-mail: plants@glasshouseworks.com
Website: http://www.glasshouseworks.com
Amaryllids, aroids, gesneriads, gingers, oxalis,
    etc.; catalog $2.00

Kelly's Plant World
10266 E. Princeton
Sanger, CA 93657
Telephone 559/294-7676; fax 559/294-7626
E-mail: hkellyjr2@aol.com
Website: http://members.aol.com/hkellyjr2
Crinums, lycorises, cannas; descriptive list $1

Louisiana Nursery
Route 7, Box 43
Opelousas, LA 70570
Phone 318/948-3696; fax 318/942-6404
Louisiana irises, crinums; catalogs: $4.00 for
    daylilies and irises; $6.00 for other plants

McClure & Zimmerman
P.O. Box 368
Friesland, WI 53935-0368
Telephone 800/883-6998 (8:00 A.M. to
    4:30 P.M. M–F CST)
Fax 800/374-6120
E-mail: info@mzbulb.com
Website: www.mzbulb.com
Eclectic and standard Dutch bulbs; free
    catalog

Hugh McDonald
Neglected Bulbs
P.O. Box 2768
Berkeley, CA 94702
Calochortus, Fritillaria, Erythronium,
    Brodiaea, etc.
Website: http://members.aol.com/Nglctdblbs

Mitsch Daffodils
P.O. Box 218
Hubbard, OR 97032
Telephone 503/651-2742;
    fax 503/651-2792
E-mail: havensr@web-ster.com
Website: http://www.web-ster.com/havensr/
    mitsch
Catalog $3 (deductible on order)

Old House Gardens Heirloom Bulbs
Scott Kunst
536 Third St.
Ann Arbor, MI 48103-4957
Telephone 734/995-1486;
    fax 734/995-1687
E-mail: OHGBulbs@aol.com
Website: www.oldhousegardens.com
Heirloom daffodils, *Hippeastrum* x *johnsonii*,
    Rhodophiala bifida, and other rare antique
    bulbs from the 1200's to the 1950's, includ-
    ing many grown in the South rather than
    in Holland; catalog $2.00

Oregon Trail Daffodils
41905 SE Louden
Corbett, OR 97019
Telephone 503/695-5513;
    fax 503/695-5573
E-mail: daffodil@europa.com
Free catalog

Park Seed
1 Parkton Ave.
Greenwood, SC 29647-0001
Telephone 800/845-3369; fax 864-941-4206
E-mail: info@parkseed.com
Website: www.parkseed.com
Standard hardy bulbs; free catalog

Plant Delights Nursery, Inc.
9241 Sauls Rd.
Raleigh, NC 27603
Telephone 919/772-4794; fax 919/662-0370
Website: http://www.plantdelights.com
Zephyranthes, aroids, lycorises, etc.; for catalog,
    send 10 stamps or 1 box of chocolates

The Plumeria People
910 Leander Dr.
Leander, TX 78641
Telephone 512/254-0807
Gingers, bulbs, irids, cannas; catalog $3.00

John Scheepers, Inc.
23 Tulip Drive
Bantam, CT 06750
Telephone 860/567-0838; fax 860/567-5323
E-mail: catalog@johnscheepers.com
Website: www.johnscheepers.com
Standard Dutch bulbs, alliums; free catalog

Skittone Bulb Co.
1415 Eucalyptus
San Francisco, CA 94132
Eclectic bulbs

Southern Exposure
35 Minor at Rusk
Beaumont, TX 77702-2414
Telephone 409/835-0644
Aroids; catalog $5

Southwestern Native Seeds
Sally Walker
P.O. Box 50503
Tucson, AZ 85703
Seeds only; catalog $2

TyTy Plantation Bulb Co.
P.O. Box 159
TyTy, GA 31795
Telephone 800/972-2101;
    fax 912/388-8108
Website: www.tytyga.com; see also
    www.chulaga.com, www.aaronscanna-
    amaryllis.com
Crinums, cannas, aroids, gingers, etc.; free
    catalog

Van Bourgondien Bros.
P.O. Box 1000
Babylon, NY 11702-9004
Telephone 800/622-9997;
    fax 800/327-4268
E-mail: blooms@dutchbulbs.com
Website: www.dutchbulbs.com
Standard Dutch bulbs; free catalog

Van Engelen Inc.
23 Tulip Drive
Bantam, CT 06750
Telephone 860/567-8734;
    fax 860/567-5323
E-mail: catalog@vanengelen.com
Website: www.vanengelen.com
Dutch bulbs mostly in wholesale quantities;
    free catalog

Mary Mattison van Schaik Imported
    Dutch Bulbs
P.O. Box 188
Temple, NH 03084
Telephone 603/878-2592
Free catalog

Wayside Gardens
1 Garden Lane
Hodges, SC 29695-0001
Telephone 800/845-1124;
    fax 800/817-1124
Website: www.waysidegardens.com
Standard Dutch bulbs; free catalog

William R. P. Welch
P.O. Box 1736
Carmel Valley, CA 93924-1736
Telephone and fax 831/659-3830
E-mail: bulbbaronbill@aol.com
Best list of daffodils for warm climates,
    including tazettas, jonquils, permanent old
    standards from other divisions, etc., plus
    Amaryllis belladonna; free list

M & C Willets
P.O. Box 446
Moss Landing, CA 95039
Telephone 831/728-BULB
E-mail: mandcw@ccnet.com
Website: http://www.bulbmania.com
Eclectic list of South African bulbs, etc.;
    catalog $1 (refundable on order)

Guy Wrinkle Exotic Plants
11610 Addison St.
North Hollywood, CA 91601
Telephone 310/670-8637; fax 310/670-1427
E-mail: GuyWinkle@RareExotics.com
Website: www.RareExotics.com
Eclectic South African and Andes bulbs;
    catalog $1

Yucca Do Nursery, Inc.
Route 3, Box 104
Hempstead, TX 77445
Telephone 979/826-4580
E-mail: yuccado@nettexas.net
Northeast Mexico bulbs, *Zephyranthes,* etc.;
    catalog $4.00

GLOSSARY

Actinomorphic: regular; symmetrical; shaped equally on all sides.

Acuminate: tapered to a point.

Acute: sharp, ending in a point.

Adnate: grown to or organically united with another part, as the base of the tepals to the staminal cup in some *Hymenocallis*.

Aestivate: to be dormant in summer.

Alliaceous: onion- or garlic-like, usually referring to the odor or flavor.

Allopatric: occupying different habitats or areas.

Androecium: the stamens.

Anther: the pollen-bearing part of the stamen.

Anthesis: the act of flowering.

Apomictic: producing seeds or plants without fertilization.

Arcuate: arching, curved.

Articulated: jointed.

Ascending: directed upward.

Asexual propagation: propagation from plant tissues by other means than the union of sex or germ cells.

Backcross: to cross a hybrid with one of its parents.

Basal plate: the solid, corm-like bottom of the bulb that holds the scales together and from which roots emerge.

Bifid: two-cleft.

Biflabellate: fan-shaped.

Blade: the flat part of a leaf or flower segment.

Bract: a reduced leaf.

Bulb: a fleshy, bud-like stem-base; a swollen storage organ, usually underground, emitting roots from below, composed of one or more scales or leaf bases, attached to a basal plate, and enclosing the growing point.

Bulbiferous: bearing bulblets as offsets.

Bulbiliferous: bearing bulbils.

Bulbils: miniature bulbs produced asexually in the umbel, in the leaf axils, or above the bulb.

Bulblets: small bulbs produced around the parent bulb.

Bulbous: swollen or enlarged.

Calcareous: growing on chalky or limestone soil.

Campanulate: bell-shaped.

Canaliculate: with a channel or groove.

Capitate: head-like.

Carinate: keeled.

Cauline: placed on the stem.

Cernuus: drooping, nutant.

Character: feature or peculiarity by which individuals of a variety, species, genus, or other category can be recognized or differentiated.

Chimera: an inherited variegation in which the variegation is top to bottom or lengthwise, splitting the plant into two or more sections.

Chromosome number: the number of chromosomes in the nucleus of a specific plant cell; usually constant in each species.

Chromosomes: the rod-like structures of the cell nucleus which carry the genes.

Ciliate: edged with hairs.

Clone: an individual plant, genetically and phenotypically unique, reproduced vegetatively and duplicating its parent.

Colony: a group of individuals of one species.

Compressed: flattened.

Connate: fused or joined, as at the base.

Connivent: adherent, converging but not fused.

Cordate: heart-shaped.

Corm: a solid, swollen underground basal plate, not having scales, with the embryonic bud-like growing point at its summit or sides.

Cormel, cormlet: a small corm produced by a mature corm.

Corona: an extra organ formed between the perianth and the stamens, as in daffodils, or joining the filaments to form a membranous crown, as in *Hymenocallis.*

Costate: having lateral ribs in addition to the central midrib.

Crest: elevated, toothed, or irregular ridge of tissue.

Cucullate: hooded.

Cultivar: a cultivated variety of a natural or artificial hybrid, sport, or selection. The written name of a cultivar is enclosed in single quotation marks, as in *Crinum* cv. 'Carnival.'

Cyme: a flat-topped determinate inflorescence, with the central flowers opening first.

Deciduous: losing foliage seasonally, as opposed to evergreen.

Declinate: turned downward, forward, or to one side, the tips often recurved, as in flowers of *Habranthus.*

Decumbent: lying upon the ground.

Dehiscence: the method or process of opening a seedpod or anther to release the contents.

Dentate: indentations (teeth) perpendicular to the margins.

Denticulate: finely dentate.

Dicot: plant that initially produces two seed-leaves.

Dimorphic: occurring in two forms.

Diploid: a plant with the normal genetic complement of two complete sets of chromosomes (2n).

Distichous: two-ranked, with leaves on opposite sides of a stem and in the same plane, as in bearded irises.

Diurnal (of flowers): remaining open during daylight hours.

Double: full; having two or more times the usual number of petals.

Elliptical: more or less oblong, with pointed ends; oval in outline.

Endemic: native to a definitive area or region.

Ensiform: sword-shaped.

Ephemeral: short-lived, fugacious, beginning and ending in a day.

Epipetal: borne on the petal.

Epiphyte: a plant growing on another, or on some other elevated support.

Erect: upright.

Exerted: sticking out.

Falcate: curved, like a sickle.

Falls: in irises and certain other irids, the outer three perianth parts, falling downward or outward.

Fasciculate: clustered.

Filament: staminal stalk.

Filiform: thread-like.

Fistulous (of leaves): tubular, hollow in the center, like a soda straw; terete.

Floret: one of the numerous small flowers forming an umbel, as in *Allium.*

Floriferous: flower-bearing.

Form: the lowest rank given to plants by botanists, and referring to slight variations within a species or variety. Also the individual shapes of flowers, leaves, etc.

Fugacious: ephemeral, fleeting, lasting but a short time.

Funnel-form: funnel-shaped.

Genotype: a type determined by genetic characters.

Genus: a closely related group of plants including one or more species. Plural: genera.

Geophyte: a name for plants having subterranean bulbous rootstocks.

Gibbous: swollen on one side, usually basally, as in a snapdragon corolla.

Gland: an organ secreting oil, nectar, etc.

Glandular zone: a gland-like zone bearing secreting organs.

Glaucescent: slightly glaucous.

Glaucous (of leaves): covered with a powdery or waxy bloom that can be wiped off, serving as a sunscreen. The foliage is then bluish or grayish.

Globose: globe-shaped.

Grex name: A Latinized name for a group of similar plants from crossing two species with one another.

Gynoecium: the female element of a flower, or a collective term used for several pistils of a single flower used as a unit.

Gynophore: a stalk supporting the gynoecium.

Habitat: the location in which a plant naturally grows wild.

Haploid: having one set of chromosomes.

Hardy: able to survive winter or extreme climatic or environmental conditions.

Herbaceous: deciduous and non-woody, dying back to the ground and then reappearing seasonally.

Herbarium: a collection of dried plant specimens.

Hirsute: clothed with stiff hairs.

Hybrid: progeny of genetically different parents.

Hypocratiform: salver-form.

Hysteranthous: flowering before leaves appear; precocious.

Imbricate: overlapping in a scale-like manner.

Incumbent: turned inward.

Inferior (of ovaries): positioned beneath or below the perianth.

Inflorescence: the entire flower cluster of a scape.

Invasive: applied to noxious weeds, voluntarily intrusive with an overabundance of seeds, bulblets, or bulbils.

Keel: a prominent rib, ridge, or crease on the undersurface.

Laciniate: deeply and narrowly slashed and cut.

Lanceolate: lance-shaped, narrow, tapering to a point.

Lectotype: the original type specimen in a selected herbarium.

Limb: the blade of a leaf or petal.

Linear: narrow, with the edges more or less parallel.

Locule: compartment or cell of an ovary.

Lorate: strap-shaped.

Midrib: the main rib of a leaf or floral segment, usually on the interior or upper surface; the reverse side of a keel.

Monocot: plant that has a single seed-leaf, such as grass.

Monograph: a special treatise on a subject of limited range.

Monotypic genus: one comprised of a single species.

Mutation: sudden genetic alteration in form or qualities; a sport.

Naturalized: not native but reproducing and colonizing as if wild, without human intervention.

Nectary: a gland that secretes nectar.

Nerve: prominent vein.

Nocturnal (of flowers): opening at night and closing during the day.

Nutant: pendant, drooping.

Oblanceolate: inversely lanceolate, and broader in the middle.

Obovate: inversely ovate, wider above the middle.

Obtuse: blunt.

Offset: a lateral bulblet from the base of another bulb.

Ovary: the ovule-bearing structure at the base of the flower, which develops into a seedpod after fertilization.

Ovate: egg-shaped.

Ovoid: oval in outline.

Ovule: the embryonic egg.

Palmate: with several lobes, spreading like the digits of a hand.

Panicle: branched inflorescence.

Papillate: covered with nipple-like protuberances.

Patent: widely spreading.

Pedicel: the stalk of an individual flower.

Pedicellate: having pedicels.

Peduncle: flower stalk.

Pendant: nutant, nodding.

Perennial: lasting for more than two seasons.

Perianth: the showy outer part of a flower.

Perianth segment: in monocots, one of the segments comprising the flower, usually six in number, similar to the petals and sepals of dicot flowers.

Perianth tube: the tubular connection between the ovary and the perianth segments.

Perigone: surrounding the reproductive organs, as in the segments.

Persistent: lasting.

Petiolate: having a petiole.

Petiole: leaf stalk.

Phenotype: a type determined by its appearance, as opposed to a genotype.

Pistil: the complete female reproductive part of the flower, consisting of the stigma, style, and ovary.

Plicate: pleated.

Pollen: male sex cells from the anthers of the flower.

Polyploid: having more than two sets of chromosomes.

Proteranthous: leafing prior to flowering.

Pseudopedicel: a false joint where perianth tube and perianth merge.

Pubescent: hairy or downy.

Pustulate: minutely blistered.

Putative: reputed, supposed.

Raceme: an elongated peduncle with the flowers carried on pedicels.

Recumbent: reclining, lying.

Recurved: bent or curved downward or backward.

Reflexed: abruptly recurved downward or backward.

Reticulated: netted.

Revolute: rolled backward.

Rhizomatous stolons: deciduous elongated horizontal rhizomes terminating in a small bulb or corm.

Rhizome: a horizontal or vertical underground stem.

Rootstock: a root-like underground stem.

Rosette: leaves arranged in a circular pattern at or near ground level.

Rosulate: in rosettes.

Rotate: wheel-shaped, flat and circular.

Rugose: wrinkled.

Scabrous: with minute projections, rough to the touch.

Scale: one of the fleshy tunications of a bulb.

Scape: a leafless flower stalk arising from the ground.

Section: division. *Narcissus* used to be divided into "sections" before the current system of "divisions" was set up.

Segment. *See* Perianth segment.

Serotine: late to leaf or flower, or to appear.

Sessile: lacking a pedicel, growing directly from the peduncle; stemless.

Sexual propagation: propagation involving the

union of sex cells or gametes to form seeds.

Sp.: species (singular).

Spadix: the thick finger-like organ inside the spathe of aroids, carrying the flowers at its lower end and elongated into a pollen-bearing appendix at the apex.

Spathe: a modified small leaf or bract subtending the inflorescence.

Spatulate: spoon-shaped.

Species: a natural grouping of related and freely interbreeding plants in a fundamental classification unit, contained within a genus.

Spike: an elongated peduncle with the flowers unbranched and sessile.

Sport: mutation; a spontaneous deviation from the type.

Spp.: species (plural).

Staminal cup: a false corona formed by the union of the stamens, as in *Hymenocallis*.

Staminode: a sterile, enlarged stamen.

Standards: in irises and certain other irids, the inner three perianth parts, which often stand erect.

Stellate: star-shaped.

Stigma: the tip of the style (female part) receiving the pollen.

Stipitate: borne on a short stalk.

Stolon: a horizontal stem, underground or at ground level, terminating in new plants, bulbs, or corms.

Striate: with fine longitudinal lines.

Style: the female organ between the ovary and stigma.

Sub-: prefix, meaning almost.

Subequal: nearly equal.

Suberect: almost erect.

Subgenus. *See* Subspecies.

Subglobose: almost globe-shaped.

Subpetiolate: having a minimal petiole.

Subsp.: subspecies.

Subspecies, subgenus: a subdivision of a species or genus insufficiently distinct to merit species or generic rank, often reflecting a special geographic range.

Subtend: to be beneath or lower than.

Superior (of ovaries): above the perianth.

Sympatric: occupying the same habitat.

Synanthous: having flowers contemporary with the leaves.

Synonym: another name for a taxon that already has a valid name.

Taxon: a taxonomic category, such as a genus or species.

Tepals: perianth segments of monocots, usually six in number, equivalent to the petals and sepals of dicots.

Tepal tube: the tube formed by tepals joined together at their bases.

Terete: cylindrical; circular in transverse section.

Terrestrial: of the ground; a land plant.

Tetraploid: having four sets of chromosomes (4n).

Trifid: three-cleft.

Trigonous: three-angled.

Triploid: having three sets of chromosomes (3n). Usually sterile.

Tuber: a swollen, solid underground rootstock capable of producing roots and shoots from dormant buds.

Tunics: bulb coats; the covering of bulbs and corms.

Umbel: an inflorescence in which all flowers radiate from a common center at the apex of the scape, like spokes in a wheel.

Undulate: wavy.

Urceolate: urn-shaped.

Valve: one of the pieces into which a capsule or bract splits.

Variety: a plant division below the rank of species or subspecies, differing enough to merit a varietal name.

Ventricose: with a one-side swelling or inflation, more pronounced than when gibbous.

Versatile: attached at the center and swinging free.

Vestigial: imperfectly developed, usually smaller and less complex than the prototype.

Vittate: striped longitudinally.

Widespread: distributed over a wide area, but not necessarily common.

Xerophyte: plant adapted to very dry conditions.

Zygomorphic: bilaterally symmetrical, as in *Sprekelia.*

BIBLIOGRAPHY

Ajilvsgi, Geyata. *Wild Flowers of the Big Thicket, East Texas, and Western Louisiana.* College Station: Texas A & M University Press, 1979.

Bailey, Liberty Hyde, and Ethel Zoe Bailey. *Hortus Third.* New York: Macmillan, 1976.

Baker, J. G. *Handbook of the Amaryllideae.* London: George Bell & Sons, 1888. Reprint, New York: Stechert-Hafner, 1972.

Barre, Peter. *Ye Narcissus or Daffodyl Flowere, and Hys Roots.* Reprint, Washington, D.C.: American Daffodil Society, 1968.

Baumgardt, John Phillip. *Bulbs for Summer Bloom.* New York: Hawthorn Books, 1970.

Belin, G. *Les Plantes bulbeuses.* Paris: J. B. Baillière et Fils, 1952.

Bird, Richard. *Lilies.* Secaucus, N.J.: Chartwell Books, 1991.

Bryan, John E. *Bulbs.* 2 vols. Kent: Christopher Helm; Portland, Ore.: Timber Press, 1989.

Caillet, Marie, and Joseph K. Mertzweiller. *The Louisiana Iris.* Waco: Society for Louisiana Irises/Texas Gardener Press, 1988.

Cassidy, G. E., and S. Linnegar. *Growing Irises.* London and Canberra: Croom Helm, 1982.

Correll, Donovan Stewart, and Marshall Conring Johnston. *Manual of the Vascular Plants of Texas.* Richardson: University of Texas at Dallas, 1979.

Crockett, James Underwood. *Bulbs.* New York: Time-Life Books, 1971.

Davies, Dilys. *Alliums.* London: B. T. Batsford; Portland, Ore.: Timber Press, 1992.

de Graaff, Jan. *The New Book of Lilies.* New York: M. Barrows & Co., 1951.

de Graaff, Jan, and Edward Hyams. *Lilies.* London: Thomas Nelson & Sons, 1967.

Doutt, Richard L. *Cape Bulbs.* Portland, Ore.: Timber Press, 1994.

Duncan, G. D. *The Lachenalia Handbook.* Kirstenbosch, South Africa: National Botanic Gardens, CTP Book Printers, 1988.

Du Plessis, Niel, Graham Duncan, and Elise Bodley. *Bulbous Plants of Southern Africa.* Cape Town: Tafelberg Pub., 1989.

Eliovson, Sima. *Namaqualand in Flower.* Johannesburg: Macmillan, 1972.

———. *Wild Flowers of Southern Africa.* 6th ed. Johannesburg: Macmillan, 1980.

Everett, T. H. *The American Gardener's Book of Bulbs.* New York: Random House, 1954.

Fell, Derek. *Essential Bulbs.* New York: Crescent Books, 1989.

Genders, Roy. *Bulbs: A Complete Handbook.*

Indianapolis and New York: Bobbs-Merrill Co., 1973.

———. *Miniature Bulbs.* New York: St. Martin's Press, 1963.

Germishuizen, Gerrit, and Anita Fabian. *Transvaal Wild Flowers.* Johannesburg: Macmillan South Africa, 1982.

Glattstein, Judy. *The American Gardener's World of Bulbs.* Boston and New York: Little, Brown and Co., 1994.

Grace, Julie. *Bulbs and Perennials.* Wellington, New Zealand: A. H. & A. W. Reed; Beaverton, Ore.: Timber Press, 1984.

Graf, Alfred Byrd. *Exotica 3.* East Rutherford, N.J.: Roehrs Co., 1963.

Grey, C. H. *Hardy Bulbs.* 3 vols. New York: E. P. Dutton & Co., 1938.

Grey-Wilson, Christopher, and Brian Matthew. *Bulbs: The Bulbous Plants of Europe and Their Allies.* London: William Collins and Sons, 1981.

Hannibal, Les S. *Garden Crinum. Bulletin of the Louisiana Society for Horticultural Research,* vol. 3, no. 5, 1970–1971.

Harrison, Richmond E. *A Handbook of Bulbs and Perennials for the Southern Hemisphere.* Palmerston North, New Zealand: R. E. Harrison & Co.

Haskin, Leslie L. *Wild Flowers of the Pacific Coast.* Portland Ore.: Binfords & Mort, 1934.

Herbert, William. *Amaryllidaceae.* London: James Ridgeway and Sons, 1837.

Herbertia (yearbook of the International Bulb Society, formerly the American Plant Life Society), vols. 1–50. Pasadena, Calif., 1934–1994.

Herwig, Rob. *128 Bulbs You Can Grow.* New York and London: Macmillan, 1975.

Hill, Lewis and Nancy. *Bulbs: Four Seasons of Beautiful Blooms.* Pownal, Vt.: Garden Way Publishing, 1994.

Hobbs, Jack, and Terry Hatch. *Best Bulbs for Temperate Climates.* Portland, Ore.: Timber Press, 1994.

Hulme, Mairn. *Wild Flowers of Natal.* Dieter Maritzburg, Natal, South Africa: Shooter & Shuter, 1954.

Jackson, W. P. U. *Wild Flowers of Table Mountain.* Cape Town: Howard Timmins, 1977.

———. *Wild Flowers of the Fairest Cape.* Cape Town: Howard Timmins Publishers, Cape & Transvaal Printers, 1980.

Jefferson-Brown, Michael. *Narcissus.* Portland, Ore.: Timber Press, 1991.

Jeppe, Barbara. *Spring and Winter Flowering Bulbs of the Cape.* Cape Town: Oxford University Press, 1989.

Johnston, Marshall C. *The Vascular Plants of Texas: A List, Up-dating the Manual of the Vascular Plants of Texas.* 2d ed. Austin, 1990.

Jones, Stanley D., Joseph K. Wipff, and Paul M. Montgomery. *Vascular Plants of Texas.* Austin: University of Texas Press, 1997.

Killingbeck, Stanley. *Tulips.* Secaucus, N.J.: Chartwell Books, 1991.

Koopowitz, Harold, and Hillary Kaye. *Plant Extinction: A Global Crisis.* Washington D.C.: Stone Wall Press, 1983.

Lawrence, Elizabeth. *The Little Bulbs.* New York: Criterion Books, 1957.

Lawrence, George H. M. *Taxonomy of Vascular Plants.* New York: Macmillan, 1951.

Lee, George S. "Daffodil Handbook." *American Horticultural Magazine,* vol. 45, no. 1, January 1966.

Lodewijk, Tom. *The Book of Tulips.* New York: Vendome Press, 1978.

Mathew, Brian. *The Crocus.* Portland, Ore.: Timber Press, 1982.

———. *Dwarf Bulbs.* London: B. T. Batsford, 1973.

———. *The Iris.* New York: Universe Press, 1981.

———. *The Larger Bulbs.* London: B. T. Batsford, 1978.

———. *The Smaller Bulbs.* London: B. T. Batsford, 1987.

Mathew, Brian, and Turhan Baytop. *The Bulbous Plants of Turkey.* London: B. T. Batsford, 1984.

Mathew, Brian, and Philip Swindells. *The Complete Book of Bulbs, Corms, Tubers, and Rhizomes.* Pleasantville, N.Y.: Readers Digest Association, 1994.

McFarland, J. Horace, R. Marion Hatton, and Daniel J. Foley. *Garden Bulbs in Color.* New York: Macmillan, 1941.

McNair, James K. *All about Bulbs.* San Francisco: Ortho Books, 1981.

McQueen, Sally. *The Complete Guide to Growing Bulbs in Houston.* Houston: River Bend Co., 1978–1985.

McVaugh, Rogers. *Flora Novo-Galiciana,* vol. 15. Ann Arbor: University of Michigan, 1989.

Miles, Bebe. *Bulbs for the Home Gardener.* New York: Grosset & Dunlap, 1976.

———. *The Wonderful World of Bulbs.* Princeton, N.J.: D. Van Nostrand Co., 1963.

Mitchell, Sydney B. *Iris for Every Garden.* New York: M. Barrows & Co., 1960.

Molseed, Elwood. *The Genus Tigridia (Iridaceae) of Mexico and Central America.* University of California Publications in Botany, vol. 54. Berkeley and Los Angeles: University of California Press, 1970.

Mueller, Charles H. *Bulbs for Beauty.* New York: M. Barrows & Co., 1947.

Ogden, Scott. *Garden Bulbs for the South.* Dallas: Taylor Publishing Co., 1994.

Ownbey, Marion. *The Allium canadense Alliance.* Research Studies of the State College of Washington. Monographic Supplement 1, vol. 23, no. 4: 1–106, 1955.

———. *The Genus Allium in Arizona.* Research Studies of the State College of Washington, vol. 15, no. 4, 1947.

———. *The Genus Allium in Texas.* Research Studies of the State College of Washington, vol. 18, 1950.

Ownbey, Marion, and Hanna C. Aase. *Cytotaxonomic Studies of Allium.* Pullman: Washington State College, 1955.

Pearse, R. O. *Mountain Splendour: The Wild Flowers of the Drakensberg.* Cape Town: Howard Timmins, 1978.

Peters, Ruth Marie. *Bulb Magic in Your Window.* New York: M. Barrows and Co., 1954.

Phillips, Roger, and Martyn Rix. *The Bulb Book.* London: Pan Books, 1981.

———. *The Random House Book of Bulbs.* Edited by Brian Mathew. New York: Random House, 1989.

Polunin, Oleg. *A Concise Guide to the Flowers of Britain and Europe.* Oxford and New York: Oxford University Press, 1987.

Quinn, Carey E. *Daffodils, Outdoors and In.* New York: Heathside Press, 1959.

Reilly, Ann. *Taylor's Bulbs for Summer.* Chanticleer Press Edition. Boston: Houghton Mifflin Co., 1989.

Reynolds, Marc, and William L. Meachem. *The Garden Bulbs of Spring.* New York: Funk and Wagnalls, 1967.

Rix, E. Martyn. *Growing Bulbs.* London and Canberra: Croom Helm; Portland, Ore.: Timber Press, 1983.

Rockwell, F. F. *The Book of Bulbs.* New York: Macmillan, 1927.

Rockwell, F. F., and Esther C. Grayson. *The Complete Book of Bulbs.* Philadelphia and New York: J. B. Lippincott Co., 1977.

Rockwell, F. F., Esther C. Grayson, and Jan de Graaff. *The Complete Book of Lilies.* New York: Doubleday & Co., 1961.

Royal Horticultural Society. *The New Royal Horticultural Society Dictionary of Gardening.* Editor-in-chief Anthony Huxley;

editor Mark Griffiths. London: Macmillan
Press; New York: Stockton Press, 1992.

————. *The New Royal Horticultural Society
Manual of Bulbs.* Consultant editor
John Bryan. Portland, Ore.: Timber
Press, 1995.

Scheider, Alfred. *Park's Success with Bulbs.*
Greenwood, S.C.: Geo. W. Park Seed
Co., 1981.

Schulz, Ellen D. *Texas Wild Flowers.* Chicago:
Laidlaw Brothers, 1928.

Scott, George Harmon. *Bulbs: How to Select,
Grow, and Enjoy.* Tucson: HP Books,
1982.

Shinners, Lloyd H. *Spring Flora of the Dallas–
Fort Worth Area, Texas.* Dallas: Southern
Methodist University, 1958.

Schulz, Peggie. *Amaryllis, and How to
Grow Them.* New York: M. Barrows
and Co., 1954.

Slate, George L. *Lilies for American Gardens.*
New York: Charles Scribners & Sons, 1939.

Stearn, William T. *Botanical Latin.* 3rd ed.,
rev. London: David & Charles, 1983.

Sunset Books. *How to Grow Bulbs.* Menlo
Park, Calif.: Lane Books, 1975.

Synge, Patrick M. *The Complete Guide to
Bulbs.* Edinburgh: R. & R. Clark, 1961.

Traub, Hamilton P. *The Amaryllis Manual.*
New York: Macmillan, 1958.

————. *The Genera of Amaryllidaceae.* La Jolla,
Calif.: American Plant Life Society, 1963.

Traub, Hamilton P., and Harold N. Moldenke.
Amaryllidaceae: Tribe Amarylleae. La Jolla:
American Plant Life Society, 1949.

Vance, Ronald. *The Home Gardener's Guide to
Bulb Flowers.* New York: Abelard-
Schuman, 1967–1974.

Verdoorn, I. C. "The Genus Crinum in
Southern Africa." *Bothalia,* vol. 11, nos. 1–2,
pp. 27–52, 1973.

Warburton, Bee, and Melba Hamlin, eds.
The World of Irises. American Iris Society.
Salt Lake City: Publishers Press, 1978.

Wilder, Louise Beebe. *Adventures with
Hardy Bulbs.* New York: Dover Publications, 1936.

Weathers, J. *Beautiful Bulbous Plants.* London:
Simpkin, Marshall, Hamilton, Kent &
Co., n.d.

Weston, T. A. *All about Flowering Bulbs.*
New York: A. T. De La Mare Co., 1931.

————. *Bulbs That Bloom in the Spring.* New
York: A. T. De La Mare Co., 1926.

Wister, Gertrude S. *Hardy Garden Bulbs.* New
York: E. P. Dutton & Co., 1964.

Wister, John C. *Bulbs for Home Gardens.*
New York: Oxford University Press, 1948.

Wood, Allen H. *Bulbs for Your Garden.* New
York: Garden City Pub. Co., 1940.

INDEX

Boldface type indicates illustrations.